AF361592

#MeToo
AND
BEYOND

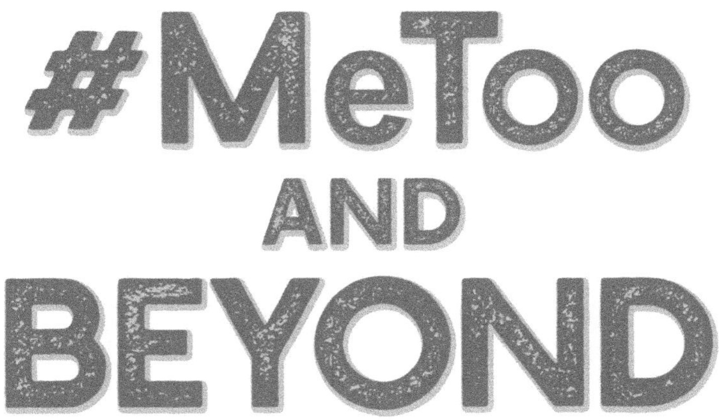

#MeToo AND BEYOND

PERSPECTIVES ON A GLOBAL MOVEMENT

EDITED BY M. CRISTINA ALCALDE AND
PAULA-IRENE VILLA

Editorial and Sales Offices: The University Press of Kentucky
663 South Limestone Street, Lexington, Kentucky 40508-4008
www.kentuckypress.com

Cataloging-in-Publication data is available from the Library of Congress.

ISBN 978-0-8131-9559-9 (hardcover : alk. paper)
ISBN 978-0-8131-9560-5 (paperback : alk. paper)
ISBN 978-0-8131-9562-9 (epub)
ISBN 978-0-8131-9561-2 (pdf)

This book is printed on acid-free paper meeting
the requirements of the American National Standard
for Permanence in Paper for Printed Library Materials.

Manufactured in the United States of America.

Member of the Association of
University Presses

Contents

Introduction

Disrupting the Familiar, Approaching #MeToo

M. Cristina Alcalde and Paula-Irene Villa

Ni una menos, vivas nos queremos! (Not one less, we want us alive!)
—*refrain from (feminist) protest movements in Latin America,
2015–present*

What history has shown us time and again is that if marginalized voices—those of people of color, queer people, disabled people, poor people—aren't centered in our movements then they tend to become no more than a footnote. I often say that sexual violence knows no race, class or gender, but the response to it does. "Me too" is a response to the spectrum of gender-based sexual violence that comes directly from survivors—all survivors. We can't afford a racialized, gendered or classist response. *Ending sexual violence will require every voice from every corner of the world and it will require those whose voices are most often heard to find ways to amplify those voices that often go unheard.*
—*Tarana Burke, "#MeToo Was Started for Black and Brown Women and Girls" (editors' emphasis)*

In 2017, #MeToo became visible on a massive, global scale. US-based *Time* magazine featured the #MeToo movement as its "Person of the Year," and the hashtag #MeToo dominated social media for months. Since #MeToo appeared to start as an outcry against sexual harassment from within the film industry, for many the movement was and may still be associated mainly with US celebrities. Alyssa Milano and Harvey Weinstein appeared as the opposing faces of #MeToo around that time as #MeToo became framed as a "red carpet" issue, especially in the international press. Far fewer people recognized the names Tarana Burke and Anastasia Melnichenko. The former is the community activist who, eleven years before the *Time* magazine feature and rise of so-called hashtag activism on Twitter, coined the phrase "me too" to make visible and demand accountability for the intersecting experiences of racism and sexual abuse of women and girls of color in communities across the United States. The latter is a Ukrainian journalist who in 2016 generated much media attention and activism on Twitter by sharing her personal account of sexual harassment through #IAmNotAfraidToSpeak (#яНеБоюсьСказати in Ukrainian). Around the same time, across Latin America mobilizations under the hashtag #NiUnaMenos (Not One Less) became among the most massive and enduring of the past decades in the region. In Germany, #Aufschrei (Outcry) and #Ausnahmslos (Without Exception) went viral in 2013 and 2016, respectively, addressing not only sexist and misogynist bullying and harassment but also the often racist and xenophobic rhetoric of antisexism in German media and society. In India, the crowdsourced #LoSHA (list of sexual harassers in academia) movement brought attention to sexual harassers in academia even before the broader #MeToo movement gained momentum there.

This book approaches #MeToo from multiple spaces, positionalities, and areas of expertise as well as from regions and contexts often overseen and understudied in the mediascapes of the Global North. We present case studies from Latin America (Peru), India, the United States, South Africa, the United Kingdom, Australia, and Israel, and we include research spanning from masculinities to trans issues to Jewish communities. Our aim is to examine both the profoundly universal and familiar experiences of sexual violence as well as the specificity of these forms of violence and mobilization against them across place, space, and participants' experiences. We heed Tarana Burke's call to center marginalized voices and experiences in varying world locations so that these experiences, instead of becoming a footnote, guide the engagement and analyses across chapters in this book as we frame polyphony as central to understanding past, current, and future forms of gendered violence and resistance.

Across the Latin American region, protesters draw on and bring together the demands of NiUnaMenos, which originated in Argentina in 2015 with the cry "Vivas nos queremos!" that started five thousand miles to the north, in Mexico, the same year to decry persistent waves of femicide and everyday forms of gendered violence. In Peru and across the region, voices unite to demand "Ni una menos, vivas nos queremos!," yet these demands do not erase the reality of multiple internal voices, tensions, and experiences that reflect diverse class, generational, racialized, and gendered positions among those protesting (Muñoz Cabrejo, chapter 10 in this volume). One such problematic issue concerns the exclusions produced by antisexist and progressive, feminist, social movements themselves: whether in Latin America, Australia, South Africa, Germany, India, the United States, or Ukraine, movements for justice have tended to exclude LGBTQ experiences (see Guadalupe-Diaz and Whalley's chapter in this volume).

In engaging with these and other so far less acknowledged experiences, we intentionally contribute to broadening the stage and discussion and enabling visibility and resonance for the nuances of gendered and sexuality-based violence as well as for the variety of political mobilizations against them. In doing so, this collection builds on previous work, especially by Bianca Fileborn and Rachel Loney-Howes (2019), in examining how #MeToo both disrupts and is limited by given understandings of gendered violence. More specifically, this volume does three things. First, it recenters precursors to #MeToo on a continuum of gendered violence as crucial for understanding #MeToo globally. The endurance and continuity of feminist mobilization against gendered violence across spaces become clear, and we can thus understand that #MeToo is by no means a singular, suddenly dynamic movement but rather part of a long and varied tradition of feminist struggles. Second, it recenters the exclusionary tendencies of a globally visible #MeToo through the voices and demands of those pushed to the margins within and across spaces to interrogate dynamics of inclusion/exclusion and to contribute to imagining alternative, more inclusive dialogue and forms of activism. Whereas previous literature has focused on exclusions within the US movement (see Gieseler 2019), this volume shows that exclusions and hierarchies are not limited to the United States. Rather, they are increasingly addressed throughout regions and institutions, generating painful yet productive conflicts within antisexist mobilizations. Third, and most broadly, this collection shifts power dynamics by centering voices from the Global South as a way to push against the "structural imbalance in the global economy of knowledge" (Banerjee and Connell 2018, 58) and the coloniality of knowledge surrounding scholarship on #MeToo (for example, Brown 2020; Collier Hillstrom 2019; Kantor and Twohey 2019; Mendes, Ringrose, and Keller 2019).

As we understand it in this collection and based on research as well as on activism in its many shades, #MeToo reflects complex fights against sexualized and gendered violence, against everyday sexism, and against toxic forms of cultural masculinity and gendered ideologies in all of their nuances and specificities. Although women remain a primary target of gendered and sexualized violence, such violence is not limited to women and girls. Boys and men suffer from sexualized aggressions and bullying as well, especially in male–male structures such as military, fraternities, and churches. Transgender, nonbinary, and queer persons are at heightened risk for gender and sexual harassment and violence. In short, violence and aggressions based on gender and sexuality serve as a display and as enforcement of institutionalized structures of power and as practices of forcing persons and entire groups into seemingly "normal" gender and sexual scripts. #MeToo and similar movements bring attention to and can help mobilize against multiple forms of gendered and sexualized violence in their various manifestations.

Through this book, it should become clear that #MeToo is not a single-issue movement. Rather, #MeToo encapsulates forms of pushback against practices, ideologies, and social structures that define certain groups as existing to please other, more powerful groups. #MeToo insists on all persons' right to make decisions about their own bodies and on all persons' dignity. #MeToo is also about the insistence to be treated with professionalism in professional settings and with respect in all situations. It is about the insistence on safety, regardless of gender, sexuality, marital and immigration status, age, ability, and other markers of identity. The multiple movements and struggles gathered around #MeToo, such as #NiUnaMenos, #Aufschrei, #Ausnahmslos, #memyös, #QuellaVoltaChe, ‏#גםאנחנו‎, #balanceTonPorc, #私も, and many more worldwide are led by women and minoritized populations responding to specific histories, goals, and challenges. Even as contributors foreground the distinctiveness of place and space, they do so against a shared global backdrop of extreme underrepresentation of women and minoritized voices at the highest levels of government and in policies and increasingly undemocratic practices that provide the context for struggles across contexts.

#MeToo and Beyond draws on a broad range of regional, topical, empirical, and theoretical perspectives to contribute to a rich dialogue among scholars and activists about the multiple ways in which #MeToo speaks to and reflects both precursors and similar movements across the globe. Rather than limit the focus to one group, generation, or national context, contributors draw attention to both similarities and differences across national contexts in order to reveal themes relevant for policy makers, nongovernmental organizations, social and political scientists, culture studies scholars, and scholars in the fields of gender, violence, family, and social movements. The chapters that follow are invitations to actively listen to and learn from perspectives that disrupt the familiar in contributing to a rich, global conversation within and around #MeToo. In the remainder of this introduction, we foreground and examine the intersecting positionalities and perspectives that inform the book's engagement with #MeToo as well as the gendered forms of violence, hierarchies of difference, and exclusionary practices discussed across chapters.

Positionalities and Intersections

In 2019, a small group of colleagues from Austria, China, Australia, Ecuador, Peru, England, Germany, India, Israel, Japan, Mexico, South Africa, and the United States came together at the University of Kentucky and were joined by the broader community for the Comparative Perspectives on #MeToo Symposium. This volume is based on the lively exchange and the learning experiences shared during this intensive symposium. Contributors, some publishing in English for the first time, come from a range of disciplines, such as anthropology, gender and women's studies, sociology, history, and literature. As a group, we identify with diverse and always intersectional gender and racialized positionalities. We represent a range of life and career stages and generations and work in a variety of institutional and national contexts. Across language, disciplinary, personal, theoretical, and generational differences, our personal, professional, and institutional commitments to immerse ourselves in a space of dialogue and learning not only held the group together but also kept us deeply engaged. It is thus also in the sense of individual positionings that we are guided by Tarana Burke's words: we must try to include as much variety as possible in our analysis of activism against sexualized and gender-based violence.

As several chapters point out, #MeToo can be both a profoundly personal experience and a thoroughly scholarly subject for analysis. The sexual violence and harassment enveloped by #MeToo enters our personal lives in academic spaces at both deeply personal levels (Basu's and McGinity's chapters in this volume) and in ways that push institutions and disciplinary associations to confront these long-standing forms of gendered violence (Sen's and Guadalupe-Diaz and Whalley's chapters). As we planned to focus on #MeToo, we determined that we, as scholars and activists, would both discuss (in the symposium) and write (through this collection) as a group. Across languages, jet-lagged, and curious about one another and the time together, we listened, discussed, asked, and supported during the course of the two-day symposium. The idea for coming together was multipronged from the start: all participants agreed to participate in person, presenting what we knew beforehand would be the basis for a book to bring these discussions beyond the constraints of the space and place in which we met. We were determined to broaden the hegemonic discourse of and on #MeToo by adding lesser-known positions in terms of both space and argument. The dynamic, generous, and multilayered challenging dialogues that our own experiences, expertise, and broader positionalities contributed to were first presented at the symposium as we imagined ways to continue and expand the discussion through this book. Rather than defining ourselves as representative of all world areas, disciplines, or identities, we sought to closely engage with specific differences and similarities across some contexts in order to learn from one another as a way to push further and disrupt our own knowledge and experience of #MeToo. Acknowledging our own positionalities also meant recognizing that some of what was shared in person could not be shared more publicly—the personal and professional costs would be too high—and respecting the necessity of those absences and silences.

As we discussed personal experiences and structural barriers to addressing the demands of movements across spaces, the connection between individual experiences and state-level governance and protection (or lack thereof) arose as a theme to which we repeatedly returned. In discussing gendered violence and femicide in South Africa, Kammila Naidoo and Denise Buiten (chapter 2) refer to a recent presidential pledge for more government action to address the high levels of violence against women, while Fanni Muñoz Cabrejo (chapter 10) examines feminist mobilization against the backdrop of government inaction to address femicides and other forms of gender violence in Peru. In examining how the demands of individuals and groups are met within specific national contexts, we discussed how minoritized experiences and voices, such as those identified as queer, were largely absent at the highest levels of government in many of our societies and in policy making. We also focused on how increasingly undemocratic practices appeared as the backdrop for struggles across contexts (Guadalupe-Diaz and Whalley's chapter).

At the time of our initial meeting, Donald J. Trump was president of the United States, and the government's policies and his personal expressions of misogyny, sexual violence, and harassment appeared in conversation and presentations, as they did in much of the media elsewhere.[1] Yet these discussions were not simply about one misogynistic president or sexism in one society. Notwithstanding differences among world leaders, it is worth noting that the strongman politics Trump exhibited and his dismissal of the complex and intersecting issues behind #MeToo resonate with similar efforts and behaviors by other world leaders. Jair Bolsonaro (Brazil), Viktor Orban (Hungary), Rodrigo Duterte (Philippines), Vladimir Putin (Russia), and Recep Tayyip Erdoğan (Turkey) have similarly consolidated and tightened their strongmen image and power as they have sought to undermine and dismantle women's sexual and reproductive rights as well as LGBTQ rights. These leaders' approaches to women's rights in particular leave little doubt of their stance on gender violence—with Duterte recommending that women guerrilla fighters be "shot in the vagina" to make them useless and Bolsonaro telling an opposition congresswoman that she was not good enough for him to rape.[2] Also, the "antigender" rhetoric and policies, including Turkey's withdrawal from the European Union's Istanbul Treaty just at the moment we are finishing this volume, display deeply authoritarian and fundamentalist politics that are systematically linked to specific forms of "political masculinity" (Hark and Villa 2015; Köttig, Bitzan, and Petö 2018; Kuhar and Paternotte 2017).

Sexism and gendered violence are, as we can witness on a global scale and as much research shows, a core element of illiberal politics.

The COVID-19 crisis has further made visible how such general toxic patterns of masculinity manifest as a heroic stance in moments of global crisis: the militarized rhetoric of "being at war," "defeating," and "winning" is symptomatic of this style of "leadership" during the pandemic. Instead of approaching the pandemic from the perspective of a generalized yet structurally unequal vulnerability and instead of addressing the pressing issues of care and infectious connectedness, the "strongmen" response echoes the bullying dynamics of gendered violence. It seeks to be unaffected, strong, autonomous, powerful, reckless. It mocks care, solidarity, and consideration as signs of weakness and brags about its own ruthlessness. As a common thread across contexts, this is precisely how those in power act and react when bullying and harassing women or other groups.

Gendered-Violence Continuum and Precursors to #MeToo

As #MeToo has made abundantly clear, and as the chapters here examine, harassment has been the norm rather than the exception for women and other marginalized persons globally. Among the most public yet understudied forms of violence against women is street sexual harassment (Kearl 2015; Vera-Gray 2016). Over the past decade and a half, research on women's experiences of fear in public spaces have brought attention to the gendering of spaces and the gendering of fear in various locations across the globe (Koskela 1999; Phadke 2012). Unwanted sexual comments, catcalls, threats, whistling, flashing, rubbing up against, touching, groping, and public masturbation are all common manifestations of harassment in public spaces (Shoukry, Hassan, and Komsan 2008; Ziets and Das 2018). Sexual harassment and sexual assault, including the sexualized deprofessionalization of women or "others" in public and professional spaces, are topics many of the contributors in this book discuss. They also address the multiple forms of resistance and the creative practices of those impacted by these forms of violence. Within a continuum of violence, street sexual harassment can be understood as an expression of pervasive gender inequality. In Paris, France, 94 percent of women using the Metro reported being harassed there

(Osez le Feminisme 2014), and in Mexico nine out of ten women similarly reported sexual harassment while using public transportation (Dunckel-Graglia 2013). In Bangladesh, approximately 90 percent of girls between ten and eighteen years old have experienced street harassment, including street sexual harassment (Kearl 2015). In the United States, sexual harassment has long been a societal problem (Collier Hillstrom 2019), with 81 percent of women and 43 percent of men reporting having experienced sexual harassment and/or assault in their lifetimes (Stop Street Harassment 2018).

Less public but no less harmful, harassment in spaces of higher education impacts both individual lives and careers and helps sustain structures of inequality upon which many universities have been built. In the United States, for example, it is worth noting that universities were created to educate the offspring of white colonizers and therefore to preserve racialized and gendered social hierarchies and inequalities (Thelin 2004). The chapters here foreground the reality that universities around the world are organizations whose formations, hierarchies, and processes are not race neutral (Ray 2019). In fact, issues of sexism (McGinity's and Sen's chapters), racism, ethnocentrism, and homophobia (Guadalupe-Diaz and Whalley's chapter) are not recent or new to institutions of higher education. Although there are distinct dynamics within various higher-education spaces across nations, social media has allowed for specific, local cases to be discussed on a global scale.

In 2017, Avital Ronell, a professor at New York University, was accused of harassing a graduate student. The case drew widespread attention because not only was the accused a well-known feminist queer scholar, but the accuser was a man. In chapter 8, Xavier L. Guadalupe-Diaz and Elizabeth Whalley approach this case to exemplify the complexities of power dynamics within academia, how queer identities challenge mainstream ideas about what constitutes sexual violence, and, most significantly, how queerness has been leveraged to normalize coercive sexual actions in a broader context in which #MeToo has largely excluded queer voices—in spite of Tarana Burke's original intent. In chapter 5, Desiree Lewis reminds us of the power of social media to expand conversations across national borders as she, too, draws on the Ronell case to examine experiences and representations of sexual harassment in North America and South Africa.

The attention to gendered power dynamics in public and private spaces as well as in spaces of work and education has been magnified by #MeToo, but these experiences and the mobilization against them are far from new. As several chapters in this volume stress, #MeToo landed in regionally specific constellations that are the result of multiple previous mobilizations against sexualized and gender-related violence, against everyday sexism, and against rape culture. In chapter 9, Ruth Preser discusses the specific dynamics within such struggles in the Israeli context, focusing on the complex issues regarding "visibility" in public and (feminist) counterpublics and drawing on an empirical analysis of online platforms. In her chapter, Lewis discusses issues of naming and framing in the context of South Africa, linking these issues to previous and/or regional specificities of context. Writing from and speaking to the same context, in chapter 2 Naidoo and Buiten analyze #MeToo in light of "local activism, research, and debate around sexual violence [that] have long been occurring in South Africa."

In chapter 4, Srimati Basu focuses on the ambivalent character of the law in feminist politics and situates her analysis in the very different tensions between feminist protests and legal policies in the United States and India. Part of this discussion is how sexual and gender aspects of everyday life are legally "policed" as private or public. The seemingly overpoliticization and legal regulation of what are traditionally considered intimate and private aspects of life are in fact the main anxieties of antifeminism, which traditionally defends the (often enough sexist and unequal) status quo against equality and legal rights. Again, #MeToo addresses precisely this issue by demanding the corresponding legislation, political support, and public acknowledgment of structural sexism and sexuality-based harassment in all its forms, from microaggressions to overt violence. It is precisely this "scandal" that makes #MeToo so powerful and effective. It once again and much in line with the plethora of feminist traditions all over the globe unmasks the political dimension of the seemingly private or individual. And it demands political answers. In chapter 1, Rachel Loney-Howes stresses this dimension and discusses the specificities of political-public dynamics and #MeToo in Australia: "If the ultimate goal of movements such as #MeToo is to prevent violence against women, then the recognition and subsequently a complete overhaul of the discursive frameworks governing social, cultural, legal, and political structures is needed—structures that include but are not limited to patriarchy, colonialism, racism, heterosexism, and capitalism." From a different angle yet arriving at similar conclusions in chapter 6, Keren McGinity weaves together the political and personal, showing the public aspects of the private in her personal account of how she publicly denounced sexual misconduct by a prominent colleague in the US Jewish studies community. She also discusses the corresponding media coverage.

Book Outline

This volume constitutes one substantial step in the direction of seeing, engaging with, and learning from the work of differently positioned individuals and populations in the context of global #MeToo mobilizing. In our approach to various movements under the umbrella term *#MeToo*, we recognize that the contexts and histories of these struggles may be unfamiliar to some readers. The chapters provide guiding contextual information. Although all contributors are united in approaching and making sense of #MeToo, each contributor's preferred form of presentation and sense making—from testimonial to historical analysis to legal or empirical analyses and policy recommendations—varies and reflects the multiplicity of voices within #MeToo efforts. Our commitment to recognizing multiple forms of engagement, learning, and positions necessitates providing space for these differences as part of the broader #MeToo dialogue within and across national borders even as we foreground intersections across spaces in this introduction.

In their chapters, the contributors examine how across borders of nation, religion, ethnicity, sexualities, gender, and political ideologies, the meanings of public and private are renegotiated through multiple forms of collective mobilization. In the first part, "The Politics of Inclusion, Space, and Change," chapters focus on navigating public spaces to become visible and demand justice as well as on the challenges and forms of inclusivity and solidarity that such public organizing within communities and across identities and borders can present. Writing on visibility and framings within the Australian context, Rachel Loney-Howes examines in chapter 1 the shortcomings associated with representations of survivors through #MeToo and the broader limits of the potential of #MeToo to bring about change there. In chapter 2, Kammila Naidoo and Denise Buiten point to opportunities for local and transnational organizing and solidarity as they discuss why #MeToo isn't as robust in many parts of Africa as it is in other parts of the world. As they argue, a narrow focus on #MeToo and social media erases local movements that predate #MeToo and that are at the center of decades of African feminist struggles surrounding violence against women.

Drawing on Naidoo and Buiten's analysis as well as on the ambivalent dynamics of the visibility and shadows that the politics of inclusion creates, we can ask: What, then, is lost or silenced when something is seen and highlighted? For #MeToo as a global yet always specific issue, this question can hardly be overemphasized. Focusing on the United Kingdom in chapter 3, Stephen Burrell adds yet another important lens to viewing the implications of inclusion and potential for change surrounding #MeToo: the role of men and boys in preventing violence against women. Building on feminist-standpoint epistemological approaches, Burrell examines how work with men and boys can be developed in impactful ways in the future as a way to bring about change.

In the second part, "Law, Media, and Feminist Mobilization," chapters draw attention to the limits and possibilities for understanding #MeToo and feminist mobilization as well as to the possibilities for accountability through law and media. In chapter 4, delving into the sometimes blurred lines of ethics and law that individuals and movements negotiate and demand in seeking justice, Srimati Basu examines #MeToo's ambivalent relationship to law, analyzing how in both India and the United States the movement calls upon yet moves beyond the law as individuals and groups seek to express grievances and demand justice in areas where laws have previously failed them.

In chapter 5, Desiree Lewis focuses on the mediascape of #MeToo in North America and South Africa as a way to understand the politics of representation of #MeToo across continents. She reminds us that while expanding the conversation and visibility of gendered violence, media representations can also limit and undermine these discussions and deeper understandings of the dynamics by transforming the political subject of sexual violence into a familiar and often superficial tabloid narrative.

The third part, "Higher Ed and the Disruption of Everyday Violence and Exclusions," concentrates on academia as one institutional space in which hierarchies and sexism (as well as other forms of sexual- and gender-based harassment) are structurally entangled. In chapter 6, Keren McGinity offers an intimately personal account of how she critically engaged with the US Jewish studies community when she denounced a well-known colleague in the field. In chapter 7, Rukmini Sen discusses the dynamics and responses to #MeToo in the Indian context. She links them to the increasing presence of women in (Indian) academia and the intensified efforts toward gender-equality policies in India, focusing on the complicated issue of legal regulations. Xavier Guadalupe-Diaz and Elizabeth Whalley discuss a very different multi-layered issue in chapter 8. They begin with the harassment case surrounding the queer literature scholar Avital Ronell in 2018 but refrain from exoticizing this particular case and move on to a broader analysis of queer and trans issues within #MeToo. They argue in favor of a more complex, intersectional queering of activism and research that will address academia and other institutions more broadly.

The book concludes with part IV, "Tensions and Conflicts within #MeToo." In chapter 9, Ruth Preser takes an in-depth and theory-infused look at the complexities of (politically relevant) visibility. She situates universal questions of voice, recognition, and agency via visibility within the Israeli situation, discussing the exclusion and silences produced by #MeToo itself. Preser insists on the complexity and the necessity of negotiating precisely this complexity instead of futile efforts to simplify for the sake of political effects. Based on an empirical study situated in the Peruvian context, Fanni Muñoz Cabrejo discusses in chapter 10 the intersections of gender, race, class, and ethnicity and focuses on the empirical complexities and resulting tensions in the #NiUnaMenos movement, the Latin American feminist mobilization against femicides and sexualized violence. She thoroughly interrogates how these political dynamics connect multiple feminist collectives through conflict-ridden negotiations. Her work shows that although heterogeneity in political collectives is difficult and risky, it can also be put to work productively, allowing for broad inclusion of otherwise invisibilized sectors and issues. This part foregrounds the overall point of the volume: that multiplicity and resulting conflict do not weaken massive and effective (feminist) mobilization—although this risk does exist—but rather, if addressed and negotiated, can be sources of inclusive and broad social change. We thus return to the words of Tarana Burke: "Ending sexual violence will require every voice from every corner of the world and it will require those whose voices are most often heard to find ways to amplify those voices that often go unheard" (2017).

Looking Ahead

In 2021, in the midst of the COVID-19 pandemic, the issues that fuel #MeToo are as urgent as ever throughout the globe as systemic racial, class, and gender inequalities become particularly visible and lethal. As countries respond to COVID-19 with increasingly longer shelter-in-place orders and lockdowns, women and children find themselves at heightened risk for violence as they are left with diminishing options to escape abusive partners and homes. Domestic-abuse hotlines have reported significant rises in incoming calls, ranging from 30 percent to 40 percent, across places as diverse as France, Cyprus, and Brazil.[3] Outside the home, everyday forms of violence continue, as does resistance to violence. In Mexico, where femicides have increased 137 percent over the past five years, women organized to stay home on March 9, 2020, to protest this rising tide of femicides and other forms of violence against women.[4] Femicides and protests against them continue as well in other parts of the world. Struggles for LGBTQ rights persist in response to the continued efforts to delegitimize, devalue, and disenfranchise those individuals and identities. For those escaping from their home countries to seek refuge in neighboring countries, sexual abuse continues to be a reality in migrant detention centers.

This book shows how #MeToo is very much about how we as individuals, as organizations and institutions, and as entire societies structure and value intimacy and bodies within systems of dominance and hierarchies of differences. This might, in fact, be one of the most important lessons to take from this book and to lay out a path for us to walk from here: we need much more conversation on how to address this unequal "value" further in the media and in politics.

We also need more thorough research on who gets to make decisions over whose body, where, and how. This biopolitical question is not the only but certainly one of the most important questions brought up by #MeToo, and it addresses all realms: social, economic, political, legal, cultural. Whose bodies, whose affects, whose integrity belong to whom, where, how, and why?

This volume makes clear that the #MeToo conversation shares broad general, perhaps even universal, questions and issues while simultaneously making visible the situatedness of distinct contributions to the whole. The overall question seems to be the aforementioned "biopolitical" issue (i.e., Whose bodies, affects, needs, vulnerabilities, and practices count and how, to whom, where, and why?) and how this issue is intimately linked to power and structures of dominance, including social differences and inequalities. However, distinctiveness and nuances also need to be carefully addressed both in research and in (political) practices. The intimate nexus of power, sexuality, bodies, and subjects is a large and general issue, but the ways this nexus works out are highly specific. The chapters here address precisely this tension between the global and the local, between the general and the specific. We are convinced these tensions need even further attention in research and activism. So do the many dimensions and dynamics involved in #MeToo: discourses, practices, politics and policies, law, media, culture, rhetoric, the material environment, the body, identities, organizations, institutions—all are important; no single aspect holds the entire "truth" of what #MeToo is about. In this light, we hope this volume not only offers important insight into many of these issues but also inspires future research, activism, and analysis across contexts and spaces.

As we consider the contributors' analyses of persistent and harmful ways in which societies, groups, and individuals position bodies within gendered, racialized, and sexual hierarchies, we may also want to consider our own everyday practices as they intersect with hierarchies of difference and visibility. How does our own situatedness within local hierarchies of power benefit from more global forms of power? How do our individual forms of power and visibility contribute to disrupting the local and global forms of power identified in these chapters? What are the costs of these global and local forms of power for our individual gendered, racialized, and sexualized experiences? What roles do we play in holding up webs of complicity and silence that delegitimize some experiences of violence over others, while rendering some forms of resistance more legible than others? As we delve more intimately into the politics of visibility and power, what do we choose to privilege, and what do we leave unseen?

Where do we go from here? There might be a simple answer to that question, which at the same time is all but trivial and actually offers a variety of paths to take. The only seemingly easy answer is: we must stay with the trouble and keep up the polyphonic, complex, and arduous conversation that continues to emerge around #MeToo. We must insist on working through the issues at stake in research and activism, in small everyday practices, and in large-scale analysis. We must remain open to the troubling uncertainty brought by the ever-expanding and ever-deepening understanding of the increasing number of dimensions #MeToo entails.

References

Banerjee, P., and R. Connell. 2018. "Gender Theory as Southern Theory." In *Handbook of the Sociology of Gender,* 2nd ed., edited by B. Risman, C. M. Froyum, and W. J. Scarborough, 57–68. Chicago: Springer.

Brown, N. 2020. *MeToo Political Science.* New York: Routledge.

Burke, T. 2017. "#MeToo Was Started for Black and Brown Women and Girls. They're Still Being Ignored." *Washington Post,* November 9.

Collier Hillstrom, L. 2019. *The #MeToo Movement.* Santa Barbara, CA: ABC-CLIO.

Dunckel-Graglia, A. 2013. "Women-Only Transportation: How 'Pink' Public Transportation Changes Public Perception of Women's Mobility." *Journal of Public Transportation* 16 (2): 85–105.

Euronews. 2020. "Domestic Violence Jumps 30% during Lockdown in France." March 28. At https://www.euronews.com/2020/03/28/domestic-violence-cases-jump-30-during-lockdown-in-france?utm_term=Autofeed&utm_medium=Social&utm_source=Facebook&fbclid=IwAR1Ev5k.

Fileborn, B., and R. Loney-Howes, eds. 2019. *#MeToo and the Politics of Social Change.* New York: Springer.

Gieseler, C. 2019. *The Voices of #MeToo: From Grassroots Activism to a Viral Roar.* Lanham, MD: Rowman & Littlefield.

Graham-Harrison, E., A. Giufridda, H. Smith, and L. Ford. 2020. "Lock Downs around the World Bring Rise in Domestic Violence." *Guardian,* March 28. At https://www.theguardian.com/society/2020/mar/28/lockdowns-world-rise-domestic-violence?CMP=share_btn_fb&fbclid=IwAR0TwtCS4UKa ZAgtTabA4UW19r9u2KFlCS-RBBJGgcpIqmA01bzpVvDI2WE.

Guardian. 2018. "Philippines: Rodrigo Duterte Orders Soldiers to Shoot Female Rebels 'in the Vagina.'" February 13. At https://www.theguardian.com/world/2018/feb/13/philippines-rodrigo-duterte-orders-soldiers-to-shoot-female-rebels-in-the-vagina.

Hark, S., and P-I. Villa, eds. 2015. *Anti-Genderismus: Sexualität und Geschlecht als Schauplätze aktueller politischer Auseinandersetzungen.* 2nd ed. Bielefeld, Germany: transcript.

Kantor, J., and M. Twohey. 2019. *She Said: Breaking the Sexual Harassment Story That Helped Ignite a Movement.* New York: Penguin Books.

Kearl, H. 2015. *Stop Global Street Harassment: Growing Activism around the World.* New York: Praeger.

Koskela, H. 1999. "'Gendered Exclusions': Women's Fear of Violence and Changing Relations to Space." *Geografiska Annaler* 81 B (2): 111–24.

Köttig, M., R. Bitzan, and A. Petö, eds. 2018. *Gender and Far Right Politics in Europe.* New York: Springer.

Kuhar, R., and D. Paternotte, eds. 2017. *Anti-gender Campaigns in Europe: Mobilizing against Equality.* Lanham, MD: Rowman & Littlefield.

Mendes, K., J. Ringrose, and J. Keller. 2019. *Digital Feminist Activism: Girls and Women Fight Back against Rape Culture.* New York: Oxford University Press.

NPR. 2020. "Mexican Women Stay Home to Protest Femicides in 'A Day without Us.'" March 9. At https://www.npr.org/2020/03/09/813699719/mexican-women-stay-home-to-protest-femicides-in-a-day-without-us.

Osez le Feminisme. 2014. "Pourquoi cette campagne?" Web post. At http://takebackthemetro.com/.

Phadke, S. 2012. "Gendered Usage of Public Spaces: A Case Study of Mumbai." In *The Fear That Stalks: Gender-Based Violence in Public Spaces,* edited by Sara Pilot and Laura Prabhu, 51–80. New Delhi: Zubaan.

Ray, V. 2019. "A Theory of Racialized Organizations." *American Sociological Review* 84 (1): 26–53.

Shoukry, A., M. Hassan, and N. Komsan. 2008. *"Clouds in Egypt's Sky": Sexual Harassment, from Verbal Harassment to Rape.* Cairo: Egyptian Center for Women's Rights.

Stop Street Harassment. 2018. *The Facts behind the #MeToo Movement: A National Study on Sexual Harassment and Assault.* Reston: Stop Street Harassment. At https://stopstreetharassment.org/wp-content/uploads/2018/01/Full-Report-2018-National-Study-on-Sexual-Harassment-and-Assault.pdf.

Thelin, J. 2004. *A History of American Higher Education.* Baltimore: Johns Hopkins University Press.

Uchoa, P. 2018. "Jair Bolsonaro: Why Brazilian Women Are Saying #NotHim." BBC World Service, September 21. At https://www.bbc.com/news/world-latin-america-45579635.

Vera-Gray, F. 2016. *Men's Intrusion, Women's Embodiment: A Critical Analysis of Street Harassment*. New York: Routledge.

Ziets, S., and M. Das. 2018. "'Nobody Teases Good Girls': A Qualitative Study on Perceptions of Sexual Harassment among Young Men in a Slum of Mumbai." *Global Public Health* 13 (9): 1229–240.

Notes

1. In October 2016, a year before #MeToo took off, an Access Hollywood pre-interview show tape in which Mr. Trump bragged about sexually assaulting women was anonymously leaked. Within a couple of weeks of the tape release, at least twenty women had come forward to publicly accuse presidential candidate Trump of sexual misconduct. In spite of the large number of women coming forward and the behaviors they described, the following month Mr. Trump went on to win the presidential election. During the first few months of the Trump presidency and roughly a month before #MeToo's debut on Twitter in 2017, the US Department of Education's Office for Civil Rights repealed the 2011 guidance on sexual assault and harassment, which required universities to appoint a Title IX compliance officer and to prosecute sexual harassment claims under a "preponderance of the evidence" standard. The new secretary of education, Betsy DeVos, argued that the previous guidelines went too far and were unfair to the accused. By 2019, the US Department of Justice had significantly dismantled the definition of domestic violence posted on its website. Starting in early 2019, the definition of domestic violence dropped all references to sexual, emotional, economic, or psychological actions or threats of actions. The revised definition recognized only physical violence as domestic violence.

2. These comments received widespread media coverage in 2018, including in a *Guardian* article in February (*Guardian* 2018) and in a BBC report in September (Uchoa 2018).

3. Headlines in March 2020 include "Domestic Violence Jumps 30% during Lockdown in France" (Euronews2020) and "Lock Downs around the World Bring Rise in Domestic Violence" (Graham-Harrison et al. 2020).

4. See "Mexican Women Stay Home to Protest Femicides in 'A Day without Us'" (NPR 2020).

PART I

THE POLITICS OF INCLUSION, SPACE, AND CHANGE

1

#MeToo and the Future of Feminist Antiviolence Activism in Australia

Rachel Loney-Howes

When #MeToo exploded onto social media in October 2017, it exposed the widespread nature of sexual harassment and abuse around the world—although for many activists, scholars, and survivors this was not new information but rather confirmation of what they had been highlighting for decades. Nonetheless, #MeToo created a renewed opportunity for activists and survivors to interrogate and challenge the status of gender-based violence in their own local contexts as well as to broaden the parameters of recognition and representation pertaining to who can speak and under what conditions survivors can speak out (see Fileborn and Loney-Howes 2019; Fileborn and Phillips 2019). This chapter is specifically interested in examining the ways these opportunities played out in Australia, with the discussion taking a broad contextual approach that situates the arrival of #MeToo in Australia amid established and active digital feminist campaigns (McLean 2020) as well as amid existing political and policy responses to gender-based violence (Arrow 2018). Against this backdrop, it seemed possible that #MeToo would have strong resonance in Australia. Certainly, the initial responses in the form of the defunct NOW Australia[1] spearheaded by the journalist Tracey Spicer indicated that #MeToo had struck a chord there. However, my discussion suggests the response to #MeToo in Australia has been lukewarm at best.

This chapter first provides an overview of three key manifestations of #MeToo in Australia—the naming of well-known Australian media men as perpetrators of sexual harassment and assault, NOW Australia, and the Human Rights Commission into Workplace Sexual Harassment. Following this discussion, I turn to the example of #LetHerSpeak, a social media campaign that sought to challenge the limited rights of survivors of sexual assault to speak out about their cases to the media in the state of Tasmania. The notion of "speaking out" has long been a practice associated with antirape activism since the 1970s (Serisier 2018), and creating opportunities for survivors to speak out on their own terms was arguably the main goal of #MeToo.[2] However, "speak-outs" have been heavily criticized for the problematic ways particular survivors' voices and experiences have been mobilized for instigating social, institutional, and structural change. In this sense, I use #LetHerSpeak to point to some of the complexities surrounding the nature and position from which Grace Tame (the survivor behind #LetHerSpeak) was able to speak, placing the discussion in dialogue with critiques of the politics of recognition and representation surrounding survivors of gender-based violence. These issues of recognition and representation manifested elsewhere in Australia's response to #MeToo, despite the opportunity that the movement created to actively engage with and prioritize the efforts, voices, and experiences of Aboriginal and Torres Strait Islander women (Ryan 2019). Ultimately, I suggest that although #MeToo had some success initiating policy responses and enabling some survivors to speak out, the manifestations of #MeToo in Australia reinforced certain privileges associated with representation and recognition that limit the scope of change.

Addressing Gender-Based Violence in Australia

Since at least the 1970s, on the back of second-wave feminism, Australia has been engaged with seeking to address the issue of gender-based violence. In 1974, for example, the Whitlam government initiated the Royal Commission into Human Relationships, with the terms of reference being broadly to "investigate the family, social, legal and sexual aspects of male and female relationships" (Arrow 2018, 82).

Although gender-based violence, such as domestic and family violence as well as sexual harassment and assault, were not the specific focus of the commission, it provided a public platform for women as well as support services to discuss the prevalence of these issues around the country (Arrow 2018). The Royal Commission was thus a significant turning point for establishing feminist vocabularies of gender-based violence in public and social policies (Arrow 2018). The fifteen recommendations that emerged in relation to domestic violence and the two subsequent studies commissioned by the inquiry into men's violence against women in the home have served as the backbone for Australian policy responses to violence against women (Arrow 2018; Murray and Powell 2011).

Despite this long trajectory of political recognition of and attempts to address the prevalence of gender-based violence in Australia, at least one woman dies at the hands of her current or former partner every week there (Bryant and Bricknell 2017). When I was preparing this chapter for publication in October 2019, five women were violently murdered by their current or former partner or by someone well known to them in the space of seven days (Dent 2019). In October 2018, ten women in the space of twenty-two days had been murdered under the exact same circumstances (Dent 2018). The frequency of such events seems to have engendered a banality about them—or at least rendered the public apathetic to the reality of gendered-based violence in Australia—despite a strong history of feminist and policy efforts to address this issue.

These staggering numbers, which are conservative compared to those in other parts of the world, are not just faceless but represent mothers, partners, sisters, friends, neighbors, members of the community, as well as the wide-reaching impact of their deaths.[3] The personalization of these figures in Australia has been made visible to the public through the Counting Dead Women campaign on Facebook and Twitter, which records and publishes the number of femicides nationally. The campaign goes to painstaking efforts to document and detail the circumstances of their deaths, utilizing publicly available data to ascertain information about the victim, the perpetrator, and the incident, giving them context and bringing the gendered nature of these crimes into clear view (McLean 2020). Research undertaken by Patricia Cullen and her colleagues (2019) has further corroborated the material published by the Counting Dead Women project, identifying that the majority of these women killed by their current or former partners had histories of documented violence against them, suggesting that stronger early-intervention policies could have prevented their deaths.

Beyond the number of femicides in Australia, the prevalence of violence against women is reflected in data collected by the Australian Bureau of Statistics. The findings from the most recent Personal Safety Survey (2016) highlighted that one in three women have experienced at least one form of gender-based violence in their lives since the age of fifteen, with one in five women indicating that this experience occurred in the previous year (Bryant and Bricknell 2017).[4] These acts of violence include domestic and family violence, intimate-partner violence, and sexual assault. Yet, despite this knowledge, the existence of gender-based violence continues to be treated with suspicion, and women who speak out are routinely accused of exaggerating, misinterpreting, and lying about what happened and are blamed for being raped or for inciting intimate-partner violence (see Fileborn and Loney-Howes 2019). These challenges are exacerbated for Aboriginal and Torres Strait Islander women in Australia, with Aboriginal women approximately five times more likely to experience domestic and family violence than non-Aboriginal women and thirty-five times more likely to be hospitalized as a result (Blagg et al. 2018).[5] The responses to and recognition of Aboriginal and Torres Strait Islander women's experiences of violence are even further undermined in Australia than they are for non-Aboriginal women. Like many First Nations women around the world, Aboriginal women in Australia in the colonial period were historically treated as highly sexualized and fetishized objects for the services of white men in ways that reinforced colonial entitlement, dominance, and ownership over their bodies (Conor 2013; Moreton-Robinson 2000; Ryan 2019). Sexual violence has long been a tool of colonization and imperialism. Aboriginal women's bodies, like African/African American and First Nations women's bodies around the world, are positioned as disposable and expendable—collateral damage necessary for advancing the project of colonization or slavery and establishing white European dominance. These tropes remain, with media reporting on Aboriginal women's experiences of sexual violence—in particular—in Australia continuing to position them in ways that render them unrapable or responsible for their victimization (Ryan 2019).

Such attitudes, including victim blaming and the disbelief of survivors, persist despite decades of feminist activism seeking to dispel these myths (Loney-Howes 2019; Serisier 2018). Although the latest National Community Attitudes to Violence against Women Survey (NCAS) from 2017 indicates that attitudes toward and knowledge about violence against women are shifting, problematic perspectives remain.[6] For example, 40 percent of respondents to the NCAS survey indicated they felt many women exaggerate their unequal treatment in Australia, and 32 percent believed that victims who do not leave their abusive partners are partly responsible for the violence if it continues. Attitudes toward sexual violence also continue to reflect strong beliefs in rape myths. For instance, 16 percent of respondents believed that women routinely lie about being raped. A further 31 percent agreed that women who claimed to have been sexually assaulted had "led the man on and later regretted it," and 42 percent of people who completed the survey believed that accusations of sexual assault were made as a way of getting back at men (Webster et al. 2019). These statistics and attitudes remain reasonably stagnant, despite a significant number of national, state, and territory efforts to engage in effective primary prevention as well as to implement evidence-based secondary and tertiary prevention strategies to better support women leaving violent relationships.

I mention these statistics as a backdrop to the arrival of #MeToo in Australia to demonstrate an already-existing yet contentious public dialogue, whether generated through efforts such as the Counting Dead Women project and the NCAS or not. In addition to these public efforts to demonstrate the prevalence of gender-based violence as well as the enduring problematic attitudes underpinning people's perceptions, it is important to note the political landscape prior to the emergence of the #MeToo movement. As mentioned earlier, since at least the 1970s there has been (some) political will to be seen to be doing *something* at the federal, state, and territory levels to address violence against women and children. Suellen Murray and Anastasia Powell (2011) offer a detailed analysis of the changes to Australian policy and legislation in this area from the 1980s until 2009. However, there came a significant turning point in 2010, when the federal government released the National Plan to Reduce Violence against Women and Their Children, which was to be reviewed every four years until its completion in 2022 (Nancarrow

2010). At the time the plan was drafted, states and territories had inconsistent strategies in place to respond to domestic and family violence as well as sexual assault. As such, the National Plan was developed to foster a deeper collaborative and consistent approach to addressing gender-based violence as well as to further fulfill Australia's obligations under international law and human rights legislation (Nancarrow 2010).

Beyond this particular policy landscape, other efforts to investigate the harms of gender-based violence emerged after 2010. In late 2012, for example, the Gillard government announced a Royal Commission to investigate institutional responses to child sexual abuse, which ran from 2013 to 2017 (Wright, Swain, and McPhillips 2017). Although this Royal Commission was not explicitly examining gender, it generated significant public dialogue about sexual abuse and institutional efforts to cover up and deny the levels of violence experienced by children in faith-based organizations, sporting clubs, and other care facilities. During the time this Royal Commission was sitting, Rosie Batty emerged as a national advocate for better responding to and addressing the causes of domestic and family violence (Hawley, Clifford, and Konkes 2018).[7] Following the widespread media coverage of and public response to the murder of Rosie's son Luke, perpetrated by his father, her former husband, the state of Victoria announced the Royal Commission into Family Violence, which ran from 2015 to 2017 and made 227 recommendations—all of which the state premier agreed to implement.

At the same time that there was increased policy attention directed at addressing domestic and family violence, reforms were being made in a number of states and territories to legislation regarding sexual offenses. Most recently, the state of Victoria introduced reforms to the Crimes Amendment Act of 2014, making a number of improvements to law on sexual offending, specifically the introduction of affirmative consent as well as additional support for judges to give jury directions in order to curtail rape myths and victim blaming from influencing decisions in rape trials (Larcombe et al. 2015).[8] Finally, as the Royal Commission into Family Violence in Victoria was wrapping up, the Australian Human Rights Commission released the findings from a nation-wide survey of more than thirty thousand university students at thirty-nine institutions in August 2017 about their experiences of sexual harassment and assault on campus (Henry 2019). The *Change the Course* report revealed that more than 50 percent of respondents had experienced sexual harassment at least once in 2016, 26 percent of which took place in a university setting and were predominantly perpetrated by someone known to the survivor (Gebicki et al. 2017). Against the backdrop of these policy reforms, legislative changes and public inquires have been substantial primary prevention frameworks developed by the research and advocacy groups Our Watch and Australia's National Research Organisation for Women's Safety (ANROWS), which have made significant progress in advocating for the recognition of sexual violence as caused by gender inequality.

Harnessing #MeToo in Australia

The aforementioned activist, political, policy, and legislative responses are not an exhaustive list—individual states and territories in Australia have crafted their own responses to the issue of gender-based violence, in particular family and domestic violence, that are beyond the scope of this chapter to address. Yet these responses are indicative of the social and political climate at the time #MeToo emerged. The release of the findings from the *Change the Course* report (Gebicki et al. 2017) investigating sexual harassment and assault on university campuses could not have been timelier for the arrival of #MeToo in October 2017, following Alyssa Milano's rallying call to get people to tweet "Me Too" in response to the allegations of abuse perpetrated by Harvey Weinstein.

Arguably, #MeToo in Australia manifested in three direct ways: (1) the naming of high-profile men in the entertainment industry; (2) the setting up of a "one-stop shop" to support survivors in the form of NOW Australia; and (3) the announcement of the National Inquiry into Workplace Sexual Harassment. However, the response to these approaches has been mixed, illustrating the contentious nature of #MeToo as well as the enduring challenges associated with addressing gender-based violence in Australia more broadly.

Naming and Shaming

In terms of the response to the individual cases of naming—or outing perpetrators—that emerged in the wake of #MeToo in Australia, there was significant resistance. Popular media presenters and actors Don Burke, who hosted a popular gardening television show, and Craig McLachlan, who gained public notoriety for his performance of Frank-N-Furter during the stage production and tour of the *Rocky Horror Picture Show* in 2014, were accused of sexual harassment following the emergence of #MeToo. Prior to the allegations, Burke had been earmarked by a number of people within the Australian media industry as someone to avoid, with journalist investigations revealing claims of sexual harassment as far back as the 1980s—although formal action was never taken (Knowles and Branley 2018).

Unlike Burke, McLachlan did not have an established reputation as a perpetrator of sexual harassment; however, both men denied any wrongdoing and sued the Australian Broadcasting Company (ABC), Fairfax Media, and the women who publicly accused them for defamation following the publication of the alleged offenses. In November and December 2017, shortly after the public outing of Burke and McLachlan, the *Daily Telegraph* published two articles claiming that the celebrated Australian actor Geoffrey Rush had sexually harassed a young female costar during the Sydney Theatre Company's production of *King Lear* in 2015. The articles, it was later claimed by Chief Justice Michael Wigney, were "highly speculative," and so the backlash was substantial. Rush sued the *Daily Telegraph* for defamation, seeking more than $25 million in damages. After a highly publicized trial in which Justice Wigney described the survivor as "not an entirely credible witness . . . prone to exaggeration and embellishment," Rush was awarded $850,000 in compensation for damages resulting from the loss of income (Whitbourn and Mitchell 2019); however, the decision was highly problematic both legally and politically (Ailwood 2019). I do not have the capacity to provide a detailed analysis of the case in this chapter, but it is worth noting that Justice Wigney's decision and subsequent description of the complainant relied on piecemeal documents that may not necessarily have met the rules of evidence (Ailwood 2019). Moreover, the survivor herself had not wished to go public with her experience in the first place and as a result lost control over the way her experience as well as her identity as a survivor were represented and responded to in the public sphere (Ailwood 2019). The upshot of this case is that the survivor's reputation rather than the alleged perpetrator's suffered irreparable damage.

At the same time, this example also illustrates the complexities associated with who can speak out about sexual harassment and assault and under what conditions. The response to the previous complaint is markedly different from the response to another claim made about harassment/inappropriate behavior allegedly perpetrated by Geoffrey Rush. I am referring to the testimony given by the Australian actress Yael Stone, star of the Netflix television series *Orange Is the New Black*. On December 17, 2018, an interview with Stone aired on ABC in which she spoke out about her own experiences of "inappropriate sexual behavior" perpetrated by Geoffrey Rush early in her acting career (Sales and Denness 2018). Unlike with the first allegations against Rush, which were made without the survivor's consent, Stone had significant control over her narrative, choosing to go public on her own terms while at the same time being very careful not to publicly accuse Rush of sexual harassment. Indeed, in her testimony Stone does not describe her experience retroactively as sexual harassment but rather frames it as a matter of public interest to talk about experiences like hers to highlight the power imbalances and specific vulnerabilities that create the conditions for sexual harassment to take place. In other words, Stone's interview and discussion of her experience offer an invitation to critically reflect on the boundaries of inappropriate behavior in the workplace rather than to incite a so-called witch hunt against individual men.[9] Unlike in the case published in the *Daily Telegraph*, there was little pushback against Stone—and, indeed, there has been much silence on her testimony since the interview aired, although Rush issued a formal public statement of apology in response to the allegations. He did not do this for the other complainant.

NOW Australia

Unlike in the United States, defamation laws in Australia heavily restrict survivors of sexual violence from naming offenders, and the response from the aforementioned accused celebrities illustrates the extent to which the law fails to take seriously the experiences of survivors. In addition, the cases highlighted the problems associated with power relations as well as lack of support systems and avenues of redress for survivors in the entertainment industry in Australia. Thus, when #MeToo emerged on social media, Tracey Spicer—a well-known journalist, media presenter, and self-proclaimed feminist—launched NOW Australia in collaboration with volunteers to help address and prevent harassment and assault in the workplace, primarily but not exclusively the Australian media industry.

Shortly after Milano encouraged survivors to tweet #MeToo, Spicer released the following statement on Twitter: "Currently, I am investigating two long-term offenders in our [Australian] media industry. Please, contact me privately to tell your stories."

Positioned as Australia's version of #TimesUp, NOW Australia was intended as a one-stop shop for survivor support-and-referral system and offered legal advice and connections to trusted journalists should survivors wish to take their stories public. NOW Australia was instrumental in highlighting the long-standing sexually inappropriate behaviors perpetrated by Don Burke, mentioned earlier as one of the "scalps" during the initial outing of offenders in the Australian entertainment industry. However, despite the well-intentioned approach by Spicer and those who joined the NOW Australia team, the project was relatively short-lived. In October 2019, a feature-length article was published on *BuzzFeed News* revealing that Spicer and the NOW movement quickly became overwhelmed with the number of submissions they received (Ryan and Rushton 2019). Spicer was quoted as saying she had expected to only receive "12 to 14 responses, not thousands" when she launched the movement (quoted in Mollard 2019), indicating just how unprepared the organization was to support survivors. The article also highlighted a lack of consultation from existing support services as well as the replication of existing services already financially stretched and underfunded rather than the offer of something new or different (Ryan and Rushton 2019). Furthermore, it was revealed that the organization had not been transparent with information about where the raised funds were being spent and on whom (Funnell 2019).

In addition, questions emerged over representation in relation to board members and others involved or associated with the organization. In June 2018, for example, on the cover of *Latte* magazine the image of those leading the charge of "dismantling discrimination" in Australia—specifically those involved in NOW Australia—featured only white women.[10] As mentioned earlier, in Australia the voices and faces of women of color have been markedly absent from public discussions of gender-based violence outside of a deficit approach that highlights the prevalence of violence experienced by Aboriginal and Torres Strait Islander women. Recognition of the prevalence of violence experienced by Aboriginal women is absolutely vital, and the whitewashing of #MeToo in Australia through this image in *Latte* magazine is illustrative of the continual erasure of Aboriginal women who work tirelessly on the ground to support and advocate for their communities (Ryan 2019). The erasure is not dissimilar to the way Milano's tweet, however well intentioned it might have been, marginalized the work of Tarana Burke, with NOW Australia entrenching white, corporate feminism as the face of #MeToo and thus leaving untouched the colonial, neoliberal, patriarchal structures that create the conditions for sexual harassment and assault to occur (Gill and Orgad 2018; Loney-Howes 2019).

Institutional Responses

Beyond the entertainment industry, the significant public response to #MeToo in Australia has driven interest in addressing institutional barriers to reporting and preventing sexual harassment in the workplace. In Australia, workplace sexual harassment is addressed as a civil legal matter under the Sex Discrimination Act of 1984, which was implemented on the grounds that sexual harassment affected productivity and to solidify Australia's commitment to the United Nations Convention on the Elimination of all Forms of Discrimination against Women (CEDAW) of 1979 (Thornton 1991). The effectiveness of the legislation has been questionable (see Thornton 2002, 2010), with #MeToo revealing how weakly it has addressed sexual harassment in the workplace as well as the widespread shortcomings and cover-ups within organizations and workplaces in their prevention strategies and responses to claims of sexual harassment. As a result, the Australian Human Rights Commission announced a National Inquiry into workplace sexual harassment, Respect@Work, as a direct result of #MeToo. The inquiry began in mid-2018, and the most recent update in July 2019 revealed that submissions indicate gaps in existing laws and legislation as well as inconsistences across different states and territories for reporting and providing redress for claimants (Australian Human Rights Commission 2019).

It is, of course, significant that #MeToo prompted the Human Rights Commission to investigate the deep-seated challenges associated with the prevalence of workplace sexual harassment. The Terms of Reference stipulated an emphasis on investigating the drivers of workplace sexual harassment, such as age, gender, sexual orientation, cultural background, disability, and Aboriginal and/or Torres Strait Islander identity. However, the inquiry is not due to conclude for some time, and it is impossible to determine at this point what the outcomes will be—or indeed whether the recommendations will be taken up and how successful they will be at instigating cultural changes within institutions. Moreover, it is unclear to what extent the inquiry is accommodated to workplaces beyond corporations and established institutions or to more precarious forms of labor that exist on the peripheries of the formal labor market, casual employees, or, indeed, small businesses or places of employment. For instance, to what extent has or will the commission investigate, address, and make recommendations for contexts in which women are situated in dangerous or isolating working conditions where power relations are structured in ways that make it impossible for them to report harassment or abuse? It is unlikely that the outcomes of an inquiry of this type will address the structural elements, such as neoliberal capitalism, that render women vulnerable to abuse and exploitation in the first place.[11]

In addition to Respect@Work, the most recent update to the National Plan to Reduce Violence against Women and Their Children has an increased focus on sexual assault following the impact of #MeToo. The latest plan (the Fourth Action Plan) endorsed by the Council of Australian Governments in August 2019 and due to run until the end of 2022, for example, repeatedly mentions the need to better prioritize the processes and policies in place when responding to sexual assault and makes the primary prevention of sexual violence a specific priority area. However, much of the discussion in relation to addressing sexual assault is lumped in with domestic and family violence. The contextual dynamics of sexual violence and harassment can and do differ from those underpinning domestic and family violence and require a spectrum of specific targeted responses in criminal justice settings, health care, and support services that address issues relating to the way first respondents treat survivors. Beyond institutional responses, the latest

National Plan acknowledges the role #MeToo has played in necessitating the importance "of survivors of sexual harassment and assault being able to come forward, tell their stories and be believed" (Commonwealth of Australia 2019, 32). However, the recognition, representation, and acceptance of a broad spectrum of survivors and their experiences are needed to break down the stigma, myths, and attitudes associated with sexual violence and to create opportunities for survivors to tell their stories in ways and forums they find meaningful.[12]

#LetHerSpeak

While the aforementioned direction responses to #MeToo in Australia have had mixed results, there is one clear example of an indirect yet tangible outcome, illustrating the opportunity #MeToo created for activists in specific local contexts to develop an interventionist framework or discourse and to pursue a more targeted agenda. The case of #LetHerSpeak emerged in 2018 on the back of #MeToo, seeking to challenge the laws preventing survivors from speaking out about their case, even after it has settled in court, in the state of Tasmania. The survivor Grace Tame initiated #LetHerSpeak, seeking to speak out about her experience of sexual assault perpetrated by her high school math teacher in 2010. The perpetrator was sentenced to two years and ten months in prison (he was released early) and served an additional four months in prison for creating and disseminating child-exploitation material after "bragging" online that Australian men envy him for having a "sexual relationship" with a girl seventeen years his junior (Knowles 2019). During the initial trial, newspaper reports and headlines sensationalized the case, with some suggesting that Grace, unnamed at the time, was complicit in the abuse and that it was consensual.[13] The issue of Grace wanting to speak out (or at the very least *speak back*) about her experience was further fueled following an interview given by the perpetrator to Bettina Arndt—an Australian woman who is notoriously antifeminist—in which he claimed to be the victim because he lost "absolutely everything" as a result of his conviction. This interview was then posted online, which Grace saw, but because of the journalism gag laws in Tasmania she could not speak out to challenge his retraumatizing and defamatory comments—despite having already waved her right to anonymity.

In response, Grace teamed up with the Australian feminist journalist Nina Funnell and started the #LetHerSpeak campaign, stating: "There can be no MeToo Movement in Tasmania" because of the persistence of elements within the Evidence Act of 2001 that prevent survivors from speaking out. At the same time, Grace had been fighting the Tasmanian Supreme Court to obtain a special exemption to speak out—to the cost of $10,000. The social media campaign led by Funnell attracted the support of the "leader" of the #MeToo movement, Alyssa Milano. Grace also gave an emotional yet powerful interview on the *7:30 Report*—the same program on ABC that aired Yael Stone's interview about Geoffrey Rush—on August 12, 2019. The campaign was incredibly successful: on October 20, 2019, the Tasmanian government announced that changes would be made to the legislation enabling survivors older than eighteen to share their stories, provided they have written authorization to do so (Blackwood 2019). Arguably, these legislative changes would not have been possible without the momentum behind #MeToo, and the #LetHerSpeak campaign is an indirect yet concrete success story of #MeToo in Australia.

#MeToo, #LetHerSpeak, and Addressing
Violence against Women in Australia

Grace Tame and Yael Stone's interviews as well the campaign #LetHerSpeak are exemplary of long-standing practice in antirape and speak-out advocacy—indeed, #MeToo more broadly is the latest iteration of public speak-outs since the 1970s (Fileborn and Loney-Howes 2019; Loney-Howes 2019; Serisier 2018). However, although #LetHerSpeak was indeed a "success" story of #MeToo in Australia, we should be cautious in our celebrations. In particular, we should be mindful of the privileges and conditions afforded to those who are given public space to speak out about sexual violence. Some of these critiques are reflective of the issues underscoring #MeToo more broadly as well as of other specific challenges that have arisen in relation to #MeToo in Australia.

One of the key foundations of antirape politics is that speaking out about personal experiences and breaking the silence will end the violence (Serisier 2018). In other words, speaking out does transformative political work in terms of preventing sexual violence as well as support-ing and validating survivors who speak out. Yet decades of speaking out has not reduced sexual violence or domestic violence, nor has it had a significant impact on shifting public perceptions about the harms of gender-based violence and the underlying political causes of violence against women. If anything, the response to and impact of survivor speech have become increasingly polarized (Serisier 2018), even more so in the wake of #MeToo (Rosewarne 2019). The backlash against #MeToo and survivors who have spoken out, in particular those who have targeted, with or without evidence, powerful men for their inap-propriate behavior, has culminated in suggestions that #MeToo has gone "too far" (see Fileborn and Phillips 2019 for a critique of this posi-tion). Some commentators have accused the movement of producing a sense of feminist hysteria and irrationality (Sommers 2017) and that it generated a sex panic by placing seemingly less serious offenses such as sexual harassment on par with sexual assault and rape and by advocating for new and more punitive laws to address the problem (Matthews 2019).

Overall, survivor speech is typically treated with suspicion rather than accepted as truth, and the response to the ways some survivors in Australia spoke out in public and within legal settings resulted in sig-nificant damage to their credibility. This was particularly evident in the experience of the survivor whose testimony was heavily (and unneces-sarily) scrutinized in Geoffrey Rush's successful defamation lawsuit. Yet she did not want to be publicly named or identified as a survivor, illus-trating to some extent why gag laws, such as those Grace Tame sought to amend, exist.[14] The case also highlights the great risks survivors take in going public with their experiences. However, Yael Stone and Grace Tame did not seem to experience the same level of trepidation in shar-ing their stories as the survivor outed in the *Daily Telegraph*, and, indeed, both advocated for increasing public discussion about women's experi-ences of sexual harassment and violence as well as greater acceptance of and support for survivors who speak out. Once a survivor's narrative enters into the public sphere, that person ultimately loses control of the story. Clearly, however, there are certain characteristics of survivor speech that render some more credible than others and therefore wor-thy of public support and powerful enough to engender structural reforms. Typically, these elements of recognition are afforded to survivors whose experiences fit within a specific subjectivity—namely, women who are white, young, cisgendered, heterosexual, able-bodied, and capable of telling a story of sexual suffering in a clear, coherent, and consistent way (see Fileborn and Loney-Howes 2019). Indeed, one of the key issues cited by Justice Wigney in Geoffrey Rush's defamation case was the inconsistency of the claimant's testimony across different sources of evidence, which he used as grounds for maintaining his position that she was an unreliable witness (Ailwood 2019). The real story of #MeToo and its origins in the activism of Tarana Burke and her work with African American communities in Alabama and other parts of the United States are now well documented. However, it took a white, powerful female celebrity's voice to draw attention to the issue, thus bringing into stark relief the long history of the erasures of women of color and their experiences of violence (hooks 2000) as well as of their role in antirape advocacy (Matthews 1994). We see the same logics governing recognition in relation to instances of speaking out about gender-based violence in the Australian context.

Given these ongoing challenges associated with recognition and representation, I question the extent to which Stone and Tame would have been as successful in publicizing their experiences and initiating legal reforms had they been Aboriginal women, queer women, or even simply white women with less social, cultural, and economic capital. A further issue is the way the example of Grace Tame reinforces the power of the law as the central site of judgment over the validity of experiences of sexual violence. Survivor speech acts directed at the legal system are often paradoxical.

On the one hand, they have sought to expose legal fictions and the law's ability and capacity to judge the "truth" of rape (Serisier 2018, 48). On the other hand, at the same time that activists dispute the authority of the law to pronounce judgments about sexual violence, they simultaneously turn to it as the site of reform whereby a "rewritten criminal justice discourse" remains the most appropriate place to hear, evaluate, and respond to stories of sexual violence (see Serisier 2005, 2007). Given that Tame's experience had already been validated as legitimate by the law, her turn to the law as a site of reform and change, even if for the purposes of speaking out, fails to acknowledge that very few survivors formally report sexual assault and that among those who do even fewer will receive a conviction that favors them (see Millsteed and McDonald 2017). Tame therefore occupies an elevated position of privilege given that the weight of the law is on her side, having already delivered a verdict in support of her.

In terms of public advocacy, the failure of NOW Australia to include women of color on its board of directors and the lack of the diversity in *Latte* magazine's story about the "Business Chicks," as mentioned earlier, is illustrative of the ongoing erasure of Aboriginal and Torres Strait Islander women's contributions to preventing violence against women in their communities (Ryan 2019). As I outlined earlier in this chapter, Aboriginal women are five times more likely to experience domestic and family violence, yet the public and political recognition of this violence is sidelined in favor of the voices and experiences of white women in Australia. For instance, the public face of domestic and family violence has been Rosie Batty—a white, middle-class woman, not an Aboriginal woman. #MeToo created an opportunity to intervene in shifting the conditions upon which survivors in particular could speak out and, more specifically, challenge normative assumptions about harassment and violence as well as the politics of recognition (Fileborn and Loney-Howes 2019). However, the uptake of #MeToo in Australia in terms of who has been seen, heard, and taken seriously has ultimately remained contained and restricted, reflecting the subjectivities, experiences, and politics of privileged white women. These issues of recognition and representation are bound up in the enduring legacy of colonialism that continues to perpetrate structural, cultural, and political violence toward Aboriginal and Torres Strait Islander women.

Voices from the queer community have also been absent in conversations about #MeToo, not just in Australia but around the world, because they are unable to speak out about experiences that challenge the heteronormative frameworks that underpin legal and cultural assumptions about sexual violence (Ison 2019). Older women, women with disabilities, and women in precarious working or financial situations have also not gained traction in public responses to sexual violence in the era of #MeToo in Australia. In this sense, #MeToo in Australia suffers from many of the same shortcomings it has throughout the world and in historical interventions that seek to shed light on the prevalence of gender-based violence. It is unclear to what extent the responses to address gender-based violence in Australia following #MeToo will also attempt to explore these intersectional issues of recognition and representation as well as to tackle the underlying structural frameworks that create the conditions for sexual harassment and assault to occur in the first place. Activists and advocates should continue to use the momentum generated by #MeToo in Australia and elsewhere to ensure that the parameters of recognition and responses to violence are diverse and intersectional.

The long-standing political investment in addressing violence against women since the 1970s as well as the strong presence of domestic and family violence on the public and political agenda upon the arrival of #MeToo in Australia suggested that there was a strong opportunity for the movement to make substantive headway. However, the responses to #MeToo in Australia have been mixed. The process of social change and legislative reform is often slow, and measuring the impact of social movements such as #MeToo is incredibly difficult beyond moments of mass mobilization. It will be some time until the effects of #MeToo become evident in social, political, and legal spheres. Indeed, the examples presented in this chapter point to the problems associated with knee-jerk reactions to complex social problems, illustrating the time and financial resources needed to properly and appropriately investigate effective approaches to addressing gender-based violence as well as to implement and evaluate prevention and intervention strategies. In this sense, reading the impact of social movements through the lens of "success" or "failure" or in temporal terms overlooks the broader context in which movements emerge as well as the politics of recognition and representation that underscores mobilization and response (Loney-Howes 2020). Although digital social movements such as #MeToo can incite outrage and quickly mobilize crowds to call for change (Papacharissi 2015), in order to address gender-based violence in the long term we need measured, evidence-based, ecological, and intersectional responses.

This chapter has attempted to wrestle with these complexities in relation to the impact of #MeToo in Australia by offering a broad contextual framework that sets the scene in which the movement arrived and made its presence felt in Australia. I then charted three specific ways in which the movement manifested in Australia: the public outing of men accused of sexual harassment in the entertainment industry, the development and subsequent shortcomings of NOW Australia in its attempt to help support survivors, and the championing of the National Inquiry into Workplace Sexual Harassment by the Human Rights Commission. I then turned to a discussion about the campaign #LetHerSpeak as an indirect example of the potential of #MeToo to instigate meaningful and tangible changes. However, we should be cautious in celebrating these "successes" of the movement. Although this chapter has not provided a detailed discussion about the complexities of these examples, it nonetheless raises some important questions about the challenges and limitations of both "speaking out" as a practice and about the positioning of institutions as the site of social, cultural, and political change.

#MeToo has had an undeniable impact in igniting a renewed consciousness about sexual harassment and violence around the world. However, the more painstaking task of social, cultural, institutional, and political change requires far more than survivors speaking out about their experiences. The privileges afforded to certain survivors with seemingly more authentic or curated stories in the public sphere will continue to stymie any efforts to broaden the parameters of recognition and representation not just in Australia but also around the world. Inquiries into workplace sexual harassment as well as the strengthening of existing violence-prevention and intervention frameworks are a good start. However, if the ultimate goal of movements such as #MeToo is to prevent violence against women, then the recognition and subsequently a complete overhaul of the discursive frameworks governing social, cultural, legal, and political structures is needed—structures that include but are not limited to patriarchy, colonialism, racism, heterosexism, and capitalism. All of these particular discourses intersect in ways that make tackling the issue of gendered violence in Australia challenging and heavily resisted, ultimately illustrating some of the reasons why #MeToo has been contentious in Australia.

References

Ailwood, S. 2019. "The Perversion of Consent in the #MeToo Era." Paper presented at the conference "Positioning the Politics of Consent in Law and History," University of Technology, Sydney, November 7–8.

Arrow, Michelle. 2018. "Making Family Violence Public in the Royal Commission on Human Relationships, 1974–1977." *Australian Feminist Studies* 33 (95): 81–96.

Australian Human Rights Commission. 2019. "Everyone's Business: National Workplace Sexual Harassment Inquiry." At https://www.humanrights. gov.au/our-work/sex-discrimination/projects/national-inquiry-sexual-harassment-australian-workplaces.

Australian Institute for Health and Welfare (AIHW). 2019. *Family, Domestic, and Sexual Violence in Australia: Continuing the National Story 2019.* Cat. no. FDV 3. Canberra: AIHW. At https://www.aihw.gov.au/reports/domestic-violence/family-domestic-sexual-violence-australia-2019/contents/data-sources-for-monitoring-family-domestic-and-sexual-violence/national-community-attitudes-towards-violence-against-women-survey-ncas.

Blackwood, F. 2019. "Let Her Speak: Tasmanian Government Announces Sexual Abuse Victims Will Be Able to Tell Their Stories." *ABC News,* October 21. At https://www.abc.net.au/news/2019-10-20/tasmania-government-sexual-assault-victims-law-change-grace-tame/11621164.

Blagg, H., E. Williams, E. Cummings, V. Hovane, M. Torres, and K. N. Woodley. 2018. *Innovative Models in Addressing Violence against Indigenous Women.* Sydney, Australia: ANROWS.

Bryant, W., and S. Bricknell. 2017. *Homicide in Australia 2012–13 to 2013–14: National Homicide Monitoring Program Report.* Canberra: Commonwealth of Australia. At https://aic.gov.au/publications/sr/sr002.

Commonwealth of Australia. 2019. *Fourth Action Plan to Reduce Violence against Women and Their Children (2019–2022).* Canberra: Department of Social Services, Commonwealth of Australia.

Conor, L. 2013. "'Black Velvet' and 'Purple Indignation': Print Responses to Japanese 'Poaching' of Aboriginal Women." *Journal of Aboriginal History* 37:51–76.

Cullen, P., G. Vaughan, Z. Li, J. Price, D. Yu, and E. Sullivan. 2019. "Counting Dead Women in Australia: An In-depth Case Review of Femicide." *Journal of Family Violence* 34 (1): 1–8.

Dent, G. 2018. "We Despair: 10 Women Murdered in 22 Days." Women's Agenda, October 26. At https://womensagenda.com.au/latest/we-despair-10-women-murdered-in-22-days/.

———. 2019. "Five Women Were Murdered in Australia in Seven Days." Women's Agenda, September 30. At https://womensagenda.com.au/latest/five-women-were-murdered-in-australia-in-seven-days/.

Fileborn, B., and R. Loney-Howes, eds. 2019. *#MeToo and the Politics of Social Change.* New York: Springer.

Fileborn, B., and N. D. Phillips. 2019. "From 'Me Too' to 'Too Far'? Contesting the Boundaries of Sexual Violence in Contemporary Activism." In *#MeToo* *and the Politics of Social Change,* edited by B. Fileborn and R. Loney-Howes, 99–115. New York: Springer.

Funnell, N. 2019. "MeToo Movement's Where to Moment." *Saturday Paper,* October 19–25. At https://www.thesaturdaypaper.com.au/opinion/topic /2019/10/19/me-too-movements-where-moment/15714036008953.

Garibotti, M. C., and C. M. Hopp. 2019. "Substitution Activism: The Impact of #MeToo in Argentina." In *#MeToo and the Politics of Social Change,* edited by B. Fileborn and R. Loney-Howes, 185–200. New York: Springer.

Gebicki, C., R. Pomering, G. Flynn, N. Grogran, E. Hunt, J. Bell, K. N. Raman, and A. Meagher. 2017. *Change the Course: National Report on Sexual Assault and Sexual Harassment at Australian Universities.* Canberra: Australian Human Rights Commission.

Gill, R., and S. Orgad. 2018. "The Shifting Terrain of Sex and Power: From the 'Sexualization of Culture' to #MeToo." *Sexualities* 21 (8): 1313–324.

Hawley, E., K. Clifford, and C. Konkes. 2018. "The 'Rosie Batty Effect' and the Framing of Family Violence in Australian News Media." *Journalism Studies* 19 (15): 2304–323.

Henry, N. 2019. "Universities Have Made Progress on Responding to Sexual Assault, but There's More to Be Done." *The Conversation,* February 11. At http://theconversation.com/universities-have-made-progress-on-responding-to-sexual-assault-but-theres-more-to-be-done-111343.

hooks, b. 2000. *Feminism Is for Everybody: Passionate Politics.* New York: Pluto Press.

Ison, J. 2019. "'It's Not Just Men and Women': LGBTQIA People and #MeToo." In *#MeToo and the Politics of Social Change,* edited by B. Fileborn and R. Loney-Howes, 151–67. New York: Springer.

Knowles, L. 2019. "Finally, She Can Speak: Her Abuser Could Speak Out. And He Did. Now, She Can Too." *ABC News,* August 12. At https://www .abc.net.au/news/2019-08-12/grace-tame-speaks-about-abuse-from-schoolteacher/11393044.

Knowles, L., and A. Branley. 2018. "Don Burke Accused of Sexual Harassment, Indecent Assault during Burke's Backyard Heyday." *ABC News,* March 26. Athttps://www.abc.net.au/news/2017-11-27/don-burke-accused-of-sexual-harassment-indecent-assault/9188070.

Larcombe, W., B. Fileborn, A. Powell, N. Henry, and N. Hanley. 2015. "Reforming the Legal Definition of Rape in Victoria—What Do Stakeholders Think?" *QUT Law Review* 15:30–49.

Loney-Howes, R. 2019. "The Politics of the Personal: The Evolution of Anti-rape Activism from Second-Wave Feminism to #MeToo." In *#MeToo and the Politics of Social Change,* edited by B. Fileborn and R. Loney-Howes, 21–35. New York: Springer.

————. 2020. *Online Anti-rape Activism: Exploring the Politics of the Personal in the Age of Digital Media.* Wagon Lane, Bingley, UK: Emerald Press.

Matthews, H. 2019. "#MeToo as Sex Panic." In *#MeToo and the Politics of Social Change,* edited by B. Fileborn and R. Loney-Howes, 267–83. New York: Springer.

Matthews, N. A. 1994. *Confronting Rape: The Feminist Anti-rape Movement and the State.* London: Routledge.

McLean, J. 2020. "Australian Feminist Digital Activism." In *Changing Digital Geographies: Technologies, Environments, and People,* edited by J. McLean, 203–28. New York: Springer.

Millsteed, M., and C. McDonald. 2017. *Attrition of Sexual Offence Incidents across the Victorian Criminal Justice System.* Melbourne, Australia: Crime Statistics Agency.

Mollard, A. 2019. "Tracey Spicer: '#MeToo Isn't about Me.' *Daily Telegraph,* October 28. At http://dailytelegraph.com.au/lifestyle/stellar/tracey-spicer-metoo-isnt-about- me/news-story/85817c220d5c33ef2e008b71cd26d20b.

Moreton-Robinson, A. 2000. *Talkin' Up to the White Woman: Aboriginal Women and Feminism.* Brisbane, Australia: University of Queensland Press.

Murray, S., and A. Powell. 2011. *Domestic Violence: Australian Public Policy.* North Melbourne: Australian Scholarly Publishing.

Nancarrow, H. 2010. "Time Is of the Essence: Progress on the National Council's Plan for Australia to Reduce Violence against Women and Their Children." *University of New South Wales Law Journal* 33 (3): 836–53.

New South Wales Law Reform Commission. 2018. *Consent in Relation to Sexual Relations: Consultation Paper 21.* Sydney: New South Wales Government.

Papacharissi, Z. 2015. *Affective Publics: Sentiment, Technology, and Politics.* London: Oxford University Press.

Rosewarne, L. 2019. "#MeToo and the Reasons to Be Cautious." In *#MeToo and the Politics of Social Change,* edited by B. Fileborn and R. Loney-Howes, 171–84. New York: Springer.

Royal, K. 2019. "Journalist Guidelines and Media Reporting in the Wake of #MeToo." In *#MeToo and the Politics of Social Change,* edited by B. Fileborn and R. Loney-Howes, 217–34. New York: Springer.

Ryan, H., and G. Rushton. 2019. "The Leaders of Australia's 'Time's Up' Movement Made Big Promises They Couldn't Keep." *BuzzFeed News,* October 18. At https://www.buzzfeed.com/hannahryan/metoo-movement-now-australia-tracey-spicer.

Ryan, Tess. 2019. "This Black Body Is Not Yours for the Taking." In *#MeToo and the Politics of Social Change,* edited by B. Fileborn and R. Loney-Howes, 117–32. New York: Springer.

Sales, L., and C. Denness. 2018. "*Orange Is the New Black* Star Yael Stone Makes Explosive Allegations about Geoffrey Rush." *ABC News,* December 18. At https://www.abc.net.au/news/2018-12-17/yael-stone-explosive-allegations-about-geoffrey-rush/10625916.

Serisier, T. 2005. "'Remembering Anita': Rape and the Politics of Commemoration." *Australian Feminist Law Journal* 23 (1): 121–45.

———. 2007. "Speaking Out against Rape: Feminist (Her)Stories and Anti-rape Politics." *Lilith* 16:84–95.

———. 2018. *Speaking Out: Feminism, Rape, and Narrative Politics.* New York: Springer.

Sommers, C. 2017. "A Panic Is Not an Answer: We're at Imminent Risk of Turning This #MeToo Moment into a Frenzied Rush to Blame All Men." *New York Daily News,* November 26. At https://www.nydailynews.com/opinion/panic-not-answer-article-1.3651778.

Thornton, Margaret. 1991. "Feminism and the Contradictions of Law Reform." *International Journal of the Sociology of Law* 19 (4): 453–74.

Webster, K., K. Diemer, N. Honey, S. Mannix, J. Mickle, J. Morgan, A. Parks, et al. 2019. *Australians' Attitudes towards Violence against Women and Gender Equality: Findings from the 2017 National Community Attitudes towards Violence against Women Survey (NCAS).* Sydney, Australia: ANROWS. At https://ncas.anrows.org.au/findings/#target_dl.

Whitbourn, M., and G. Mitchell. 2019. "Rush Set to Receive Millions in Defamation Victory against the *Daily Telegraph*." *Sydney Morning Herald,* April 11. At https://www.smh.com.au/national/geoffrey-rush-wins-defamation-case-against-the-daily-telegraph-20190329-p518ze.html.

Wright, K., S. Swain, and K. McPhillips. 2017. "The Australian Royal Commission into Institutional Responses to Child Sexual Abuse." *Child Abuse and Neglect* 74:1–9.

Notes

1. The name "NOW Australia" is not connected to the National Organization for Women but rather simply emphasizes the term *now.*

2. It is worth noting that the goals of the movement were never clearly articulated, which makes defining the #MeToo movement through a traditional social movement lens problematic (see Fileborn and Loney-Howes 2019).

3. See Garibotti and Hopp 2019 for a discussion about the NiUnaMenos (Not One [Woman] Less) campaign, a fourth-wave grassroots feminist movement that started in Argentina in 2016 in response to the number of femicides in the country and spread quickly to surrounding countries, such as Mexico, Chile, and Peru. Also see Muñoz Cabrejo's chapter in this volume.

4. The Personal Safety Survey has been run every four years since 2012 and collects information about the "nature and extent of violence experienced by men and women since the age of 15" from people ages eighteen and older in private residences across Australia. The survey captures experiences of intimate-partner violence, stalking, physical assault and sexual abuse, and general feelings of safety (Australian Institute for Health and Welfare 2019).

5. Although the terms *domestic violence* and *family violence* are often used interchangeably, in Australia it is important to note the distinction, particularly when describing violence experienced by Aboriginal women and girls. Whereas *domestic violence* tends to refer to acts of violence that encompass physical, emotional, sexual, or psychological abuse between two intimate partners, *family violence* is used to capture experiences of violence that happen in broader kinship relationships.

6. The NCAS is distributed every four years in Australia among adults ages sixteen years and older. It is the world's longest-running survey of community attitudes toward violence against women.

7. In 2015, Rosie Batty was named "Australian of the Year" for her advocacy work in relation to speaking out about domestic and family violence and was instrumental in shifting conversations about domestic and family violence away from being a "private matter" toward a discussion about gender inequality.

8. The Law Reform Commission in New South Wales also recently handed down the draft of proposed reforms to its rape laws in order to improve the reporting process and amendments to the legal requirements for establishing consent, as influenced in part by the #MeToo movement (New South Wales Law Reform Commission 2018).

9. Many public figures and journalists have described the #MeToo movement as a "witch hunt" (see Fileborn and Phillips 2019).

10. *Latte* magazine is a bimonthly publication produced by the networking organization Business Chicks.

11. Since the completion of this chapter, the Human Rights Commission has wrapped up the Respect@Work inquiry, releasing its final report in March 2020, which included fifty-five recommendations—none of which is binding, and all of which focus mostly on better education and training (https://humanrights.gov.au/our-work/sex-discrimination/publications/respectwork-sexual-harassment-national-inquiry-report-2020#0UPQW).

12. As of October 2020, the consultation phase for the next National Plan was under way; however, it remains unclear whether the federal government will *listen* to survivors and advocacy groups respectfully and translate their voices into substantive and meaningful policy reforms. If the past is anything to go by, this outcome seems unlikely.

13. The issue of media reporting on sexual violence has come under intense scrutiny since the advent of #MeToo, particularly for the ways in which jour-

nalism draws on particular myths and assumptions about survivors to make salacious claims that undermine their experiences (see Royal 2019).

14. Tracey Spicer came under further scrutiny for inadvertently revealing the names of survivors who reported their experiences to NOW Australia during a televised interview of her about the organization on ABC in November 2019.

2

Tackling Gender-Based Violence in South Africa

Organizing, Calling Out, Embracing #MeToo

Kammila Naidoo and Denise Buiten

South Africa has for some time held the unenviable position as a nation with one of the highest rates of sexual violence in the world, highest of any country not at war (Du Toit 2014). Although discussion of what has been labeled as "a war against women" has built over the years to achieve relatively ongoing media attention, analysis, and grassroots activism, its central space in public debate, political discourse, and mass action has been relatively uneven (Buiten and Naidoo 2016). Public debate has intensified in bursts, usually in response to particularly brutal or high-profile cases. The latter have included cases of baby rape (Posel 2005), the rape trial of then vice president Jacob Zuma in 2006 (Motsei 2007), and the horrific gang rape and murder of seventeen-year-old Anene Booysen in 2013 (Boonzaier 2017; Buiten and Naidoo 2016). However, political responses to these issues have been dishearteningly low, with government attention around key media cases initially erupting but soon simmering down. Further, although especially violent and brutal cases have tended to act as flashpoints for public attention on sexual violence, broader issues of sexual harassment have remained relatively marginalized as a lesser issue in the context of other forms of violence against women.

In the past three years, however, and in tandem with the global #MeToo movement and prosecutions in the United States, potentially significant shifts have begun to emerge. Local activism, research, and debate around sexual violence have long been occurring in South Africa (Gouws 2016). At a broader level, though, South Africa's public spaces have only recently engaged more fully with discussions and exposés of sexual harassment (Farber 2018; Madia 2019). As an illustration, in a dramatic moment in South Africa's labor history, 290 Lanxess Chrome mineworkers went on strike in June 2019, remaining underground for nine days in freezing temperatures, in protest against the long-standing sexual harassment of one of their colleagues. Their main demand, which management promised to accede to, was that the perpetrator of the abuse be suspended and face charges (Emdon 2019). Moving from the struggles of underground workers to the distresses of the corporate world, a study of sexual harassment in South Africa's formal business sector found that approximately one-third of businesswomen have been victims of unwanted sexual advances in the workplace (Columinate 2018).

In addition to growing attention to sexual harassment, the year 2019 saw the issue of rape and femicide explode into public spaces. On June 20, 2019, in offering his State of the Nation address, President Cyril Ramaphosa referred to the extreme levels of violence against women in South Africa and pledged to take more decisive action than ever before to turn the tide (Kgosana 2019). Soon after he gave this address and following a spate of documented femicides of women and girls during national Women's Month as well as a series of brutal rapes and murders of young women and girls, broad-based public attention to and action around gender-based violence intensified considerably. President Ramaphosa once again reiterated the government's commitment to curbing and reducing the high levels of gender-based violence. This time, though, emergency action plans were advocated, and 1.1 billion Rand (US$73.5 million) were set aside from state coffers to make these action plans work. As a show of solidarity, the president canceled his scheduled international trips (including one to the United Nations General Assembly), stating his intention to focus on the resolution of violence afflicting the country. At the same time, protest action intensified, and social media groups dedicated to issues of violence against women swelled at unprecedented rates. Media reporting on cases of sexual violence and femicide grew. Although these are significant signs, it remains to be seen whether and how such civil and political action will be sustained and implemented.

This chapter describes some of the kinds of violence experienced by women and girls in South Africa, drawing attention to the ways this violence is shaped by context. It focuses on selected realities that hinder progress in addressing violence against women and girls and that challenge the development of collective solidarities capable of pushing hard enough to effect change in this context. Part of this hindrance, we argue, is the tense relationship between local and global networks. #MeToo isn't "big" in many parts of Africa or, indeed, in South Africa because it is largely perceived as led and popularized by middle-class celebrity (white) women (Gouws 2019). However, we suggest that, despite political hindrances and tensions between local and international movements, public and networked practices of confronting or "calling out" violence and harassment are swelling, supported and emboldened by (though not indebted to and still distinct from) the international #MeToo movement. We suggest that an invigorated, feminist-informed, and networked set of solidarities and campaigns (local and global) within and outside social media can effectively create stronger prospects for change and gender transformation. To fully understand or implement change strategies, though, stronger contextually specific understandings are required (Buiten and Naidoo 2016; Gouws 2019), and this goal can best be achieved by recognizing and supporting locally specific movements. Above all, the point of the chapter is to emphasize that, despite challenges, much has been happening in South Africa to expose, confront, and address violence against women. These actions predate #MeToo and continue to strengthen against violent realities significant for South African women. Thus, even if there is currently no strong following of #MeToo in South Africa, there are vital and growing areas of synergy and connection. Locally informed movements draw from decades of African feminist struggle as well as from the experiences, networks, and wider set of debates enabled by the international #MeToo movement. As such, there are opportunities for both local particularities and transnational solidarities.

Key Issues Driving the Persistence of Gender-Based Violence in South Africa

In September 2019, protest marches throughout South Africa led by universities and nongovernmental organizations displayed the strongest solidarity and offered the harshest condemnation of gender-based violence after the body of University of Cape Town student Uyinene Mrwetyana was discovered. She had been raped and killed by a postal worker on the premises of a post office on a Friday afternoon, August 30. Within a few weeks of this event, multiple murders and rapes of women and girls were reported in the media: they included youth advocate and University of Western Cape student Jesse Hess, who was raped and murdered in her home; fourteen-year-old Janika Mallo, who was found raped and murdered in her grandmother's backyard; boxing champion Leighandre "Baby Lee" Jegels, who was shot dead by her former partner; twenty-one-year-old student Precious Ramabulana, who was raped and stabbed to death; and Lynette Volschenk, who was murdered allegedly by a man living in her apartment building. Throughout the period of the protests, the following question was frequently raised: Why do so many women continue to face violent assaults and insecure lives despite public condemnations and despite considerable educative and legislative work on gender, sexuality, and violence against women and children? The hashtag #AmINext, initially developed to draw attention to the high levels of missing and murdered Indigenous Canadian women, trended in South Africa and reflects the state of fear many women live in.

The most recent South African Demographic and Health Survey (*South African* 2016) reveals that one in five women older than eighteen has reported domestic violence. It has been reported elsewhere that the murder rate for women increased by 117 percent during the 2015–2016/2017 period and that sexual offenses in the same period rose by 53 percent (South African News Agency 2018). South Africa's femicide rate is said to be five times greater than the global average, and its rate of rape is among the highest in the world. Statistics from 2018–2019 show that one woman is murdered every three hours in South Africa. These annual police statistics also show that more than forty thousand rapes were reported in this period, one every thirteen minutes. Although reporting rates are notoriously difficult to ascertain, activists in the field suggest they are extremely low, some studies suggesting that as few as 3.9 percent of rapes are reported (Machisa et al. 2011). Further, the rape of children occurs at distressingly high levels, with 15,790 cases reported to police in 2015–2016 alone, approximately one every thirty-three minutes. Where research has been undertaken with men, it has revealed that a startlingly high number of men admit to committing sexual and other forms of violence against women (Gqola 2015; Jewkes et al. 2010). These kinds of statistics reveal how normalized sexual violence has become (Gqola 2007).

Various and complex factors may explain the extent and persistence of gender-based violence, but at least four can be highlighted. The first concerns prevailing *gendered public discourses.* "Women's empowerment" discourses in relation to the public sphere are not matched by gendered public discourses that reference the "private sphere" of, for example, home, sexuality, and family (Gqola 2007). South Africa's post-apartheid legislation and policy are firmly in line with the most progressive of international conventions designed to protect women's rights and entitlements. However, despite "women's empowerment" discourses, affirmation of rights "on paper," and the public visibility of women in Parliament, at universities, in the corporate sector, and in all spheres of society, media reports frequently remind the public of senior state officials who have engaged with impunity in violent acts and violent talk against women (Naidoo 2018). These officials include Jacob Zuma, who subsequent to his acquittal in a rape trial in which he actively espoused a series of rape myths (Motsei 2007) went on to become president for nine years, and current ministers of the country, accused of sexual assault and physical abuse. Whether in civil society or among leadership, "gender based violence is very ordinary: it is everywhere, commonplace, made to seem normal" (Gqola 2007, 118). Further, reporting and addressing violence are inhibited by a macrosocial context in which male-dominated practices, systems, and ways of operating linger and where women who fall foul of them are not afforded sufficient empathy or support (see, for example, Motsei 2007). Many women's groups thus call for more vigorous engagement with sociocultural practices and institutions that maintain male dominance, misogyny, predatory, and abusive practices as well as homophobia and heteronormativity. As Pumla Dineo Gqola has articulated, "The discourses of gender in the South African public sphere are very conservative in the main: they speak of 'women's empowerment' in ways that are *not* transformative, and as a consequence, they exist very comfortably alongside overwhelming evidence that South African women are *not* empowered: the rape and other gender based violence statistics, the rampant sexual harassment at work and public spaces, the siege on Black lesbians and raging homophobia, the very public and relentless circulation of misogynist imagery, metaphors and language" (2007, 115, emphasis in original).

Gendered public discourses can extend to the existence of mutated cultural practices that serve to oppress women and that persist particularly in some rural areas of South Africa. These practices raise complex issues around the role of contemporary patriarchies in shaping the ways cultural practices are manifested today and around the tensions inherent in addressing this role in light of strong historical reasons for distrusting the targeting of "culture." Here, one can mention the practice known as *ukuthwala* (coerced union), which entails the abduction or mock abduction of a young girl by a man and his associates with the intention to pressure her family into conceding to a marriage. Although in its original precolonial form the practice was regarded as a kind of elopement, necessitating mutual consent, it is often not so in its contemporary form, wherein it frequently involves the abduction of young girls for marriage to older men. In 2016, Statistics South Africa revealed that ninety thousand girls between the ages of twelve and seventeen had been married to or were in some kind of union with older men. *Ukuthwala* cases are often complex and reflective of a tension between legal requirement of consent and age of majority, on the one hand, and community views and rights to culture, on the other (Mwambene and Kruuse 2017). Further, these practices often throw up complexities and mixed messages in relation to consent within relationships (Mwambene and Kruuse 2017). However, given the number of cases that appear to involve coercion and lack of consent, the low number of convictions of abductors of young women and girls suggests toleration of this version of *ukuthwala*. There has been no strong criticism of the practice, even in its most coercive forms, from state officials, suggesting careful avoidance so as to not offend rural hierarchies. This is reflective of what Hannah Britton describes as a need to "walk the delicate line of working *with, within* and *against* the state to create change" (2006, 150, emphasis in original). The gendered politics around potentially problematic mutated cultural practices and problematic actions by leaders are indicators of entrenched contemporary patriarchies at the state level as well as of the tensions thrown up in addressing these patriarchies in light of colonial and apartheid processes that denigrated African cultures. These issues are compounded by the dearth of both research and public attention to the problem of gender-based violence committed by white South African men (Buiten and Naidoo 2016), which perpetuates the racialization of gendered violence and therefore also the tensions that exist around calling out violence in a postcolonial context.

A second reality pertains to what many graduate students frequently uncover in the course of their fieldwork: *dependency entrapments.* As indicated by the Centre for the Study of Violence and Reconciliation (2016), more than half of the women in the Gauteng province have referred to experiences of violence in their intimate unions, and about 80 percent of men in these studies admit to being violent toward a partner. Married women with children seem to be a high-risk category, but so too are all women who find themselves dependent on male support. In social ecological models, violence is viewed as more likely when rigid gender roles *intersect* with social isolation and male-dominated decision making and control of finances (Mpani and Nsibande 2015). Rendani Tshifhumulo and Pilot Mudhovozi (2013) refer both to social and economic dependencies that trap women in violent relationships as well as to the power of the socialization process in entrenching women's absence from key decision making around finances.

Transactional sex, or sex in the context of exchange for money or gifts, is also common in many parts of South Africa for a range of complex social and economic reasons (Mampane 2018; Masvawure 2010). Although women's agency must be acknowledged in this context, transactional sex is often characterized by male dominance (Zembe et al. 2013). It has also been associated with higher risk of violence due to the dependencies and power dynamics it relies on and fosters. Recent research on migrant women in Cape Town (Giorgio et al. 2016), for example, has shown that violence is more likely in the context of transactional sex and that levels of social support or isolation of those engaging in transactional sex play a key role in either protecting women from violence in these situations or increasing their vulnerability. Dependency entrapments are also evident in relationships based on transactional sex. Transactional relationships between younger women and older men (or "blessers") are fairly common and linked to short-term financial support. When violence occurs in these relationships, it can be particularly difficult for the women to speak out, not only because of the financial dependencies inherent in the relationship but also because of assumptions regarding the women's own culpability for the violence perpetrated against them in this context.

Religious and community leaders have recently also come under fire from some quarters for entrenching relationships of social dependency through conservative discourses around marriage and heterosexual relationships. Domestic violence is in many cases justified by religious or community leaders on the basis of a woman's inadequate performance as "a good wife" or of a woman's "rebellion" in not acquiescing to male leadership in a household. Domestic violence is normalized as indicative of a relationship in need of healing and reconciliation, including changed behavior on the part of the woman, and women are counseled to forgive and reconcile with perpetrators (Bassadien and Hochfeld 2005; Boonzaier and De la Rey 2003; Mshweshwe 2019). This kind of advice from authority figures can deepen social dependencies not only within the relationship but within the wider community, creating a powerful pull factor for remaining in a violent relationship.

A third problem involves the *inhibiting effects of scrutiny* that women fear when laying a complaint against an abuser and, simultaneously, the reticence and dismissive attitudes of service providers and law enforcement agencies. This is not new or unique to African settings but remains a deterrent in getting women, in particular those from rural or working-class backgrounds, to break their silence. The Tshwaranang Legal Advocacy Centre (2009) found upon investigation that the police in parts of the country were usually either not recording domestic violence or recording it poorly. Poor documentation has led to perceptions in some centers that the rate of sexual violence has in fact decreased. The police have also been found to be noncompliant and inconsistent in serving notices and warrants on perpetrators. Apart from the police, clinic and health workers attending to rape victims in public institutions are often described as unsympathetic and highly judgmental. Importantly, however, this factor varies according to the intersection of other social forces. As Tarana Burke, the woman who first used the phrase "me too," claimed, "Sexual violence knows no race, class or gender, but the response to it does" (quoted in United Nations Women 2017). The South African media have indeed focused to a far greater degree on urban, middle-class victims than on rural, working-class, or poorer women. Some younger, professional, or university-based women have found the confidence to make claims via the media, especially social media platforms, and these platforms have responded more empathetically and strongly to them. However, for most South African women, speaking out is met with intensified scrutiny, at times even contempt, and this response has had a chilling effect on calling out violence against women at a larger scale.

Inadequate legal protections for victims of gender-based violence who are brave enough to go through the courts contribute to the silencing of women. In late 2018, the rape trial of a pastor, Timothy Omotoso, remained headline news for weeks. Pastor Omotoso was charged with raping and sexually abusing Cheryl Zondi, a twenty-two-year-old student, from the time she was fourteen. Zondi is one of South Africa's first victims of rape to agree to have her testimony broadcast live on television. In the weeks leading up to the trial, she had to be protected by security personnel because there were numerous threats to her life. She was subjected to extremely tough and highly invasive cross-examination, giving the public full insight into how victims are scrutinized. Defense attorney Peter Daubermann asked her many times about Omotoso's penis and to explain how many centimeters she was penetrated. Interviewed after Zondi was cross-examined, one activist maintained: "They see what's happening with the Daubermanns of the world, re-victimizing you on the stand, not listening to you when you answer your questions honestly. . . . We're trying to say, 'stop dehumanizing us on the stand, listen to us when we speak'" (quoted in Gajanan 2018). Thirteen years earlier, too, South Africa had faced a similar scenario when Deputy President Jacob Zuma was accused of rape. His accuser, Fezekile Kuzwayo (Khwezi), offered painful testimony and faced a hostile reception from Zuma's supporters outside of court, some holding placards that read "burn the bitch" (Motsei 2007). Khwezi was interrogated about her sexual past and presented as mentally unhinged. Despite evidence that multiple sexual assaults are a reality for many South African women, Khwezi's assertion that she had endured rape on more than one previous occasion was met with accusations from the defense that she had a history of making up false rape claims (Motsei 2007). Her life in danger, she was eventually forced into exile after Zuma was acquitted, while Zuma went on to become president. Harsh and often misogynistic legal and public scrutiny of victims acts as a deterrent, inhibiting survivors from coming forward. In this context, the calling out of violence by *individual women,* who become public targets, is not likely to lead to change.

A further and most difficult problem to highlight is the relative absence in South Africa of a broad-based women's movement guided by feminist principles. This is not to suggest that activism and civil action in this space have been absent; instead, the problem is that feminist-informed action has to date lacked the necessary broad-based, popular appeal and critical mass to effect change in the face of the challenges outlined earlier. This absence of mass appeal, in part, has its roots in South Africa's political history, where nationalist movements centered race and class over gender as priority areas and where feminism has been regarded with skepticism as a form of cultural imperialism. In this national struggle, women's liberation was largely rendered a subordinate and potentially internally divisive issue, subsidiary to the larger quest for enfranchisement and emancipation from racial and class oppression (Britton and Fish 2009; Buiten 2016). Further, although there had been a rich history of women's political movements in South Africa, the "feminist" movement was skeptically regarded as Western-centric, and Western feminist movements were regarded as another source of racialized and classed oppression (Britton and Fish 2009; Buiten 2016). After 1994, when one of the world's most democratic constitutions was put in place by President Nelson Mandela's government, women's rights and representation in all institutions of the society were argued to be assured. What the Constitution did not ignite, however, were significant shifts in patriarchal ideologies. Addressing these ideologies requires redress to the historical position of gender and women's movements.

Civil society advocacy has historically always been strong in South Africa. A number of social justice groups were central to the drafting of the Domestic Violence Act (DVA) put in place in 1998 to protect women against all forms of violence—physical, verbal, emotional, economic—and to the incorporation of action against various configurations of abusive behavior, such as stalking, harassment, and intimidation. Although such acts and the policy put in place have been commendable, implementation has been weak. As an illustration, Shereen Usdin and her colleagues, writing two years after the DVA was implemented, acknowledged that "while the campaign achieved its major goal, numerous attempts by civil society organizations to impact on the content of the national instructions, guidelines and training of police and justice officials were less successful" (2000, 63). The challenge to effectively implement rights on paper can also be read as a challenge to muster a political will to champion the gender-based violence agenda. Cuma Limekaya stated in a report submitted to the president: "Political will is critical for an effective response to [gender-based violence]. It refers to the degree to which political leaders actively give attention to the issue and back up that attention with financial, technical and human resources. There is a perception of political weakness in South Africa to take effective measures to address [gender-based violence], meaning political leaders are not perceived to express strong commitment to [its] prevention or response" (2016, 68). The necessity, thus, for organized feminist actions to drive the implementation of policy on gender-based violence cannot therefore be underestimated.

As mentioned earlier, a range of historical and contemporary civil society action and activism, including related to gender-based violence, has existed in South Africa. However, organizations working in this space, although making important strides, have found eking out their role within the new dispensation to be challenging in particular ways.

The key challenges for gender-based violence organizations working with the state, according to Hannah Britton (2006), include accessing leadership, fostering political will while maintaining autonomy and an agenda capable of transforming the status quo, and avoiding becoming "technocratic handmaidens" of the state. Women's activism against gender-based violence in South Africa has also engendered varying levels and forms of feminist orientation. Amanda Gouws (2016), for example, has contrasted the Shukumisa campaign (a network of organizations addressing sexual violence) with the work of the African National Congress's Women's League, showing that although both worked substantially against gendered violence, the former presented a more feminist-informed lens and the latter a more nationalist-culturalist lens to understand the issue.

The International and the Local: #TotalShutdown and #MeToo

Organized protest actions led by women have been occurring in South Africa since the 1950s. They have almost always—during and after apartheid—been organized to protest against unfair legislation, socio-political inequities, or a lack of delivery of housing, water, or electricity provisions. Although networked women's organizations around gender-based violence, such as Shukumisa, have been active for some time (Gouws 2016), it is primarily since 2018 that women-led public demonstrations on a very large scale have been directed against violent men and have called on men in government to become proactive. In August 2018, at the start of what South Africans refer to as Women's Month, women in all provinces participated in #TotalShutdown marches intended to bring the country to a standstill. This organized action was a concerted attempt to draw public attention to the very high levels of gender-based violence endured in the country. The slogan that gained immediate popularity was "Enough is enough," which emphasized the need for strong and meaningful collective action, for solid leadership, for government to ensure that no men implicated in acts of violence against women be given positions in state structures, and for perpetrators of domestic violence, assault, rape, and femicide to be apprehended and sentenced. Couched in feminist vocabulary, the marchers' call was for an invigorated political will and for the president himself to be a visible agent of change, to be more vocal on the topic of gender-based violence, and to pay attention to the demands on the ground. It was argued that the amorphous patriarchal edifice would be difficult to dislodge (see Bennett 2001, 90) but possibly could be disrupted if identified and loudly tackled on all sites, whether in the home, the workplace, on campuses, or in public arenas. Thousands of women marched to the offices of the president to hand over their petition, but the president was at first not there to receive it. They were angered by his absence, insisted that he turn up and receive their petition, and waited until he did so. When he did arrive later in the evening, he promised to set up a summit before the year was over. He did so later in November 2018, and he has since then been regularly called to account for progress made; he has also been kept alert to incidences of violence on university campuses and in communities. When he addressed the protesting women in 2018, he reflected on the postapartheid democratic transition and lamented the persistence of violence against women in South Africa, suggesting that it represented a failure on the part of the state. A few days later he remarked: "The assault on the dignity and integrity of women has reached unprecedented levels. . . . [T]here is a real danger that because violence against women has become so pervasive . . . as a society we have gradually become unmoved and stopped seeing it [as abhorrent]" (Ramaphosa 2018, also quoted in Africa News Agency 2018).

The #TotalShutdown marches were precisely an attempt to resist the tendency to see the ongoing brutality of gender-based violence as "normalized," a reality to be shuddered at and then shrugged off. The National Summit against Gender-Based Violence and Femicide that the president was urged to organize was held in partnership with civil society groups. The summit created a convenient space for diverse groups of women to come forward and discuss their experiences and to openly refer to the ways they have been abused or suffered trauma. This difficult and complex process had many emotionally charged and defiant moments. It did, however, mark a new phase in feminist organizing in the country. Sinmi Akin-Aina refers to this feminist organizing as characterized by continuous efforts at "self-definition and re-definition" (2011, 66, 73). A redefinition seemed apparent in the way the broad but committed membership of supporters exposed selected cases of violence emanating from different settings and different women in the country but similar problematic experiences with regard to state and other institutional responses. In her writing, Akin-Aina (2011) raises fundamental differences among women seeking to work together—including nationality, race, class, and other identities. An intersectional women's struggle, as #TotalShutdown sought to present itself, offers an opportunity for mass-based and very different sisterly networks to come together with common purpose. A broad-based engagement would network with women across a large spectrum, acknowledging and recognizing their unique struggles and contexts and understanding that there would be constraints and possibilities with regard to how solidarities can be built and sustained. On September 24, 2019, South Africa's Heritage Day, protests were held in different parts of the world as South Africans abroad, women's groups, and their supporters joined to condemn the murder of Uyinene Mrwetyana. Thus, there seems to be opportunity in the current context for genuine and renewed feminist, networked sets of solidarities and campaigns crossing all boundaries but crafted in a way that is mindful of ongoing struggles and certainly of "respect for the paradigms and strategies that people of [different] areas have established" (Nnaemeka 2005, 57). Strategically, as already intimated, in the local South African scenario the preference has been for collective action, as in the form of country-wide marches and petitions to the state, to draw attention to the "generalized" problem and not to pinpoint or name and shame perpetrators on a large scale, as has happened through #MeToo in the United States and elsewhere.

Despite the challenges presented by difference, it would be vital to seek to build strong networked solidarities. Resilient, autonomous, feminist-informed movements against gender-based violence have been shown in various contexts to be more effective in creating change than women's representation in government (Weldon and Htun 2013). Gouws (2016) argues that this is certainly the case for South Africa, where the fact that 42 percent of government positions are filled by women has seemingly had little effect in creating substantive change in relation to gender-based violence. Working outside of or even alongside government has its challenges. As Laura Hartmann shows, "Women activists [in South Africa] are torn between publicly demanding their rights and jeopardizing the organizations they are running" (2019, 74). More "radical" agendas that call out and robustly challenge the status quo in this context may threaten or alienate government and affect financial and other forms of support, thus placing women's activism in a precarious and carefully negotiated position (Hartmann 2019). The support of networks, then, is ever more important.

Naming and shaming require confidence that is often linked to privilege and middle- to upper-class support bases. South Africa has had a few publicized #MeToo moments inspired by the global movement of 2017 and 2018. None of them resulted in the alleged perpetrators facing any consequences, and none received visible or substantial support from the #TotalShutdown mobilizations. Three prominent cases can be referred to. First, in 2017, the celebrated singer and songwriter Jennifer Ferguson called out Danny Jordaan, president of the South African Football Association, accusing him of sexually assaulting her in 1994. A second woman then came forward with allegations of rape against Jordaan. Jordaan defended himself, was not convicted of any charges, mustered enormous support from the South African Football Association, and eventually was unanimously reelected as its president. Second, in 2018 Nerisha Singh, director for risk advisory at the corporation Grant Thornton, laid a charge of sexual harassment against the company's CEO, Paul Badrick. Singh's charge led to further accusations of sexual harassment at Grant Thornton. After a drawn-out investigation, Singh was forced to resign, and the CEO was cleared of all charges. Third, a series of women, including Palesa Letlaka, Rosie Motene, Ingeborg Lichtenberg, and Nico Athene, accused the renowned film director Khalo Matabane of sexual assault, rape, and harassment. The various incidences of violence implicating Matabane have been covered in the media, but as yet no formal charges have been laid, and he continues to function as a celebrity. The grassroots activism that exemplified the start of #TotalShutdown efforts in August 2018 did not support individual women taking on very powerful men in national sports, the corporate sector, and the film industry. #TotalShutdown activists successfully raised the specter of violent husbands, gangsters, and criminals in largely working-class communities but stopped short of displaying the same unambiguous support for the middle-class women taking on high-profile men. The role of various identities of victims and perpetrators—in terms of class, race, ethnicity, age, educational status, sexual orientation, religion—is significant in defining attitudes and feeding into the gendered public discourses.

Titilope Ajayi suggests that "spotlighting movements like #MeToo has a way of obstructing our vision of longstanding mobilizations on the ground in various parts of the world against the same issues. . . . [T]here have been many significant movements tackling the same issues—even long before #MeToo" (2018). In addition to #TotalShutdown and #AmINext, we can mention #NakedProtests, led mainly by Black African women students who protested against university authorities' inaction on campus rapes. Further, although not yoked to the #MeToo hashtag, emerging solidarities via social media are demonstrating the capacity for networked action. Facebook groups set up to discuss issues of gender-based violence—some with memberships in the hundreds of thousands—have begun to organize around issues such as parole of sexual and domestic homicide offenders, mobilizing portions of their networks to turn up to court, sign petitions, and engage in other forms of action. These kinds of digital networks must be considered in the context of the #MeToo movement, which has heightened awareness around the visibility of and increased legitimation of gender-based violence as well as the possibilities of digital activism and has encouraged wider women's engagement with these issues. However, these networks are not derived from #MeToo but rather are locally contextualized networks shaped by not only transnational but also, in important ways, context-specific histories. As Gouws suggests, "The visibility of #MeToo makes it easy to overlook the very powerful campaigns against sexual violence that go on in Africa" (2019), and although most of these campaigns are happening outside the digital space, many are increasingly drawing on the possibilities of digital networking. This is something that can be strengthened if there is increased connection and synergy between existing social movements and digital campaigns, while still maintaining the connection to the specific contexts that have birthed and sustained the existing movements. #TotalShutdown, for instance, quite effectively drew on social media strategies popularized in other contexts to mobilize women into action for short periods of time. More uniquely, however, the original advert publicizing the countrywide marches that went out, via both traditional and new forms of media, declared the action to be "the Intersectional Women's March against Gender-Based Violence" and was supported by women of all races, ages, nationalities, and sexual orientations. This feature of the campaign was important in terms of garnering support and presenting a case for its local relevance and legitimacy.

As shown, state responses have indeed recently shifted due to the pressure applied by such collectivities. However, it is not so clear whether a more resilient digital activism that links up with transnational, global movements such as #MeToo can have a more fundamental impact on encouraging more effective and accountable law enforcement bodies that will result in the punishment of perpetrators. "Calling out" and speaking assertively require a sturdy network of support that many South African women have simply not previously had. The South African activist Makganwana Mokgalong wrote that revelation alone doesn't bring change—persistent on-the-ground confrontations of violence and misogyny do (International Association of Women in Radio and Television 2017). Globally, the #MeToo movement has indeed empowered many women in various parts of the world; it has captured imaginations and has given some women the confidence to speak up and direct attention to their own plight and to the magnitude of gender-based violence and harassment. Sporadic moments, though, are not enough to disrupt the edifices and embedded cultures that allow gender-based violence to continue. Energized and sustained networks of feminist scholars and activists are required to be active in theorizing, strategizing, and connecting across boundaries if there is to be any impact at all in addressing the scourge of violence (all forms of violence) against women today.

This chapter takes the position that although #MeToo has not been a major force or movement in South Africa, it has been inspirational for many and has prompted some women to speak out against sexual harassment and sexual assault. Gender-based violence has long been a serious and disturbing problem in South Africa, and a range of more radical actions against such violence has been taken up at different points, so we can challenge the need to measure South Africa's engagement with gender-based violence against the #MeToo yardstick. South Africa has had and continues to reveal its own local forms of mobilizing and activist organizing (see, for example, Gouws 2016; Michell, de Lange, and Moletsane 2018). Nonetheless, particularly in the context of implicitly sanctioned impunity around gender-based violence in political discourse and the severe backlash against whistleblowers and accusers for a number of reasons specific to the South African context, these actions and the calling out of violence have not been as strong as they could be. There is a reluctance to engage in transnational activism due to the issues identified—the nationalist struggle, struggles against racism, nonintersectional and elite feminist action against gender-based violence, and so on. The current strategy of calling on and demanding that the president of the country put mechanisms in place to deter violence and apprehend abusers is powerful, but there is much that South African activists can also learn from the #MeToo movement. Among the many lessons is the importance of further using digital platforms and other forums to tackle sexual harassment and other forms of gender-based violence and to support victims by helping to counteract backlashes, pushing for convictions of perpetrators, and improving policies and laws. Global networks of feminist scholars, connecting in a resilient and energetic fashion, will present new possibilities for intervening and effecting change. These transnational strategies and synergies, however, need to be embedded within locally birthed and sustained networks and understandings of gender-based violence to be both effective and legitimate.

References

Africa News Agency. 2018. "#Womensday: National Gender Summit Will Be Held End of August—Ramaphosa." At https://www.iol.co.za/news/south-africa/western-cape/womensday-national-gender-summit-will-be-held-end-of-august-ramaphosa-16477929.

Ajayi, T. F. 2018. "#MeToo, Africa, and Politics of Transnational Activism." Africa Is a Country, July. At https://africasacountry.com/2018/07/metoo-africa-and-the-politics-of-transnational- activism/.

Akin-Aina, S. 2011. "Bread, Butter, Culture, and Power." *Nokoko* 2 (Fall): 65–88.

Bassadien, S. R., and T. Hochfeld. 2005. "Across the Public/Private Boundary: Contextualising Domestic Violence in South Africa." *Agenda* 66:4–15.

Bennett, J. 2001. "'Enough Lip Service!' Hearing Post-colonial Experience of Gender-Based Violence." *Agenda* 50:88–96.

Boonzaier, F. 2017. "The Life and Death of Anene Booysen: Colonial Discourse, Gender-Based Violence, and Media Representations." *South African Journal of Psychology* 47 (4): 470–81.

Boonzaier, F., and C. De la Rey. 2003. "'He's a Man and I'm a Woman': Cultural Constructions of Masculinity and Femininity in South African Women's Narratives of Violence." *Violence against Women* 9 (8): 1003–29.

Britton, H. 2006. "Organising against Gender Violence in South Africa." *Journal of Southern African Studies* 32 (1): 145–63.

Britton, H., and J. Fish. 2009. "Engendering Civil Society in Democratic South Africa." In *Women's Activism in South Africa: Working across Divides*, edited by H. Britton, J. Fish, and S. Meintjies, 1–42. Scottsville, South Africa: University of Kwa-Zulu Natal Press.

Buiten, D. 2016. "South African Feminisms." In *The Wiley-Blackwell Encyclopaedia of Gender and Sexuality Studies*, edited by N. Naples, R. C. Hoogland, M. Wickramasinghe, and W. C. A. Wong. Milton, Australia: Wiley-Blackwell.

Buiten, D., and K. Naidoo. 2016. "Framing the Problem of Rape in South Africa: Gender, Race, Class, and State Histories." *Current Sociology* 64 (4): 535–50.

Centre for the Study of Violence and Reconciliation (CSVR). 2016. *Mapping Local Gender-Based Violence Prevention and Response Strategies in South Africa.* Johannesburg, South Africa: CSVR. At https://www.csvr.org.za/pdf/Mapping-gender-based-violence-prevention-and-response-strategies.pdf.

Columinate Insites Consulting. 2018. "Too Much #MeToo: Sexual Harassment in the South African Workplace." At https://www.columinate.com/2018/09/04/too-much-metoo-sexual-harassment-in-the-south-african-workplace/.

Du Toit, L. 2014. "Shifting Meanings of Postconflict Sexual Violence in South Africa." *Signs* 40 (1): 101–23.

Emdon, E. 2019. "Numsa Strike against Sexual Harassment Is a 'Powerful Moment in Labour History.'" *Mail and Guardian,* July 4. At https://mg.co.za/article/2019-07-04-numsa-strike-against-sexual-harassment-is-a-powerful-moment-in-labour-history.

Farber, T. 2019. "Half of Women in Science and Medicine Sexually Harassed." *Times Live,* June 30. At https://www.timeslive.co.za/news/south-africa/2018-06-30-half-of-women-in-science-and-medicine-sexually-harassed/.

Gajanan, M. 2018. "South Africans Rally for Rape Accuser After She Endured a Grueling Cross-Examination during Televised Trial." *Time,* October 18. At http://time.com/5428303/cheryl-zondi-omotoso-trial-south-africa-cross-examination/.

Giorgio, M., L. Townsend, Y. Zembe, S. Guttmacher, F. Kapadia, M. Cheyip, and C. Mathews. 2016. "Social Support, Sexual Violence, and Transactional Sex among Female Transnational Migrants to South Africa." *American Journal of Public Health* 106 (6): 1123–129.

Gouws, A. 2016. "Women's Activism around Gender-Based Violence in South Africa: Recognition, Redistribution, and Representation." *African Review of Political Economy* 43 (149): 400–415.

———. 2019. "#MeToo Isn't Big in Africa. But Women Have Launched Their Own Versions." *The Conversation,* March 7. At http://theconversation.com/metoo-isnt-big-in-africa-but-women-have-launched-their-own-versions-112328.

Gqola, P. D. 2007. "How the 'Cult of Femininity' and Violent Masculinities Support Endemic Gender Based Violence in Contemporary South Africa." *African Identities* 5 (1): 111–24.

———. 2015. *Rape: A South African Nightmare.* Johannesburg, South Africa: MFBooks Joburg.

Hartmann, L. 2019. "'Los my poes af': The Fine Line between Being Radical Enough and Being Too Radical." *Agenda* 33 (2): 74–83.

International Association of Women in Radio and Television. 2017. #MeToo South Africa. At https://iawrt.org/news/metoo-south-africa.

Jewkes, R., Y. Sikweyiya, R. Morrell, and K. Dunkle. 2010. "Why, When, and How Men Rape: Understanding Rape Perpetuation in South Africa." *SA Crime Quarterly* 34 (1): 23–31.

Kgosana, C. 2019. "10 Highlights of Cyril Ramaphosa's State of the Nation Address." *Times Live,* June 20. At https://www.timeslive.co.za/politics /2019-06-20-10-highlights-of-cyril-ramaphosas-state-of-the-nation-address/.

Limekaya, C. 2016. *Report on Diagnostic Review of the State Response to Violence against Women and Children.* Johannesburg, South Africa: Departments of PME and Social Development, KPMG.

Machisa, M., R. Jewkes, C. Lowe Morna, and K. Rama. 2011. "The War at Home: Gender Based Violence Indicators Research Project—Gauteng Report." *Genderlinks,* August 16. At https://genderlinks.org.za /wpcontent/uploads/imported/articles/attachments/13452_be gin_war_ at_home.pdf.

Madia, T. 2019. "Former PA Accuses ANC's Pule Mabe of Sexual Harassment." *News 24,* January 10. At https://www.news24.com/SouthAfrica /News/not-true-that-ive-chickened-out-of-sexual-harassment-hearing-pule-mabes-former-pa-20190110 (no longer online).

Mampane, J. N. 2018. "Exploring the 'Blesser and Blessee' Phenomenon: Young Women, Transactional Sex, and HIV in Rural South Africa." SAGE Open. At https://doi.org/10.1177/2158244018806343.

Masvawure, T. 2010. "'I Just Need to Be Flashy on Campus': Female Students and Transactional Sex at a University in Zimbabwe." *Culture, Health, & Sexuality* 12:857–70.

Michell, C., N. de Lange, and R. Moletsane. 2018. "Addressing Sexual Violence in South Africa: Gender Activism in the Making." In *What Politics? Youth and Political Engagement in Africa,* edited by E. Oinas, H. Onodera, and L. Suurpää, 317–36. Leiden, Netherlands: Brill.

Motsei, M. 2007. *Kanga and the Kangaroo Court: Reflections on the Rape Trial of Jacob Zuma.* Melbourne, Australia: Spinifex Press.

Mpani, P., and N. Nsibande. 2015. *Understanding Gender Policy and Gender-Based Violence in South Africa.* Johannesburg, South Africa: Soul City.

Mshweshwe, L. 2019. "Support for Abused Rural Women in the Eastern Cape: Views of Survivors and Service Providers." PhD diss., University of Johannesburg.

Mwambene, L., and H. Kruuse. 2017. "The Thin Edge of the Wedge: Ukuthwala, Alienation, and Consent." *South African Journal on Human Rights* 33 (1): 25–45.

Naidoo, K. 2018. "Confronting the Scourge of Violence against South Africa's Women." *New Agenda* 71:40–44.

Nnaemeka, O. 2005. "Bringing African Women into the Classroom." In *African Gender Studies: A Reader,* edited by Oyeronke Oyewumi, 51–65. New York: Palgrave.

Posel, D. 2005. "The Scandal of Manhood: 'Baby Rape' and the Politicization of Sexual Violence in Post-apartheid South Africa." *Culture, Health, & Sexuality* 7 (3): 239–52.

Ramaphosa, C. 2018. "Presidential Address at Summit on Gender-Based Violence and Femicide." November. At https://www.gov.za/speeches/president-cyril-ramaphosa-gender-based-violence-and-femicide-summit-1-nov-2018-0000.

South African Demographic and Health Survey (SADHS). 2016. Pretoria: Statistics South Africa.

South African News Agency. 2018. "Gender Based Violence on the Rise." June 19. At https://www.sanews.gov.za/south-africa/gender-based-violence-rise.

Tshifhumulo, R., and P. Mudhovozi. 2013. "Behind Closed Doors: Listening to the Voices of Women Enduring Battering." *Gender and Behaviour* 11 (1): 5080–88.

Tshwaranang Legal Advocacy Centre. 2009. "Implementing the Domestic Violence Act in Acornhoek, Mpumalanga." January. At http://www.tlac.org.za/wp-content/uploads/2012/01/Research-Briefimplementing-the-Domestic-Violence-Act-in-Acornhoek.pdf.

United Nations Women. 2017. "Executive Director's Blog Series: #MeToo Has Made Us All Responsible for Change—Sexual Harassment in the Workplace." At http://www.unwomen.org/en/news/stories/2017/11/op-ed-ed-phumzile-16days-day2.

Usdin, S., N. Christofides, L. Malepe, and A. Maker. 2000. "The Value of Advocacy in Promoting Social Change: Implementing the New Domestic Violence Act in South Africa." *Reproductive Health Matters* 8 (16): 55–65.

Weldon, S. L., and M. Htun. 2013. "Feminist Mobilisation and Progressive Policy Change: Why Governments Take Action to Combat Violence against Women." *Gender and Development* 21 (2): 231–47.

Zembe, Y. Z., L. Townsend, A. Thorson, and A. Mia Ekström. 2013. "'Money Talks, Bullshit Walks': Interrogating Notions of Consumption and Survival Sex among Young Women Engaging in Transactional Sex in Post-apartheid South Africa. A Qualitative Enquiry." *Globalization & Health* 9 (28): 1–16.

3

Changing Men and Masculinities in the United Kingdom and Beyond in the Wake of #MeToo

Stephen R. Burrell

#MeToo in the United Kingdom

The #MeToo movement has had a significant impact on public discourses in the United Kingdom. From the entertainment industry to politics, sport, and the workplace, it has highlighted the pervasiveness of sexual violence and harassment across British society and the extent to which it is embedded in its institutions. In the process, the voices of victim-survivors have been heard more widely perhaps than ever before, and public awareness of the problem appears to have been growing as a result (Fawcett Society 2018). This growth has helped to bring into question influential sexual and relationship norms based on male dominance, which prioritize men's needs and desires over women's. This chapter considers how the impacts of the #MeToo movement in the United Kingdom relate to developing efforts to engage men and boys in the prevention of sexual violence and other forms of men's violence against women.

Even before #MeToo rose to international prominence in 2017, after first being initiated by Tarana Burke in the United States in 2006, interest had been growing within policy and practice in the United Kingdom and around the world toward stopping violence and abuse from being enacted in the first place by working with men and boys (Flood 2015; Tolman et al. 2019). These efforts seek to address the roots of violence against women based on the recognition that the vast majority of violence in society is perpetrated by men and is closely connected to constructions of masculinity and men's structural dominance within patriarchal social orders (Flood 2019a).

The growth of work of this kind is directly influenced by feminist social movements such as #MeToo, which have challenged victim-blaming framings of men's violence against women, placed the focus on its root causes, and encouraged men to play a role in its prevention (Flood 2015). One example of this is how, in response to #MeToo and the #TimesUp campaign that followed it, a group of men in the US film industry, along with antiviolence activists, initiated a campaign entitled #AskMoreofHim. It called for men to "support survivors, condemn sexism wherever we see it and hold ourselves and others accountable" (Representation Project 2018). Another example is the conversations generated through the hashtag #HowWillIChange, which emerged in response to #MeToo and encouraged men to consider the role they play in helping to sustain rape culture (PettyJohn et al. 2018).

There has also been increasing public discussion in the United Kingdom in recent years about the harmful behaviors that rigid expectations of masculinity contribute to. This emphasis can be seen in the increasingly popular use of the term *toxic masculinity* to describe such harms (Gavey 2019) and in public interventions and writings by male celebrities, such as Robert Webb (2017) and Grayson Perry (2017). These conversations have arisen with a focus on a range of different issues—not least how expectations about what it means to be a man hold back men and boys themselves, such as by contributing to poor mental health and difficulties in seeking support (Ragonese, Shand, and Barker 2019). However, they have been particularly prominent in relation to men's use of violence, harassment, and abuse toward women, and in this respect #MeToo has played a significant role. For instance, Gillette's viral advertising campaign "The Best Men Can Be," launched in January 2019, sought to address harmful masculine norms and made explicit reference to the #MeToo movement.

To some degree in the United Kingdom, #MeToo does appear to have led more men to reflect on their own connections to issues such as sexual violence. For instance, a Fawcett Society (2018) survey found that more than half of people ages eighteen to thirty-four, including 58 percent of young men, said they were more likely to speak up against sexual harassment after #MeToo. Meanwhile, 53 percent of respondents felt that in the twelve months after #MeToo went viral there had been changes in the behaviors that other people think are acceptable, while only 11 percent disagreed with this. Yet there remains a sense that many of the people who most need to have these conversations—that is, men—are still not paying anywhere near enough attention. For instance, in the Fawcett Society (2018) survey, 43 percent of respondents were aware of #MeToo, thus indicating that more than half of respondents (particularly in older age groups) had not even heard of the movement. The survey found that 28 percent of men had had conversations with other men about sexual harassment in the past twelve months—a not insignificant number, but still only a minority. Meanwhile, there has been backlash from some men toward #MeToo (Flood 2019b), with, for example, the aforementioned Gillette campaign receiving considerable reactionary responses in the media and online. Calls for men to speak out, such as #AskMoreofHim, have also been relatively marginal and do not appear to have led to significant expansions in antiviolence activism among men to date.

This means that efforts to engage men and boys in the prevention of men's violence against women have much work to do to achieve serious and long-lasting change. This chapter is based on observations from research carried out between May 2016 and June 2017, while the #MeToo movement was rapidly starting to grow in the United Kingdom and many other countries. The study investigated the contemporary landscape of work with men and boys to prevent violence against women in the United Kingdom through fourteen expert-informant interviews with influential activists as well as eight focus groups with forty-five young men in university sports teams, exploring how they make sense of violence-prevention campaigns. These focus groups were facilitated with videos from campaigns to prevent violence against women, with the goal of enhancing understandings of how this work can be developed in the future.

The Political Dynamics of Violence-Prevention Work

Several organizations in the United Kingdom work with men and boys to prevent violence against women and to build gender equality, such as

White Ribbon (whiteribbon.org.uk) and Beyond Equality (beyonde-quality.org), and are connected to the global MenEngage Alliance (menengage.org) (Burrell 2018). This work forms part of wider violence-prevention efforts that women's organizations have been leading the way in developing—in schools, for example. However, compared to the size of the problem, work with men and boys in the United Kingdom remains piecemeal, localized, and underresourced. In one important step forward, relationships and sex education became mandatory for schools to teach in 2020, although it remains to be seen how effectively this vital part of the curriculum will be supported and delivered. The picture does vary significantly across the United Kingdom, with Scotland leading the way in developing work to prevent violence against women based on a gender-informed approach (Lombard and Whiting 2018).

Experts interviewed as part of this research highlighted a number of obstacles to building work to prevent men's violence against women in the United Kingdom. First of all, the influence of ongoing neoliberal government austerity measures has had a highly detrimental impact on antiviolence work, such as in the closure of domestic-violence refuges (Ishkanian 2014). By extension, it becomes even more difficult to fund prevention work if frontline services are struggling to survive. Compounding this issue has been the influence of "gender-neutral" framings of the problem (based on the notion that because men can be victims of abuse, too, services should simply cater to everyone in the same degendered way), which delegitimizes and depoliticizes specialist services for women (Ishkanian 2014). If there is a lack of recognition of the gendered roots of violence in the first place, it is also harder to justify specifically working with men and boys.

Finally, beyond some strong words, there remains an absence of serious commitment to or ambition for prevention work at the policy level, connected to the underprioritization of violence against women more broadly (Gadd 2012).

Achieving Structural Transformations

These obstacles point to a broader struggle facing violence-prevention work—that it is not sufficient to focus only on changing the attitudes and behaviors of individual men and boys. Although doing so is undoubtedly vital, it will not have lasting and deep-rooted impacts if the wider society and the structures in which we live our lives are not changing along with individuals' attitudes and behaviors (Salter 2016). This is a particularly sizable challenge for antiviolence work, given that these same structures obstruct the expansion of the activist work in the first place. It is therefore important to be realistic about what singular prevention initiatives can achieve. Although any opportunity should be seized upon, one-off, short-term, or single-level interventions are generally likely only to be able to create limited impacts on their own (Flood 2019a). Furthermore, they risk being tokenistic by enabling institutions and organizations to say they are doing something to address the problem even while they avoid making any serious changes to the gender inequalities embedded within their own structures.

The need for holistic, multilevel, systemic change therefore applies to organizations and institutions in the same way as to society as a whole (Peacock and Barker 2014). Although prevention campaigns, education, and training are important first steps, they must be ongoing and in-depth, involve the whole community wherever possible, and be accompanied by transformations in the systems and structures of organizations in terms of building gender equality in them and transforming the masculinized logics within that help to legitimize violence against women. For instance, in recent years in the United Kingdom universities have started taking steps to prevent sexual violence on campus as a result of pressure from students and staff (Chantler et al. 2019). This process has included introducing workshops on consent and bystander intervention, for example. However, institutions have typically failed to recognize a number of key factors in the issue: that there are connections between sexual violence and other forms of violence against women, such as intimate-partner abuse; that university staff can also perpetrate or be subjected to violence and abuse, which can be facilitated by university hierarchies; that violence and abuse are gendered phenomena in that they are predominantly perpetrated by men against women; and that they are perpetuated by dominant gender norms and systemic gender inequalities within the institution. Effective prevention work requires addressing all of these factors in order to truly be able to move toward university cultures that no longer tolerate or enable violence toward women.

This does not mean that engagement work with men and boys on its own is futile or unnecessary—quite the opposite. Indeed, critiques of work focusing on attitudes and behaviors can sometimes ignore the question of how structural change is actually achieved. How else can we cultivate transformations in social systems if not through the efforts made by collectives of individuals? It is therefore valuable to analyze the dynamic relationships between social action and societal structures in order to develop prevention work that can bring about real social change (Messerschmidt 2013). Furthermore, engagement work can play a crucial role in encouraging individuals to come together and collectively play a role in bringing about transformations, not only in themselves but in the social structures that shape their lives, as well as in illuminating how this is possible.

Building a Pro-feminist Movement of Men

Thus, a key focus for men involved in antiviolence efforts should be campaigning for considerably more serious and ambitious steps to be taken across the institutions of society toward ending men's violence against women. For those in the field of engaging men, it is vital not to lose sight of the roots of that work in social movement building and activism. Although the increasing professionalization of men's antiviolence work (Messner, Greenberg, and Peretz 2015) can in some ways be seen as a beneficial development (such as by enabling the work to be scaled up), this work must be combined with broader efforts to create and support feminist political and social change if the antiviolence movement is to achieve the kind of far-reaching impacts that are needed. Indeed, one of the central goals of engaging men and boys could be seen as recruiting them to a pro-feminist movement, which works in support of and solidarity with feminist efforts such as #MeToo to end men's violence against women.

It could be argued that #MeToo has helped place greater attention on the structures that underpin violence against women by illustrating not only how pervasive and normalized sexual violence and harassment are but also how embedded they are within many of society's institutions, which condone and facilitate that behavior (Gill and Orgad 2018).

However, it has also been suggested that #MeToo has been limited primarily to holding to account individual abusive men and that although this is important, it does not necessarily do much to change the underlying patriarchal structures that make abuse possible (Gavey 2019). Furthermore, the media focus primarily on the most extreme and high-profile cases, such as that of Harvey Weinstein, may help to reproduce the idea that sexual violence and harassment are enacted by individual "monstrous others" rather than being connected to the practices of men more broadly (Boyle 2019).

Reaffirming the Centrality of Gender

One crucial issue raised within the expert-informant interviews was that for work with men and boys to end violence against women to grow in the United Kingdom, the gendered dynamics of the problem need to be meaningfully recognized in policy and practice, and comprehensive prevention strategies must be devised on this basis. This means connecting violence-prevention work to a wider program of tackling gender inequality and the social norms that perpetuate it—including critical scrutiny of how these norms are embedded within and reproduced by policy itself. An important step at the policy level would therefore be placing a greater critical spotlight on the role of men and masculinities in a range of different public-health problems (Hearn and McKie 2008). We cannot stop violence and abuse if we are unwilling to confront who is responsible for it and why that is the case.

This means that it is important to consider the ways in which men continue to be constructed as the default, while their practices are simultaneously left invisible and unscrutinized within different policy discourses, including around men's violence against women. Otherwise, the onus will continue to be placed on women for stopping the violence they are subjected to (Burrell 2016). However, it is vital to avoid, as Jeff Hearn has argued (2012), recentering men in the process. This shift must therefore be built around elevating and listening to women's voices and experiences. Placing the critical spotlight on men and making men's gendered positions explicit should be based on the recognition that dominant androcentric discourses leave men's practices concealed precisely because they are assumed to be the norm in the first place (Hearn and McKie 2008).

The use of men's experiences of abuse to delegitimize feminist approaches to violence against women demonstrates how explicitly gendering men can risk recentering them in the discourse and thus again marginalizing women's experiences. In the process of advocating engagement with men and boys then, this must not become an end in itself, where the focus becomes solely on the detrimental impacts of patriarchy on men (McCarry 2007). One of the expert interviewees, Carl,[1] remarked: "There's now a sense, in the sector and among policy makers, that you always have to engage men and boys, you always have to have men and boys in the room, and that I think is troubling."

#MeToo has shone a light on the gendered nature of sexual violence and harassment due to the sheer volume of women who have come forward, primarily about abuse they have been subjected to by men. At the same time, the movement has illustrated that men too can be victims of these phenomena and that they can and should be able to share their experiences and receive support as well. It is entirely possible to advocate for male victim-survivors and address the struggles they face, which are heavily influenced by dominant masculine expectations, while recognizing that sexual violence and harassment are gendered phenomena, rooted in patriarchal inequalities. Furthermore, in showing that women can also be perpetrators, #MeToo has highlighted the need for theorizing that can make sense of the intersectional complexities of violence and abuse as well as the different ways in which people's lives are shaped by violent, dehumanizing patriarchal societies based on unequal power dynamics within interpersonal and structural relations.

Complicity and Defensiveness in Men's Responses

A key finding from the focus groups carried out with young men's university sports teams related to the ways in which it can be difficult for men to recognize or accept that violence against women is personally relevant to them. In conversations about violence and abuse, men can find a variety of ways to avoid reflecting on their own lives and practices and on how they, too, might be implicated in the problem. This is a serious obstacle for violence-prevention work because such a response can also stop men from recognizing the role they can play in creating change. One significant way in which this defensiveness arose within the focus groups was when participants disassociated themselves from violence against women. This meant that the young men could simultaneously pay recognition to the seriousness of the problem and feel that they don't actually have to do anything about it by implying that it is something taking place somewhere else, separate from their lives. One example of such a response is the "not all men" statement—the perception that violence against women represents a problem only for those who directly commit it and has little to do with men more generally—and this has been one common response to #MeToo (Flood 2019b).

Methods of Disassociation

There are at least three key ways in which men distance themselves from the problem of violence against women, as demonstrated in the focus groups. First, by disassociating from the violence itself, participants suggested that although it may be horrific, it is not something that they would or could ever do and therefore has little to do with their own particular lives. Second, by disassociating from "other" men and boys, participants implied that there is something about those men who do use violence toward women that makes them different in some way (stereotypes and scapegoating are often used here to associate violence with specific groups, such as men from working-class or Black and minoritized backgrounds). For instance, in one focus group Liam remarked: "Obviously as, well, I think I can call us educated young men, we see these things and we go, yeah, obviously, common sense, don't hit women. So, I think we're actually quite fortunate in that we're exposed to this kind of, you know, moral sort of thing, so we see that and go, yeah obviously."[2] The implication of Liam's comments is that there are "other," less well-educated groups of men for whom such views are not obvious.

Meanwhile, the third form of disassociation by the young men taking part in the research was from gender inequality more broadly, not perceiving it to be something that structures their own lives and interactions (which could include downplaying its existence in the first place).

It is easy to disassociate from violence against women (including for experienced antiviolence activists) in these ways because it is difficult to accept that our lives are shaped by injustice and inequality—especially when those relations are commonly taken for granted as the normal and natural order of things. However, such responses need to be overcome for men to become invested in ending violence against women. This means that prevention work must find ways of making the issue personal to men and boys and illuminating why it is relevant to their lives. To do this, I would argue, a three-pronged approach can be useful in helping men and boys to understand the interconnections among their varied experiences as individuals, cultural constructions of masculinity and gender norms, and the patriarchal structures of society (including violence itself as a structure). It is vital to illustrate how these different components of society shape our lives both personally and politically and how we in turn contribute toward reproducing and shaping them.

Disassociating from the problem ultimately serves to consciously or unconsciously protect the status quo in terms of the patriarchal privileges and norms that one accrues and adheres to. During the focus groups, two other defensive responses of this kind were identified. The first consisted of attempts to deflect attention away from men's practices (and, by extension, one's own practices), typically by shifting the focus onto men as victims of abuse. This deflection can serve to neutralize conversations about men's violence against women and the role men can play in ending violence (Dragiewicz 2011) and was another response to #MeToo with the development of hashtags such as #HimToo (Boyle 2019). Of course, this does not mean that men's experiences of abuse are not important or that they should not be addressed. However, the frequency with which conversations about the use of violence by men were shifted in this way within the focus groups (sometimes as soon as those conversations began) suggests that this may often be a defensive response rather than necessarily representing genuine concern for male victims. For instance, Isaac commented: "My first, thought of that, and I've seen it before and I was thinking that, it's only focused on men, being the perpetrators of domestic violence. Obviously it's probably more common for physical violence to be, carried out by men, but women can just as easily, create the mental sort of stuff, that was going on. So yeah that was my sort of, view on it, and probably why it had a number of dislikes, if people thought that too."

The third main defensive response to violence-prevention messages identified in the focus groups was the construction of the problem of men's violence against women as being in some way inevitable and unpreventable. This was often articulated on the basis that phenomena such as domestic abuse are somehow biologically rooted, based on "natural" gender differences. Melanie McCarry and Nancy Lombard (2016) found similar responses in research they carried out with young people and described it as "naturalizing" the problem. This kind of response may help to explain why there can be a particular focus on or fascination with violence perpetrated by women—because unlike men's violence it is perceived to go "unnaturally" against gendered expectations.

This response also highlights some of the cognitive dissonances that can be expressed when talking to men and boys about violence against women. In the focus groups with young men, contradictory perspectives were frequently expressed. These perspectives illustrated simultaneously the impact that feminist movements such as #MeToo have had on young people's understandings and the patriarchal assumptions that young people continue to learn from many aspects of wider society. For instance, many participants recognized the centrality of emotional and psychological abuse and control to intimate-partner violence and how it does not have to involve physical violence. Yet some of those same men would go on to state that partner violence was to some degree inevitable because men are "naturally" stronger and more aggressive than women: "Obviously, physiologically, men have you know, different kinds of hormones, that would make them, perhaps act out more, in terms of aggression. And so, although they may have that built into them, that yes we are equal, at the same time, the man is more likely, we're just going to lash out, whereas a woman wouldn't do that" (Ted).

Violence-prevention work can therefore create vital dialogues with young people that can help them to move beyond some of these cognitive dissonances (Watt 2007).

Complicity

The research suggested that the concept of complicity could provide one valuable way of moving beyond some of the defensive responses that men and boys express when encountering violence-prevention messages, as Bob Pease (2015) has argued. This means helping them to understand and recognize how men's violence against women and gender inequality are not phenomena that take place somewhere "out there." They affect everyone in society, and we all are implicated in their reproduction, even if we are not directly involved in perpetrating violence itself (Pease 2015).

Men's complicity can take a number of different forms. It includes the ways in which men can (perhaps often unconsciously) contribute to the social legitimization of different forms of violence through blaming victims, excusing perpetrators, and making light of the problem. This legitimization is also cultivated through the myriad ways in which men may contribute to a wider environment of sexism and misogyny, such as through the objectification and dehumanization of women within one's peer groups. Central to this legitimization and to men's violence against women itself is the everyday reproduction of patriarchal norms of masculinity and femininity. Men can also perpetuate the problem through the enactment and normalization of unhealthy and unequal gendered practices within their own lives and relationships. Practices of male dominance may not necessarily be violent or abusive but still constitute the foundations upon which abuse is built, and if we conceptualize violence against women as a continuum (Kelly 1988), there may be occasions in which most men have engaged in behaviors that lie somewhere on that continuum (Pease 2015). Finally, all men are implicated in violence against women because of the "patriarchal dividend" they derive from it due to the role it plays in maintaining men's structural dominance over women across society (Connell 2005).

These factors, all of which implicate men in particular (although women can of course be complicit in various ways, too), mean that violence against women is relevant and personal for all men, and they also mean that all men can play a vital role in helping to ending it. At the same time, it is important to recognize that male privilege is not equally shared; some men have more power to create change than others, and many also experience some degree of subordination as a result of gendered power relations *between* men as well as other of intersecting systems of inequality.

The focus-group research indicated that complicity can provide an important lens through which to build critical consciousness among men and boys about their positions within patriarchy because it is key to understanding men's role in both perpetuating and preventing the problem (Watt 2007). Focus-group participant Bruce elucidated this point: "Because I've been in positions, obviously I think probably everyone has, where someone's said something a bit inappropriate, and you think to yourself; probably shouldn't say that, but you know, I didn't do anything to stop it at that point. So I think it also highlights that, even just for people that wouldn't do it themselves, it kind of highlights, maybe you should [do something about it]. And that can be for everyone, whether they're actively abusing someone or not, has a part to play in stopping it."

By contrast, approaches to engaging men that focus primarily on reassuring them and avoiding feelings of discomfort may in turn fail to illustrate the ways in which their lives are intertwined with men's violence against women. Pease (2015) argues that focusing on men's complicity can provide a more impactful way of reaching out to them and motivating them to become agents of change. By illuminating how all men are implicated in the problem of men's violence, an emphasis on recognizing and resisting complicity has the potential to help develop a sense of ethical responsibility among men and a personal attachment to tackling the problem.

However, this development is unlikely to be achieved through simply telling men and boys that they need to change. Violence-prevention work should instead strive to create a dialogue, which helps men and boys to develop the skills to look more critically at their own behavior and that of their peers and to understand how it is situated within a gendered social context. Pro-feminist personal change is an ongoing, lifelong process, including for experienced activists. Even in-depth prevention programs cannot expect to produce antisexist men and boys on their own. This is why it is so important to cultivate the skills through which men and boys can learn to look at the world around them from a feminist-informed perspective long after their participation in an anti-violence program has come to an end.

Raising Men's Critical Consciousness about Patriarchy

At the same time, complicity with patriarchy can be a difficult topic to discuss. It can invoke feelings of guilt and shame as men become more aware of the problem, of their own role in it, and of how they are structurally advantaged by it. There is a risk that this approach could antagonize defensiveness because it may be perceived to carry a negative or condemnatory tone toward men. Even if such a tone may be warranted at times, it could push some away. However, it is possible to frame this issue in a positive manner that can offer men a sense of hope and, crucially, opportunities for taking action. Developing a consciousness of complicity can foster a positive vision of the role that all men can play and of the social action that is needed across society in order to end men's violence against women. Violence-prevention work can thus make the case that everyone has the potential and agency to create change in our own everyday lives. Such an approach can enable a balance to be found between genuinely challenging men and engaging them in a positive way that they can relate to, without alienating them in the process.

Addressing complicity can also help men and boys to make sense of their own positionality and experiences in relation to gender and violence. Men and boys may sometimes receive mixed or confusing messages from prevention campaigns in this respect, when on the one hand to avoid alienating them they may be portrayed as being separate from the problem—as "bystanders," for example—and on the other they are encouraged to feel a sense of responsibility to do something about it. Being open with men about complicity could therefore help them to understand more clearly what the problem is and how to tackle it. Such an approach means being honest about the realities of sexism and violence within patriarchy and placing trust in men and boys and their capacity to change.

By contrast, it could be argued that some of the anxieties about alienating men within violence-prevention work are potentially patronizing. The implication is that men may to some degree be incapable of understanding and recognizing issues of structural inequality, systemic violence, and collective complicity and how they fit into these things. Patently, the existence of male agents of change such as those interviewed as part of this study demonstrates that this is not the case, and setting a low bar for men in this way risks feeding into essentialist ideas suggesting that some men are inevitably sexist or violent and that those opposed to violence are somehow "distinct" from other men.

It's also important to make clear that the purpose of violence-prevention work is not to castigate individual men for their behavior. The point is that all men are likely to be complicit in men's violence against women and patriarchy to some degree. Furthermore, rather than constructing a divide between prevention practitioners and participants, it is valuable for those who are delivering prevention work to be as honest as possible about their own complicities, too. Such an approach could help to break down barriers between practitioners and the men and boys they are engaging with by demonstrating shared positionalities and experiences, which would diminish defensiveness. For example, engagement work can be treated as an opportunity to co-create new understandings with men and boys about the myriad ways in which sexist practices and assumptions pervade everyday life and how they can be challenged. This demonstrates the need for men involved in work to end violence against women to make a concerted, ongoing effort to reflect on their own attitudes and behaviors and to model taking ownership of one's complicity. This approach has the potential to cultivate a shared feeling of solidarity and support as well as a crucial sense of collective responsibility among men and boys for building gender justice.

It could be argued that one of the achievements of the #MeToo movement in the United Kingdom has been to initiate more conversations about issues related to men's complicity. It has brought under the spotlight a wider scope of behaviors beyond sexual violence itself and has helped to illustrate the range of forms that sexual harassment, coercion, and abuse can take as well as the kinds of practices that can feed into these things. It is notable that the movement has been criticized in some quarters for this widening of the scope, with commentators suggesting that #MeToo had "gone too far" by placing attention on behaviors that are supposedly not serious enough to warrant action, as in the case of Aziz Ansari (Hindes and Fileborn 2019). Yet my focus groups with young men suggested that this is exactly the direction in which discussions about sexual violence and harassment need to go in order to bring into question the wider range of unhealthy, unequal, or coercive practices that may not be perceived as rape or sexual assault but as being within an unclear "grey area" (Hindes and Fileborn 2019). These discussions necessitate highlighting and challenging the gendered norms and power dynamics that shape sexual (especially heterosexual) interactions and the patriarchal context in which they take place (Gavey 2019). For example, we must address how men's needs and desires often continue to be prioritized over women's, how men frequently remain expected to be active initiators "in charge" of and entitled to sexual interactions, and how women are considered passive or submissive recipients. Indeed, the emphasis on the concept of consent itself can risk feeding into these discourses, with its transactional connotations that one person gives and one person (likely to be a man) seeks consent.

Constructing Masculinities in Violence-Prevention Work

Fundamental to men's complicity in violence against women is the collective construction and reproduction of masculinities, which all men participate in and are affected by to some degree. My research, together with other studies in this area, highlights that masculine norms should be a central focus for effective violence-prevention work based on a gender-transformative approach (Peacock and Barker 2014; Tolman et al. 2019). Furthermore, the harmful consequences of pressures to conform to ideas about masculinity can provide an effective entry point to conversations about preventing men's violence. Expectations surrounding what it means to be a man is something that men can relate to, as is the normalization of violence and aggression in men's lives. These notions can provide a base of understanding from which to move the discussion on to violence against women as well as a clear justification for focusing specifically on men's practices.

Examining the individual and collective dynamics of masculinities can also mediate how men and boys make sense of and respond to antiviolence messages. Indeed, this can provide one of the first hurdles for engagement work to overcome: it may not be seen as "manly" to talk about issues such as violence against women in the first place. As a result, staying silent may seem the easier course of action. This view underscores the importance of creating a safe and supportive environment in which to raise these topics with men and boys, while also being prepared to challenge group norms within such contexts where necessary (for example, if some participants are obstructing their peers from exploring these issues).

How violence-prevention work itself constructs masculinity and gender is also significant. Within both the expert interviews and the focus groups, some participants took issue with campaigns utilizing normative ideas of masculinity to get their message across. For instance, in one focus group Tyler compared two different campaigns as follows: "One tries to, basically destroy this idea of like, social gendered constructs, whereas this one is trying to, with the best intentions, it reinforces those, distinctions, and probably, does more harm than good in that sense." This might involve, for example, claiming that "real men don't hit women" (Salter 2016) or using notions of heroism and strength as ways of appealing to men. Many men may agree with these kinds of claims. Yet, as Tyler makes clear, this approach can be counterproductive because rather than bringing into question men's investments in the same masculine expectations that feed into violence and abuse, it reaffirms them based on the understanding that they should seek to be a "real man" in the first place (Flood 2015). Reaching out to men by reproducing masculine notions of "rescuing," "saving," or "protecting" women, for example, risks reinforcing the deep-rooted patriarchal assumptions that underpin violence against women, such as the idea of men having "ownership" over women and thus needing to protect their "property."

Hegemonic forms of masculinity do not necessarily involve being violent toward women; indeed, they could include vocal opposition to it, as the "real men don't hit women" claim suggests. Raewyn Connell (2005) points out that hegemonic masculinity leads to the taking of men's dominance over women for granted so that violent behavior ceases to be necessary. Meanwhile, using coercion to maintain power over women may be seen as an expression of weakness, a lack of control, and thus of emasculation in relation to other men (Hearn and Whitehead 2006), while still being viewed as necessary if that dominance is brought into question. Appealing to men's existing investments in masculinity in order to prevent violence against women can therefore risk buttressing rather than challenging the workings of these gendered power dynamics.

It is thus not enough for prevention campaigns simply to encourage men to oppose violence against women. Many men would willingly express such opposition, yet this violence remains pervasive. Rather, campaigns must get men to understand that it is the culturally instilled belief, deeply embedded within men's psyches, of superiority over women that in turn fosters the assumption that men have the right to dominate women (or to "protect" them) within different spheres. Explanations that "naturalize" men's violence fundamentally allude to this belief. This is why the social construction of gender altogether is so harmful within patriarchy: while gendered norms and expectations vary depending on context, they are ultimately founded upon a hierarchical dynamic in which the masculine is defined as superior to the feminine.

Resisting Masculinity

I would therefore argue that a key task for violence-prevention work is to engage with men and boys to dismantle masculine norms altogether rather than simply to shift toward "healthier" or nonviolent forms of masculinity. People should not be expected to conform to a certain set of practices based around gender, whatever those expectations may be. This connects to problems with some of the ways in which masculinity has been talked about in the wake of #MeToo. For instance, although the increasing discussion of "toxic masculinity" is an important positive development, there are also limitations to this popular conceptualization because it suggests that there are only certain specific forms or aspects of masculinity (and, by implication, certain men) that are the problem. I would argue instead (akin to Stoltenberg 2000) that we need to think more critically about masculinity (and gender) as a whole and about the toxicity of men being required to conform to certain ideas about manhood altogether. Otherwise, it becomes difficult to separate out which elements of masculinity are toxic for which people and which are not. Furthermore, it is simplistic to suggest that it is only those men who adhere to the more toxic forms of masculinity who need to instigate change when elements of masculine norms that contribute to social harms are likely to affect all men to some degree, albeit in different ways in different contexts.

There is a similar problem with notions of "lad culture" that have become popularly used in the United Kingdom in recent years, particularly in relation to sexual violence at university (Phipps 2016). In my focus groups, focusing on "lad culture" at times appeared to allow participants to externalize the problem and detach themselves from it. The implication was that the issue was with a specific set of practices being enacted by some "other" young men rather than a problem of masculine expectations more broadly. Of course, there are many variations in forms of masculinity constructed within different contexts by different social groups. However, sexism and misogyny on campus are not limited to students who conform to norms associated with "lad culture," such as heavy alcohol consumption and participation in university sports (Jackson and Sundaram 2021). Suggesting that the problem lies only with these specific groups or forms of masculinity does not sufficiently challenge all men's connections to patriarchy. For instance, what about violence and abuse perpetrated by male university staff? In addition, it is important not to become so fixated on particular constructions of masculinity that it is an abstract, disembodied concept that becomes problematized rather than the actual practices of men (Hearn 2012; McCarry 2007).

The research also illustrated that the reproduction of masculine norms is not a simple, one-way process. Men and boys do not simply absorb ideas about masculinity and repeat them; they have some degree of agency to challenge these ideas and in some cases choose to do so. There were instances in my focus groups where the young men would question defensive comments made by their peers or critique manifestations of gender inequality, even if doing so risked their receiving opprobrium from their teammates. Feminist movements such as #MeToo play a significant role in enabling and encouraging these expressions of resistance to dominant masculine expectations. Violence-prevention work has a vital role to play in fomenting the questioning of gender norms among men and boys, such as by illuminating that this is possible, how it can be done, and that some men are already doing so. Many of the young men I spoke to did recognize the injustices of gender inequalities in society, yet they often saw these injustices in the abstract. The key is therefore to make such injustices personal and "real" to men and boys in order to motivate and show them how they can create change.

This chapter has highlighted some of the (still ongoing) impacts that the #MeToo movement has had in the United Kingdom in relation to work with men and boys to prevent violence against women and some of the issues facing the future directions of this work as a result. It illustrates the need to make the most of the momentum built by #MeToo in order to create lasting social change, not least by advocating for a significant expansion of efforts across society to stop men's violence from being enacted in the first place. #MeToo has highlighted another vital issue to take into account in the process of building this work: how personal it is. There have been a number of cases in which men within social justice movements, including men involved in antiviolence work or identifying as pro-feminist, have been found to be perpetrating sexual violence and harassment. These cases provide a reminder that any man can enact violence toward women and demonstrate how male privilege and entitlement, deep-rooted masculinized behaviors, and sexist and misogynistic attitudes can affect all men, even those well educated in feminist ideas.

The chapter also underscores how important it is to ensure that patriarchal inequities and practices are not replicated as more men become involved in efforts to prevent violence against women (Messner, Greenberg, and Peretz 2015). #MeToo asks of all men—including those already involved in antiviolence work or pro-feminist activism—to make ourselves accountable. It asks men to look at our own lives, behaviors, and attitudes and to reflect profoundly on how they are shaped by systems of inequality, how those systems may benefit us over others, and how we may consciously and unconsciously help to maintain them—as well as on what we can do to create transformations both within ourselves and in the world around us. None of us is separate from men's violence against women or from the everyday reproduction of patriarchal social relations—but that also means we all can and should play a part in fostering social change.

References

Boyle, K. 2019. *#MeToo, Weinstein, and Feminism*. Cham, Switzerland: Palgrave Macmillan.

Burrell, S. R. 2016. "The Invisibility of Men's Practices: Problem Representations in British and Finnish Social Policy on Men's Violences against Women." *Graduate Journal of Social Science* 12 (3): 69–93.

———. 2018. "The Contradictory Possibilities of Engaging Men and Boys in the Prevention of Men's Violence against Women in the UK." *Journal of Gender-Based Violence* 2 (3): 447–64.

Chantler, K., C. Donovan, R. Fenton, and K. Bracewell. 2019. *Findings from a National Study to Investigate How British Universities Are Challenging Sexual Violence and Harassment on Campus.* Preston, UK: University of Central Lancashire.

Connell, R. W. 2005. *Masculinities.* 2nd ed. Cambridge: Polity Press.

Dragiewicz, M. 2011. *Equality with a Vengeance: Men's Rights Groups, Battered Women, and Antifeminist Backlash.* Boston: Northeastern University Press.

Fawcett Society. 2018. *#MeToo One Year On—What's Changed?* London: Fawcett Society and Hogan Lovells.

Flood, M. 2015. "Work with Men to End Violence against Women: A Critical Stocktake." *Culture, Health, and Sexuality* 17 (2): 159–76.

———. 2019a. *Engaging Men and Boys in Violence Prevention.* New York: Palgrave Macmillan.

———. 2019b. "Men and #MeToo: Mapping Men's Responses to Anti-violence Advocacy." In *#MeToo and the Politics of Social Change,* edited by B. Fileborn and R. Loney-Howes, 285–300. Cham, Switzerland: Palgrave Macmillan.

Gadd, D. 2012. "Domestic Abuse Prevention after Raoul Moat." *Critical Social Policy* 32 (4): 495–516.

Gavey, N. 2019. *Just Sex? The Cultural Scaffolding of Rape.* 2nd ed. London: Routledge.

Gill, R., and S. Orgad. 2018. "The Shifting Terrain of Sex and Power: From the 'Sexualization of Culture' to #MeToo." *Sexualities* 21 (8): 1313–324.

Hearn, J. 2012. "A Multifaceted Power Analysis of Men's Violence to Known Women: From Hegemonic Masculinity to the Hegemony of Men." *Sociological Review* 60 (4): 589–610.

Hearn, J., and L. McKie. 2008. "Gendered Policy and Policy on Gender: The Case of 'Domestic Violence.'" *Policy and Politics* 36 (1): 75–91.

Hearn, J., and A. Whitehead. 2006. "Collateral Damage: Men's 'Domestic' Violence to Women Seen through Men's Relations with Men." *Probation Journal* 53 (1): 38–56.

Hindes, S., and B. Fileborn. 2019. "'Girl Power Gone Wrong': #MeToo, Aziz Ansari, and Media Reporting of (Grey Area) Sexual Violence." *Feminist Media Studies* 20 (5): 639–56.

Ishkanian, A. 2014. "Neoliberalism and Violence: The Big Society and the Changing Politics of Domestic Violence in England." *Critical Social Policy* 43 (3): 333–53.

Jackson, C., and V. Sundaram. 2021. "'I Have a Sense That It's Probably Quite Bad . . . but Because I Don't See It, I Don't Know': Staff Perspectives on 'Lad Culture' in Higher Education." *Gender and Education* 3 (4): 435–50.

Kelly, L. 1988. *Surviving Sexual Violence.* Cambridge: Polity Press.

Lombard, N., and N. Whiting. 2018. "What's in a Name? The Scottish Government, Feminism, and the Gendered Framing of Domestic Abuse." In *The Routledge Handbook of Gender and Violence,* edited by Nancy Lombard, 171–82. Abingdon, UK: Routledge.

McCarry, M. 2007. "Masculinity Studies and Male Violence: Critique or Collusion?" *Women's Studies International Forum* 30 (5): 404–15.

McCarry, M., and N. Lombard. 2016. "Same Old Story? Children and Young People's Continued Normalisation of Men's Violence against Women." *Feminist Review* 112 (1): 128–43.

Messerschmidt, J. W. 2013. *Crime as Structured Action: Doing Masculinities, Race, Class, Sexuality, and Crime.* 2nd ed. Plymouth, UK: Rowman & Littlefield.

Messner, M. A., M. A. Greenberg, and T. Peretz. 2015. *Some Men: Feminist Allies in the Movement to End Violence against Women.* Oxford: Oxford University Press.

Peacock, D., and G. Barker. 2014. "Working with Men and Boys to Prevent Gender-Based Violence: Principles, Lessons Learned, and Ways Forward." *Men and Masculinities* 17 (5): 578–99.

Pease, B. 2015. "Disengaging Men from Patriarchy: Rethinking the Man Question in Masculinity Studies." In *Engaging Men in Building Gender Equality,* edited by M. Flood and R. Howson, 55–70. Cambridge: Cambridge Scholars.

Perry, G. 2017. *The Descent of Man.* London: Penguin.

PettyJohn, M. E., F. K. Muzzey, M. K. Maas, and H. L. McCauley. 2018. "#HowIWillChange: Engaging Men and Boys in the #MeToo Movement." *Psychology of Men and Masculinity* 20 (4): 612–22.

Phipps, A. 2016. "(Re)Theorising Laddish Masculinities in Higher Education." *Gender and Education* 29 (7): 815–30.

Ragonese, C., T. Shand, and G. Barker. 2019. *Masculine Norms and Men's Health: Making the Connections.* Washington, DC: Promundo-US.

Representation Project. 2018. "#AskMoreofHim." At http://www.therepresentationproject.org/the-movement/askmoreofhim/.

Salter, M. 2016. "'Real Men Don't Hit Women': Constructing Masculinity in the Prevention of Violence against Women." *Australian and New Zealand Journal of Criminology* 49 (4): 463–79.

Stoltenberg, J. 2000. *Refusing to Be a Man: Essays on Sex and Justice.* 2nd ed. Abingdon, UK: Routledge.

Tolman, R. M., E. A. Casey, J. Carlson, C. Allen, and C. Leek. 2019. "Global Efforts to Engage Men and Boys in Gender-Based Violence Prevention." *Global Social Welfare* 6 (4): 215–18.

Watt, S. K. 2007. "Difficult Dialogues, Privilege, and Social Justice: Uses of the Privileged Identity Exploration Model in Student Affairs Practice." *College Student Affairs Journal* 26 (2): 114–26.
Webb, R. 2017. *How Not to Be a Boy.* Edinburgh: Canongate Books.

Notes

1. All participant names used in the chapter are pseudonyms.

2. Frequent commas in quotations from research participants indicate brief pauses in speech.

PART II

LAW, MEDIA, AND FEMINIST MOBILIZATION

4

In Singular and Plural Voice

#MeToo, Law, and Solidarity

Srimati Basu

As scholars of gender-based violence, we tend to set personal stories aside from fieldwork, though we know that our professional curiosities are profoundly shaped by such confusing or disturbing moments. However, I begin here inundated by experience, remembering the many ways that our lives constitute the fields we pursue as ethnographers and feminist scholars. This chapter works through dilemmas that arise from such histories, foregrounding the vulnerability, doubt, and reflexive engagement that are critical to feminist methodology.

October 2017 seems a very long time away, but it was early in the season of #MeToo avowals, and as usual I lagged behind in keeping up with breaking trends on social media. Still, like so many others I know across the world, I joined in with wistful solidarity to say:

> But of course, "me too." (I usually avoid ALL "post x in solidarity" requests.) Standouts include: neighbor with peeing fetish [I only hope it was pee], math tutor trying to play footsie, guy seeking German-speaking helpers for an event which turned out to be a call for young female bodies handing out flyers, guy who followed us to our high school pretending he was having a painful period, not to mention innumerable buses and markets and creepy family friends and relatives. . . . In fact, I often think of the day in eighth grade where we girls had a group epiphany of "me too."

The phrase "wistful solidarity" that I used to describe this post seems to include a sort of resigned shrug at the omnipresence of rape culture, steeped in memories of (undeserved) guilt and shame at the public recognition of our sexual bodies, bravado at having navigated and survived daily creeps, and decades of insouciant laughter that mark our sarcastic recognition of seamy realities, a catharsis of group ridicule. I notice how this list could have been interminable and that I seem to have picked some markedly surreal moments with narrative punch.

These moments loomed enormously large at the time in governing quotidian mobilities and in constituting our sexual selves and yet sound inappropriately loud and privileged to me when I set them in the framework of other traumas: whether the later knowledge of a close friend's silent struggles with incest by a famous father or my academic familiarity with legal cases (such as Mathura's rape in police custody that precipitated the feminist reform of Indian rape law). As Bianca Williams says of her own reactions, "But as I thought about the stories of rape and sexual assault of those closest to me, I wondered if my 'tame' encounters with sexualized violence even *counted* in comparison to theirs" (2017), I wondered about the voices or stories that ought to be center stage. I am noticing in retrospect that the absences in my own post follow a popular script: we seek to hold the street and the neighborhood and the workplace to account, while remarking little on family and kin. It's worth noting that my experience demarcates moments of caste and class privilege (school uniform, home tutor, foreign-language classes, homes with private spaces) even while inscribing sexual harassment as a ubiquitous gendered mode of exercising or leveling power. Rebecca Traister (2017), narrating a familiar litany of experiences that she chose not to pursue formally, raises a similar doubt about the enormity of her own experiences. However, she reminds us that the pernicious ubiquity of sexual harassment infects us all and hence that every iteration of #MeToo is an acknowledgment of that infection: "So, no, I was never serially sexually harassed. But the stink got on me anyway. I was implicated. We all are, our professional contributions weighed on scales of fuckability and willingness to go along, to be good sports, to not be humorless scolds or office gorgons; our achievements chalked up to male affiliation. . . . We can rebuff the harasser; we can choose not to fuck the boss. But in a world where men hold inordinate power, we're still in bed with the guy" (2017).

I experience #MeToo stereophonically: both through the resonances of such embodied experiences that demonstrate the operations of sexuality, power, and violence in the street, home, and workplace as well as through the lens of the skill set I possess as a scholar of gender, violence, and social movements. The former leads the way: my post, like others in those early days of the hashtag, was inspired by (and in solidarity with) a group consciousness-raising wave, with little thought to concrete questions of accountability, let alone concerns with the legal-carceral. It was unclear who *could* be held accountable for what, what laws could be pertinent, and what would be gained or lost in public avowals.

But soon my professional/academic/intellectual preoccupations were on high alert. I work on the legacies of feminist legal reform (laws of property, dowry, divorce, rape, domestic violence)—that is, on the transformations or failures that arise from such reforms being institutionalized. This makes me all too well attuned to the ambiguities of putting stock in legal redress. I have found it most useful to think about law as one of the tools of cultural negotiation, with complaints and claims being diagnostic of socioeconomic tensions. I have learned to be skeptical of relying on legal solutions while aware of the strategic significance of bringing an issue to legal notice (Basu 2015; Greenhouse, Yngvesson, and Engel 1994; Sarat et al. 1998). The emergence of gender-based violence as a globally recognized category of awareness and governance, transformed and "vernacularized" in its proliferation at national and local scales (Merry 2006), has helped in negotiating through law. Putting these two parts of my reckoning together, this chapter contemplates whether #MeToo is a moment or a movement or a modality. Thinking with the nodes of law, sex, and feminism, I argue for #MeToo as an articulation of intersectional issues of sex, consent, and power in the shadow of law.

A Name, a Wave, a Whimper?

Our understandings of the scope and import of #MeToo are still inchoate and incomplete: Is it an uncoordinated set of individual pushbacks with domino effects? Or is it a transnational social movement across various professions and nations? A critique of seemingly neutral performance expectations in education or jobs? An indictment of the shortcomings of feminist interventions in law? Every piece written on #MeToo seems to seize on a different worry or triumph. In this section,

I lay out some of these pieces to give a sense of #MeToo's varied reception in feminist quarters.

Some writers appear buoyed by the very disjointedness in the affective passion of the movement, welcoming the absence of a singular organizing structure or a manifesto of demands. Supriya Nair deems the movement's very essence to be broadly revolutionary rather than narrowly legalistic: "#MeToo isn't cut and dried, and can't be. It was never simply about finding legal recourse; from the beginning, it has concerned itself with exposing a social faultline. . . . [T]he point is to lay bare the social conditions that render these misdemeanours trivial, even acceptable, even though they hurt and degrade their victims" (2018). Sarah Jaffe, in similar vein, argues for the movement as an organic critique of the failure of law and state, as a collective coming to voice: "The structures of the legal system and the workplace did not change. Instead, tens of thousands of women said yes, me too. Then, rather than wait for men to absorb that knowledge and decide whether to change or not, they started naming names. And making lists. And talking to each other. That's how organizing starts, after all. It starts with people talking about the conditions of their lives, realizing that they are common, and that they want them to change. It starts with enough people joining the conversation that they begin to believe that they can win" (2018, 81).

In these accounts, to use Nair's adjectives, #MeToo is "anarchic," "aggregative," powerful *because of* its metonymic and associational power. Some iterations of #MeToo reflect this perspective in the ways they address local specificities and call out everyday silences around work, space, body, and violence. Similarly, Farnush Ghadery's (2019) bold characterization of #MeToo as a transnational *feminist* movement dismisses critiques of it as neoliberal or individualistic and argues that it is part of histories of feminist consciousness-raising moments in various countries.

But feminist skepticism seems almost as prevalent as such buoyant faith: the wariness spans concerns about fleeting media fashion, limited inscriptions of violence, and individualized remedies. Dubravka Zarkov and Kathy Davis "do not see that things have changed for the better since the 1970s regarding the voyeuristic, sexist and misogynist nature of our societies," a failure best exemplified by victims' enduring difficulties with prosecution, new laws notwithstanding (2018, 4). They unfavorably contrast the prominence of "rich, powerful and famous celebrities" (5) and their social media following in the present moment with the mass collective protests of the 1970s, wary of the ways that sensational and sexualized detail eclipse the swath of everyday narratives. Rosalind Gill and Shani Orgad similarly critique the exclusions by race and gender identity as well as the overdetermined emphasis on workplace harassment over other forms of privatized violence, while also interrogating the nature of mediated discourse: "[The limitation] concerns the question of whether the movement's popularity and visibility are indeed due to its call for justice, or due to the salacious content of the stories it has brought to light. To put it somewhat crudely, is it sexism or sex that 'sell'? How should we understand the role of a mainstream media that suddenly seems [*sic*] to believe (some) women, after decades of trivialising and undermining us?" ([2018] 2019, 6). In contrast to those who tout the enabling possibilities of global infection through media, these scholars emphasize the difficulty of bringing to notice nuances that do not catch the sensational imagination, hence the challenges of feminist resistances setting their own terms.

The enthusiasm for seeing the downfall of the rich and famous may, indeed, be counterproductive if the (often temporary) punishment provides a salve that stalls more sustained change. Ann Pellegrini (2018) and Aswini Tambe (2017) articulate a popular feeling in the United States that Donald Trump's election, despite or because of his predatory disdain for consent to sexual behavior, precipitated the social process of women finding voice for their silence and anger, a "facilitative displacement" in Pellegrini's words (2018, 263). Pellegrini remains concerned about "what comes after #MeToo," echoing the concern expressed by Tarana Burke, who coined the concept "me too": despite occasional job losses or a few legal cases for perpetrators of violence, the worry is that such punitive measures will not result in changing norms of justice or violation and will not help process trauma. A recent poignant article in *The Cut,* "Was It Worth It?," demonstrates through twenty-five testimonials that those who spoke out now live with little improvement in their situation, with feelings of letdown at best, and with danger, harassment, and drastic effects on job stability at worst. These survivors are keenly aware of how little has shifted even when they don't second-guess their decision to speak out (Carmon and Schonbek 2019). Jia Tolentino argues that the prompt backlash that followed victims' avowals reconsolidated and strengthened patriarchal solidarities: "It will be said that [Brett] Kavanaugh was confirmed [for a seat on the US Supreme Court] despite the #MeToo movement. It would be at least as accurate to say that he was confirmed *because* of it. Women's speech—and the fact that we are now listening to it—has enraged men in a way that makes them determined to re-establish the longstanding hierarchy of power in America" (2018).

We are likely premature in diagnoses here as we try to respond and analyze in real time, but we might consider the affective salience of the phenomenon through this range of responses. Deborah Gould (2012), studying emotion in politics, emphasizes the infectious transmission of energy in the political desire to hear people speak, even when it's not clear what horizons are in view.

The Facebook statistics that "50 percent of US users are friends with someone who posted a message about experiences of assault or harassment" and that "Facebook and Twitter feeds . . . in Sweden, India, and Japan, were rocked for days" with similar posts convey a sense of this viral energy (Tambe 2018, 197). Gould contends that diffuse but visceral affect, rather than orchestrated political goals, are typical of emergent protests: "social movements as spaces of worldmaking, producing sentiments, ideas, values and practices, [the] euphoria of knowing your own and others' capacities and energies" (2012, 21). #MeToo fits Gould's characterization well both in the enthusiasm for pluralities and in the cautions and predictions of backlash. Thus, its significance may lie not in the details of outrage and redress so much as in the local and global feminist pragmatics of what it means to say "me too." As the linguistic anthropologist Anna Babel compellingly asserts, "Women are not simply remarking that it is a hard, cold world out there; we are asking you to shut the window, and the door, too. You have heard our stories and they belong to you too" (2018, 71). In Babel's view, the phenomenon may resemble a whisper campaign among friends, a familiar device across centuries "both to give other women sustenance and to arm them with information" (71) Beyond that, she contends, the iteration of #MeToo is saturated with a cumulative excess of affective mourning, a cry for cultural and structural change.

Law

What good is the law? How far can law take us? As the previous section indicates, worries about #MeToo have centered around the thorny question of translating grievances effectively and the incipient contradictions with feminist goals of justice. In this section, I consider how to think about #MeToo within a nomos of legal pluralism—that is, within a sociopolitical space in which people use existent laws as well as gaps and contradictions between legal provisions to bargain in the shadow of law (Merry 1988). The challenge is to think simultaneously about the enabling power of law, of law's privileged position in the modern state as a form of visibility and recognition, while also to be cognizant of the heavy force of law and of the carceral as a problematic solution given the disproportionate burden and effects of incarceration on communities marginalized by race, class, or citizenship.

The #MeToo movement perfectly allows us to consider what "bargaining in the shadow of law" means: accusations evoke legal infrastructures and demand better considerations of law and policy, but they also make evident the failures and limitations of existing laws. On the one hand, we have rousing cheers and thankfulness for law. The presence of laws addressing gendered harassment and violence, in no small part due to feminist pressures across the world, facilitate the hearing of grievances. Catherine Mackinnon (2019), the legal mind who was largely instrumental for formulating sexual harassment as an employment violation in the United States in terms of an equal-protection standard, justifiably points out that sexual harassment laws in various countries, often put in place as a result of feminist mobilization, form an essential resource for #MeToo. Flavia Agnes, the Indian feminist lawyer, deems that turning to law may be an advantage: "The women will be asked for proof. But as the law on sexual harassment at the workplace stipulates clearly, it is not the acts of the abuser but the perception of the violated that is relevant" (2018). Both scholar-activists, as lawyers, argue for laws as facilitative for the change in behavior or norms that can be wrested now: "The lesson learnt is that women have to stake a claim. They will not be given their rights on a platter. They have to snatch them from a patently patriarchal system of corporate governance. But it is possible to dent this structure; it is possible to bring in fresh air" (Agnes 2018).

But #MeToo also fundamentally represents the *limitations* of law as a space to redress injuries of gendered violence. The legal scholar Brenda Cossman argues that "it is also the fantastical failure of law that has led to #MeToo. Law has repeatedly refused to recognize harm after harm, with acquittals and dismissals of 'allegations' of sexual violence against women; the harm didn't happen because law has the power to define and adjudicate the harm. #MeToo can be seen as a performance of regulatory failure" (2019, 33).

Such "regulatory failures," unsurprisingly, line up with the grain of race, class, caste, and gender hierarchies. The manifestly racist outcomes of criminal justice and mass incarceration may explain why women of color do not regard carceral options with unbridled enthusiasm (Tambe 2018, 200). #MeToo activists such as the signatories to the Indian list of sexual harassers in academia (LoSHA) (Sanjana 2019), who also identify themselves as marginalized by caste and class, or to the US Shitty Media Men list (Sanjana 2019) echo a similar betrayal against legal infrastructure. These lists contend that laws have not helped them, given the intransigence of bureaucratic processes and the impunity of perpetrators. Indeed, their accusations are also leveled against those feminists who they contend have emphasized institutional reform over their care for victims, haven't sufficiently interrogated their own deep structures of social privilege (race, caste, or class), and have protected abusers who share their social locations. Some #MeToo accusations seemed to have had professional consequences for perpetrators (notably cases backed up by media investigations that uncovered records of institutional cover-ups and multiple, uncannily similar iterations of assault). Some institutions have been held to account in line with existent laws, though the transparency and robustness of these processes are far from clear. But it has become quite evident that the ability to be heard about sexual assault is highly correlated with the vulnerability and contingency of occupational categories, race, caste, and class (Carmon and Schonbek 2019; Jaffe 2018).

The relationship of feminism to law is thus at the crux of the (somewhat generational) conflict of #MeToo: the differences center around how much reliance to place on punitive or carceral solutions. Arguably, both positive and negative legal outcomes have added momentum to outrage: the group catharsis when the one case against Bill Cosby resulted in a guilty verdict or, in contrast, the way that Brett

Kavanaugh eluded repercussions despite compelling evidence against him. But feminists who long for the clarity of legal resolution—such as Davis's wistful desire: "as imperfect as the legal system is, I must admit that I really longed for a juridical procedure" in fear that men were being "blamed and shamed . . . with severe consequences" (Zarkov and Davis 2018, 6)—miss the ways that the very specter of law enables survivors to articulate their need for other kinds of reparative solutions. Rather, what we should hear in these legal cases is survivors' urges to be able to name the processes through which they were violated, the complicities of family, friends, colleagues, and institutions in denying or refusing their accounts, and a way for perpetrators to fully understand how they wounded not just bodies but psyches, affecting confidence and senses of shame and trust.

A cogent illustration is provided by the end of the Larry Nassar courtroom trial, in which he was accused of sexually abusing hundreds of gymnastics students, acts he carried out over decades by convincing them and their families that nothing was going on and that he was within bounds of medical practice (Wells and Smith 2018). The power of trial and testimony as a putative space of healing is demonstrated in the judge's decision to have Nassar's victims address him in the sentencing phase. The most remarkable moment of reckoning comes when Nassar breaks down for the first time in court upon hearing one of his friends, a primary champion of his cause, describe coming to understand her own abuse through listening to other victims. In such accounts, we see in legal testimony a space of discursive excess, where the raw effects of the abuse surface beyond the disciplinary sanctions of crime and procedure.

Sex

In recalibrating norms of sexual interaction and naming unwelcome behaviors, does #MeToo become sex-negative and conservative? How do we highlight the power to say "yes" alongside the power to say "no"? Because #MeToo calls out a range of behaviors, it may appear to conflate comedian Louis CK's egregious flashing in his office, the suggestive remarks and gazes and touches that are quotidian occurrences in the lives of feminized persons, and queasiness toward curricular content that contains references to sex and violence. Understanding how #MeToo challenges scripts of sex requires us to disentangle these strands with the goal of enhancing sexual subjectivity and agency.

Those who represent the movement as sex-negative find it to be tone-deaf to the nuances of romance and the energy of sexual exchange—that is, to be squeamish conservative feminism. The *Le Monde* letter signed by the French actor Catherine DeNeuve and ninety-nine other artists exemplifies this response, the effects amplified by DeNeuve's bona fides as a French film star and icon of smoking-hot sexuality. These artists make a case for women's "freedom" and attempt to rehabilitate gentlemanly seduction within a script of optimal gender roles: "As women, we do not recognize ourselves in this feminism, which beyond denouncing the abuse of power takes on a hatred of men and of sexuality" (quoted in Poirier 2018). The suggestion that alleged victims should toughen up and understand how erotic exchange is imbricated in normative gender binaries seems relatively easy to counter by pointing to the many examples of harassment and abuse as manifestations of power that do not even pretend to engage the objectified victim. Such so-called erotic exchanges are a means of exercising dominance, thus rendering consensual participation meaningless. Calls to toughen up in such circumstances are equivalent to asking women to accept the blatantly exclusionary structures of their professions or other social spaces.

A more explicitly political feminist stance against sex negativity poses sexuality as a zone of risk and play rather than a sacrosanct zone of safety. Cossman argues that debates in the #MeToo era are playing out the feminist "sex wars" of the 1970s if on slightly different terms, still negotiating the criteria of "pleasure vs. danger." She sees #MeToo claiming "that sexual danger for women is everywhere, and that sexual harms are real" as the identification of sexual harassment and rape as crimes of power in the 1970s did. However, she finds that detractors of the #MeToo approach don't minimize the harms of rape or harassment but rather "push back at the idea of sexuality as exclusively a site of danger . . . [and] keep space for sexual desire, for flirting and the ambivalences of sexual attraction" (2019, 30). Many of the cases in the news have been such outrageous transgressions of power and position that it is nearly impossible to think of them in the context of pleasure. But it is useful nonetheless to remember the danger of erasing women's agency around sexuality, to be wary of a turn to respectability.

Consent is a more difficult concept for feminists than our policy handbooks would have us believe, involving everyday negotiations of sexual agency and pleasure. Attraction and acquiescence and discomfort are shaped by interactions and contexts in messy ways that do not line up with legal categories, as the *New Yorker* short story "Cat Person" (Roupenian 2017) poignantly illustrates. The female protagonist's simultaneous disavowal and fleeting empowerment within a sexual encounter, neither forced nor fully joyful, exemplifies what Janet Halley designates as "constrained consent" (2016, 265). Halley argues that (university or workplace) policies attempting to be progressive become prescriptive of gender scripts and inscribe femininity as passive, infantile, and sex averse. Rather, honoring sexual adventure and exploration as positive forces (per feminist and queer theory) means also to live with disappointment and ambivalence.

To understand sexual consent and coercion within a broader framework of agency, Tambe reminds us to distinguish "predatory" abuses from the terrain of sexuality as a powerful and ambivalent cultural tool: "In many contexts—both within and outside marriage—sex is exchanged for security, affection, and money. So, a crucial point to keep in mind is that not all transactional sex is coerced. As sex positive feminists would argue, we need to guard against casting all transactions as coercion. The question is, how to discern coercion within contexts of transaction. Not all seemingly consensual transactions are free of coercion, of course. . . . But transacting in sex, or getting something in exchange for sex, does not mean that coercion is absent" (2018, 200).

Leaving space for women to be both desiring and transactional beings allows us to view survivors as people making considered or contingent decisions rather than to judge them by the failure to live up to perfect outraged victimhood.

Laws of sexual harassment or sex discrimination center upon sex as an overdetermined site of governmentality, whereas other forms of harassment or exclusion do not merit a similar weighty apparatus. In universities and other workplaces, we emphasize that occupational hierarchies invalidate any meaningful consent to sex—the onus is on those in power within the structure to be accountable for their actions. Some feminist scholars have objected to these norms as infantilization or prudery or have interrogated whether women or queer folks can be deemed powerful even when occupying those positions. *Sexual Paranoia Comes to Campus,* the subtitle of Laura Kipnis's book *Unwanted Advances,* is a prime example. Although such analyses can seem blind to the influence that professors or bosses hold over livelihoods, sexual interactions are only one form of abuse of power. The New York University professor Avital Ronell, for example, defended accusations of sexual harassment from a male graduate student with the rationale that they both consensually participated in queer camp bantering and proffered her theoretical aversion to narrow understandings of sex and consent. But to deem Ronell's behavior as harassment does not necessarily align one with prudish notions of sexual behavior, given her long record of abusive behavior toward students and colleagues that emerged. Significant, though, is that the non-sex-related behaviors were illegible to grievance processes until hooked to a set of sexualized exchanges and that these systemic humiliations, exclusions, and favoritisms lacked redressal.[1] Drishadyoti Bargi (2017) draws attention to a crucial intersectional point here, focusing on Dalit women's everyday lives in university settings to illustrate how caste, race, and class structure interaction and preference. University grievance processes on sexual harassment, often set up through the work of previous feminist generations, are so focused on law and on overt sexual approaches that they offer too little too late to remedy academic culture.

#MeToo is most immediately about unwelcome sexual overtures in the context of work or teaching. But in launching conversations about how sex operates in these realms, it has opened up debates around complex understandings of power and consent. If recognizing shades of sexualized power is one of the movement's prime contributions, one of the enduring challenges is to think about desire beyond gendered protectionism. Even as #MeToo calls out sexual coercion and violence, it wrestles with the difficulty of negotiating what sexual subjectivity might look like.

Feminism

The topics of law and sex demonstrate that #MeToo is a more contested site of feminist politics than one would have imagined. The contested territory is something like the following: Is #MeToo feminist or post-feminist? Is it the next step in an evolutionary narrative of feminist progress, or is it a move that rejects feminism as privileged and out of touch and that seeks to make its own mark in the world? It's common to ascribe the conflict to generational difference (e.g., Cossman 2019), as discussed earlier, but perhaps we might better parse the generational split as different approaches to gender-based violence: a fundamentally intersectional question or a problem pertaining to feminized bodies. The #MeToo movement indexes the changing trajectories and meanings of feminism, challenging its perceived ontology.

Many enthusiastic feminist voices fold #MeToo into the long arc of resistance against "violence against women." Mackinnon uses the evocative image of a flight of butterflies to envision a collective takeoff from a base of steady gains in legal reform:

> The world's first mass movement against sexual abuse, #MeToo took off from the law of sexual harassment, quickly overtook it, and is shifting cultures everywhere, electrifyingly demonstrating butterfly politics in action. The early openings of the butterflies' wings were the legal, political, and conceptual innovations of the 1970s, but it is the collective social intervention of the #MeToo movement that is setting off the cataclysmic transformations of which a political butterfly effect is capable. . . . As butterflies take flight from beneath the shadow of the law, imagine the first rise in women's status since the vote. Conceive a revolution without violence against domination and aggression. Envision a moment of truth and a movement of transformation for the sexually violated toward a more equal, therefore a more peaceful and just, world. It is happening all around us right now. (2019)

Mackinnon, given her background, foregrounds movements for legal change especially in US contexts, but another way to think about the US history of #MeToo genealogically is to ask how old it is. By regarding it as part of long, fraught, incomplete histories of women's resistance, including formal and informal protests against oppressive sexualization, the timeline could shift back to African American women's histories of resistance, as Cheryl Rodriguez (2018) does, rather than to the second-wave feminist organizing that Mackinnon foregrounds. Such a recalculation also pushes against the media focus on white women's narratives and on celebrity figures. It matches how #MeToo has been embraced as resistance in other locations: a "transnational feminist consciousness-raising endeavour" (Ghadery 2019, 254); the newest step in Egyptian women's fights against street harassment (Eltantawy 2019); a breaking point of generations of complaints by Indian students, Dalit workers, small-town journalists, and nongovernmental organization workers (Kurian 2018; Phillipose 2018).

But a significant motif in #MeToo is the calling out of feminists, which outpaces even the calling out of perpetrators. The media ascription of a generational catfight or even a "social vs. individual" division (Donegan 2018) often fails to capture the territorial tension: Who can lay claim to the term *feminist* when race and caste hegemonies are taken into account? If the anxiety in the United States is that #MeToo not just default to a "white women's movement" (Tambe 2018), then the anxiety in India concerns a middle-class, upper-caste domination of the terrain of feminism.

The Indian case illustrates feminist dynamics around the axes of gender and caste. In brief, #MeToo 1.0 in India started with a student's (initially private) social media list of Indian academics who are sexual harassers, which is now popularly called "LoSHA" (emerging at the same time as web lists such as Shitty Media Men). She was reprimanded by established feminist academics through a letter on a prominent blog (administered by one of the authors) for offering up a rumor network rather than relying on institutional due process and for ignoring the long history of feminist institution building and support for survivors. Supporters of the list, however, responded with a critique foregrounding the caste privilege of the letter writers, the accusation being that these (largely) upper-caste feminists were shoring up their own privileges, protecting male allies of their caste and class who loomed large on these lists, and refusing to hear how feminist institutions had failed vulnerable subjects.[2] The *distrust* of law in the latter response extends to feminists as co-conspirators in systems of privilege, wherein "feminists" are cast as a homogeneous group in a way that erases their arguments and debates. Feminist proposals for reform become conflated with legislative and administrative hurdles, thus losing the contexts that helped frame the issue (Baxi 2016).

Law was only the proximate argument in this debate. Gita Chadha describes the friction between the groups as deeply emotional: "While the older feminists, the signatories of the *Kafila* statement, communicated rage and hurt at being discredited and dismissed as 'mothers in-law,' some of the list makers felt that they were losing their feminist heroes and were being left to fend for themselves. This sense of loss was compounded by the fact that we were also losing our male allies. The sense of betrayal, hurt, and anger seems to be quite real and raw on both sides" (2017). Supporters of LoSHA wanted to look beyond law to the silent structural hegemonies of liberalism, such as quotidian processes of exclusion in jobs and schools (Bargi 2017). In contrast to the concerns that social media was highlighting only celebrities' plights, groups such as Speak Out in Kerala sought out social media for its democratizing effects: it could serve as a powerful vehicle for Dalit Bahujan Adivasi women to speak out against upper-caste or intercommunity violence by men in ways that legal process and mainstream media usually silence (Thaali 2018).

In other reckonings, however, #MeToo is a significant moment of forging feminist community anew. Kalpana Kannabiran's excellent essay "#WeToo: In the Footsteps of Bhanwari Devi" considered the events of #MeToo as "momentous in feminist politics": "It has simultaneously triggered a renewed debate on sexual violence (rejecting gradations in harm, suffering and tortuous memory), *and also called out feminist politics itself* in a graded society" (2018, emphasis in original). Kannabiran centers her intersectional analysis on Bhanwari Devi, a rural social worker in Rajasthan who was gang-raped as retaliation for her work against child marriage. Her rapists were never convicted, but her case formed the basis of sexual harassment law in India and thus has become most useful to urban and middle-class women in formal employment or education.

> With Bhanwari, we see the different simultaneous locations of the "me," defined by the specific "we." It's inclusive at times: community, village, the feminist collective. Or exclusionary, with the "me" standing alone at the margins, speaking truth to power. Almost always losing ground to multiple, intersecting channels of impunity bolstered by state/majoritarian power, and yet staking her rightful claim

on due process at every level in a simultaneous, integrated articulation of justice. In her self-conscious choices, she as the survivor with feminist agency transforms the "me" into a plural "we" constituted outside the frames of individual reparation/redress. (Kannabiran 2018)

Similar to Rodriguez's (2018) reinscription of the US context of feminism as tracing back to early African American women, Kannabiran defines feminism through a genealogy that emphasizes the failures and resistances of marginalized women, highlighting the forgotten futility and bravery in collective protests. She calls for a politics that is accountable to forms of harm against individuals as well as for forging alliances that recognize these profound debts. Her essay imagines multitudes within feminism without losing sight of power.

Where did we locate ourselves when we chimed in to say "me too"? The overlapping ripples and eddies of this moment or movement are located in and around law, transmitted in whispers or on social media, wary of sex as power or impatient with sex as fear, jubilant or suspicious of feminism as community. #MeToo reveals a profound unhappiness with the rules of sex and harassment in play as well as the will to disrupt those rules through whispered and shouted stories. It is a phenomenon that amplifies the categorical conflicts of law, sex, and feminism but also contains the potential to be a space for listening across differences and reimagining genealogies.

References

Agnes, F. 2018. "Taking MeToo Past the Confines of Social Media." *Tribune* (India), October 19. At https://www.tribuneindia.com/news/comment /taking-metoo-past-the-confines-of-social-media/670105.html.

Babel, A. 2018. "The Invisible Walls of the Whisper Network." *Anthrosource* 59 (3): 67–72.

Bargi, D. 2017. "On Misreading the Dalit Critique of University Spaces." *Economic and Political Weekly* 52 (50). At https://www.epw.in/engage/article /misreading-dalit-critique-university-space.

Basu, S. 2015. *The Trouble with Marriage: Feminists Confront Law and Violence in India.* Oakland: University of California Press.

Baxi, P. 2016. "'Carceral Feminism' as Judicial Bias: The Discontents around *State v. Mahmood Farooqui*." *Interdisciplinary Law* 3 (October): 1–30.

Ben-Asher, N. 2019. "Of Trauma and Power: Celebrity Sexual Misconduct Trials." *Critical Analysis of Law* 6 (1): 145–62.

Carmon, I., and A. Schonbek. 2019. "Was It Worth It?" *The Cut,* September 30. At https://www.thecut.com/2019/2009/coming-forward-about-sexual-assault-and-what-comes-after.html.

Chadha, G. 2017. "Towards Complex Feminist Solidarities after the List-Statement." *Economic and Political Weekly* 52 (50). At https://www.epw.in/engage/article/towards-complex-feminist-solidarities-list-statement.

Cossman, B. 2019. "#MeToo, Sex Wars 2.0, and the Power of Law." In *The Asian Yearbook of Human Rights and Humanitarian Law,* vol. 3, edited by J. Rehman, A. Shahid, and S. Foster, 18–37. Leiden, Netherlands: Brill Nijhoff.

Donegan, M. 2018. "How #MeToo Revealed the Central Rift within Feminism Today." *Guardian,* May 11. At https://www.theguardian.com/news/2018/may/2011/how-metoo-revealed-the-central-rift-within-feminism-social-individualist.

Eltantawy, N. 2019. "In Egypt, the MeToo Movement Is Falling Short." *Fair Observer,* November 18. At https://www.fairobserver.com/culture/me-too-movement-sexual-harassment-egypt-middle-east-womens-rights-news-61521/.

Ghadery, F. 2019. "#MeToo—Has the 'Sisterhood' Finally Become Global or Just Another Product of Neoliberal Feminism?" *Transnational Legal Theory* 10 (2): 252–74.

Gill, R., and S. Orgad. [2018] 2019. "The Shifting Terrain of Sex and Power: From the 'Sexualization of Culture' to #MeToo." *Sexualities* 21 (8): 1313–324. Eprint available through LSE Research Online, January, 1–14. At http://eprints.lse.ac.uk/91503/1/Gill_The-shifting-terrain.pdf.

Gould, D. 2012. "Occupy's Political Emotions." *Contexts* 11: 20–21.

Greenhouse, C. J., B. Yngvesson, and D. M. Engel. 1994. *Law and Community in Three American Towns.* Ithaca, NY: Cornell University Press.

Halley, J. 2016. "The Move to Affirmative Consent." *Signs* 42 (1): 257–79.

Jaffe, S. 2018. "The Collective Power of #MeToo." *Dissent,* Spring, 80–87.

Kannabiran, K. 2018. "#WeToo: In the Footprints of Bhanwari Devi." *Outlook,* November 12. At https://www.outlookindia.com/magazine/story/know-gnawing-absences-in-metoo-let-travesty-of-bhanwari-devis-trial-be-a-reminder/300835.

Kurian, A. 2018. "#MeToo Is Riding a New Wave of Feminism in India." *The Conversation,* February 1. At https://theconversation.com/metoo-is-riding-a-new-wave-of-feminism-in-india-89842.

Mackinnon, C. A. 2019. "Where #MeToo Came From, and Where It's Going." *Atlantic,* March. At https://www.theatlantic.com/ideas/archive/2019/2003/catharine-mackinnon-what-metoo-has-changed/585313/.

Merry, S. E. 1988. "Legal Pluralism." *Law and Society Review* 22 (5): 868–96.

———. 2006. "Transnational Human Rights and Local Activism: Mapping the Middle." *American Anthropologist* 108 (1): 38–51.

Nair, S. 2018. "#MeToo Is Anarchic, and That's a Good Thing." *LiveMint,* October 12. At https://www.livemint.com/Leisure/LhMn4nQG1Rmic88lB81ZDaJ/MeToo-is-anarchic-and-thats-a-good-thing.html.

Pellegrini, A. 2018. "#MeToo: Before and After." *Studies in Gender and Sexuality* 19 (4): 262–64.

Phillipose, P. 2018. "Backstory: #MeToo Is about an Individual's Rights but Is Far Larger Than a Single Person." *The Wire,* October 20. At https://thewire.in/women/backstory-metoo-movement-mj-akbar-vinod-dua.

Poirier, A. 2018. "After the #MeToo Backlash, an Insider's Guide to French Feminism." *Guardian,* January 13. At https://www.theguardian.com/world/2018/jan/2014/french-feminists-catherine-deneuve-metoo-letter-sexual-harassment.

Rodriguez, C. 2018. "Black Women and the Fight against Sexual Violence." *Anthropology News,* May–June, e91–e97.

Roupenian, K. 2017. "Cat Person." *New Yorker,* December 11. At https://www.newyorker.com/magazine/2017/2012/2011/cat-person.

Sanjana, P. 2019. "MeToo in India: Building Revolutions from Solidarities." *Decision* 46 (2): 151–68.

Sarat, A., M. Constable, D. M. Engel, V. Hans, and S. Lawrence. 1998. "Ideas of the 'Everyday' and the 'Trouble Case' in Law and Society Scholarship: An Introduction." In *Everyday Practices and Trouble Cases,* edited by A. Sarat, M. Constable, D. M. Engel, V. Hans, and S. Lawrence, 1–13. Chicago: Northwestern University Press.

Tambe, A. 2017. "Has Trump's Presidency Triggered the Movement against Sexual Harassment?" *The Conversation,* November 28. At http://theconversation.com/has-trumps-presidency-triggered-the-movement-against-sexual-harassment-88219.

———. 2018. "Reckoning with the Silences of #MeToo." *Feminist Studies* 44 (1): 197–202.

Thaali, P. 2018. "Rejecting Victimhood: The Online Speak-Out Campaign in Kerala against Harassment." GenderIT.org, October 9. At https://www.genderit.org/feminist-talk/rejecting-victimhood-online-speak-out-campaign-kerala-against-harassment.

Tolentino, J. 2018. "One Year of #MeToo: What Women's Speech Is Still Not Allowed to Do." *New Yorker,* October. At https://www.newyorker.com

/news/our-columnists/one-year-of-metoo-what-womens-speech-is-still-not-allowed-to-do.

Traister, R. 2017. "We Are All Implicated in the Post-Weinstein Reckoning." *The Cut*, November. At https://www.thecut.com/2017/2011/rebecca-traister-on-the-post-weinstein-reckoning.html#_ga=2012.267592014.1329094716.1576000941-1290738628.1576000941.

Wells, K., and L. Smith, hosts. 2018. *Believed*. Audio podcast. Michigan Radio and National Public Radio. At https://www.npr.org/podcasts/510326/believed.

Williams, B. C. 2017. "#MeToo: A Crescendo in the Discourse about Sexual Harassment, Fieldwork, and the Academy." Savage Minds, October 24. At https://savageminds.org/2017/10/24/metoo-a-crescendo-in-the-discourse-about-sexual-harassment-fieldwork-and-the-academy-part-1/.

Zarkov, D., and K. Davis. 2018. "Ambiguities and Dilemmas around #MeToo: #Forhowlong and #Whereto?" *European Journal of Women's Studies* 25 (1): 3–9.

Notes

1. See Ben-Asher 2019 for a reading of the affective discourses of gender in the case.

2. Chadha 2017 provides an account of the LoSHA debate.

5

The Language of #MeToo in South African and North American Media Discourses

Desiree Lewis

This chapter explores the global resonance of recent gender-justice discourses by reflecting on the congruence of media coverage of South Africa's #MeToo movement and reporting of the movement in North America. Any coverage of the movement cannot, of course, be equated with the actual movement's complexity. #MeToo campaigns have evolved in relation to the regional, classed, and racialized dynamics of particular contexts (see Lewis 2018). At the same time, media reporting, especially coverage that legitimates the movement, both shapes and illustrates some of the dominant narrative and rhetorical elements and strategies that have galvanized the movement at a global level.

My discussion focuses on coverage of prominent moments in the #MeToo movement in two contexts: the North American academy and South African nongovernmental organizations (NGOs) within the social justice sector. Although the movement in North America initially focused on the entertainment industry and politics, it quickly spread to college campuses. As Deborah Tuerkheimer shows, from the end of 2017 campaigns led to a situation in which "increasingly, in wide-open spaces using hashtags and mainstream media, survivors [insisted] that their violation matters" (2019, 1208). Sexual violence has characterized South African civil society and NGOs for many years. Reporting and monitoring sexual violence within these organizations have been slow because of, among other reasons, their function as champions of social justice, their leadership's reluctance to act on evidence or rumors, and staff members' dilemmas around bringing progressive organizations into disrepute. At the start of 2018, however, stories of sexual violence within these organizations erupted in the public domain. Writing that year, Nicolette Naylor described this eruption in the following way: "Over the last eight months some of the largest social justice organizations working at the forefront of human rights and dignity in South Africa, funded by social justice foundations like the Ford Foundation, have had to face a series of very public cases of sexual harassment [and] workplace bullying. . . . The first few instances of sexual harassment had a ripple effect and led to numerous other cases coming to the fore" (2018, 93).

I explore reporting on the North American academy and South African social justice sector in the *Mail and Guardian* (South Africa), the *Canadian Press,* and the *New York Times.* Because I focus qualitatively on modes of storytelling and visual representation, I analyze details in four newspaper stories in particular: two from the South African *Mail & Guardian,* one from the *Canadian Press,* and one from the *New York Times.*

The rest of this essay is divided into three parts. I start by reviewing the global significance of print-media coverage on #MeToo and introduce similarities in the content of South African and North American newspaper storytelling. Here I draw attention to how framing influences the politics of stories that legitimate the movement. The second section deepens analysis of the discursive patterns in pro-victim reporting by focusing on how stories emphasize emotionally laden dualisms that undermine attention to structural power. The third and final section focuses on some of the generic and visual conventions that unwittingly frame media interpretations of the movement.

#MeToo Print-Media Coverage

Since the movement went viral, a number of scholarly writings dealing with different countries have responded to its print-media coverage. Feminist interpretation of this coverage includes the work of Sara De Benedictis, Shani Orgad, and Catherine Rottenberg (2019), writing about the United Kingdom; of Alyssa Evans (2018), analyzing the *New*

York Times; and of Jesse Starkey, Amy Koerber, Miglena Stenadori, and Bethany Pitchford (2019), comparing the United States, Japan, Australia, and India. These writers indicate that the force of the movement resulted largely from how individual cases were communicated to audiences in print communication. It is therefore believed that media coverage often "expanded the movement's visibility beyond social media, addressing potentially new and different readerships" (De Benedictis, Orgad, and Rottenberg 2019, 718).

Writers have also drawn attention to the framing of seemingly progressive reporting, arguing that even coverage that legitimates the movement can encode narratives and conventions that undermine justice. For example, De Benedictis, Orgad, and Rottenberg show how certain positive reporting in UK newspapers confirms a popular feminism "characterized by a number of arguably limiting and problematic factors" (2019, 733). The contradictory impulses of both legitimating and suppressing gender-justice struggles are evident in the stories, all published in 2018, on which this essay focuses.

The year 2018 witnessed an explosion of media reporting on cases involving prominent figures in the South African social service sector and the North American academy. North American stories, which also filtered into South Africa, focused on academic staff in globally renowned institutions. Two examples were the accusations made against Steven Galloway, a novelist and academic at the University of British Columbia, and the investigation of Avital Ronell, a Germanist philosopher at New York University.[1] Also in 2018, stories sprung up around cases of sexual harassment in the South African social justice sector. In two widely covered cases, charges were laid against a white male employer by Black women employees at the well-known NGO Equal Education and, a few months later, also by Black women against a white male lawyer at another NGO, the Legal Resources Centre. As the print and social media coverage of all of these incidents made clear, the events exemplified #MeToo narratives in which individuals spoke out retrospectively about violation at the hands of socially prominent men (or women) in the academic and public-service sectors.

Media attention to the academy and public-service sectors is noteworthy in view of the foregrounding of more obvious contexts of patriarchal entitlement, such as the film and music industry, the corporate sector, and the political sphere. Publicly respected figures in the higher-education and social justice sectors have established reputations as champions of social justice and critical knowledge, yet these sectors are complex sites of entitlement and interpersonal domination. They are often seen as sites in which the rule of reason and justice reigns over the messiness of emotions and irrationally cruel interpersonal relationships. But the recurrence of sexual violence and the ways in which such violence is addressed in these sites expose their underbellies.

Both sites privilege patriarchal entitlement, normalizing everyday authoritarian brutalities in their institutional cultures and working relations. Both also set in place networks and physical spaces that create deep intimacies among subjects and bodies. These networks and spaces include processes such as one-on-one consultation and meetings, travel with colleagues, and work collaboration that is often outside working hours and working spaces. Of particular significance in tracing commonalities in these sectors are everyday working relations in which established academics and professionals or activists acquire authority as custodians of moral, political, and intellectual wisdom. Significantly, their powerful positions are legitimated by moral and intellectual authority. Moreover, relations of structural power are entangled with ties of intimacy and trust as well as with roles based on care, tutelage, and mentorship. These intricately intimate work relations are often forged on the basis of socially determined statuses—for example, between women and men, Black people and white people, younger employees and older ones, students and their teachers, and interns or mentees and their mentors. Media coverage of #MeToo in relation to the academy and social justice sectors therefore seems fully in line with feminist efforts to break silences about the extent of normalized violence. Commenting on the effect of this coverage in relation to the South African social justice sector, Naylor states: "Women are still not believed and are often victimized within our social justice organizations when we had always assumed secondary victimization happened 'out there' in the criminal justice system with police, magistrates and judges. No, it is happening in social justice organizations where an entire sector can vilify a woman who has spoken out against a powerful leader" (2018, 94).

The insidiously censoring impact of institutional cultures that claim to support academic freedoms and social justice is also identified in Kate

Lockwood Harris's attention to the North American academy. Focusing on students' "first-hand encounters with institutional inertia and inappropriate university responses" (2019, 2), she draws attention to the paradoxical workings of institutional environments. Although many universities may boast policies, processes, and cultures that seem to defend the rights, voices, and dignity of all campus citizens, sexual harassment cases are often drawn out and ineffectual or kept out of sight (Harris 2019, 2).

Print-media coverage of sexual violence in universities and the social justice sector has therefore supported the informal reporting, mobilization, and action that has been central to the socially transformative thrust of #MeToo. In South Africa, this support is illustrated in the lead paragraph for a South African story dealing with the social justice sector: "Civil society is supposed to be a watchdog. It's supposed to fight for what's right—but what happens when those tasked with advocating for the most vulnerable become the perpetrators?" (Raphael 2019). The forceful tone of this paragraph is echoed in a *New York Times* headline legitimating effective struggles for justice in colleges in 2019: "New Wave of Student Activism Presses Colleges on Sexual Assault" (Hartocollis 2019).

Michelle Rodino-Colocino shows how this representation works empathetically, but she also distinguishes between different forms of empathy: "Organizing movements on the basis of empathy are [*sic*] both promising and risky endeavors. It is risky because activists may mobilize . . . 'passive empathy.' . . . Passive empathy is the feeling of being in another's shoes without the risk of actually doing so . . . 'Transformative empathy' promotes listening rather than distancing or looking at speakers as 'others.' It requires self-reflexivity and potential transformation of one's own assumptions" (2018, 96).

Media coverage that seeks to legitimate the movement can promote passive empathy, with seemingly progressive messages coexisting with effects that De Benedictus, Orgad, and Rottenberg describe as "limiting rather than advancing public awareness and engagement with the larger social and structural issues that #MeToo, as a catalyst, could potentially raise" (2019, 734). In North America, among the first feminist responses to this limitation were from Margaret Atwood (2018) and Lisa Duggan (2018) in their criticisms of the media's coverage of accusations against the academics Steven Galloway and Avital Ronell.

Duggan argued that the accusations against Ronell were arbitrarily picked up by the media and generated reactive side taking rather than political engagement with injustice. She argued that accusations were "focused through the press primarily on bad individuals, rather than [on] structures of power" (2018). Advancing a similar argument about the media's role in persuading readers to empathize passively, Atwood, in commenting on the accusation against Steven Galloway, wrote: "Several years ago, the university went public in national media before there was an inquiry, and even before the accused was allowed to know the details of the accusation. . . . The public—including me—was left with the impression that this man was a violent serial rapist, and everyone was free to attack him publicly, since under the agreement he had signed, he couldn't say anything to defend himself" (2018).

Atwood also drew attention to the way that Galloway's university performatively used the media to distance itself from alleged perpetrators and thus to neglect all institutional responsibility for pursuing gendered and other social justices.

Duggan's and Atwood's attention to the dubious effects of passive empathy is echoed by other writers reflecting on the framing of seemingly positive stories. As Lisa Cuklanz shows, news media can organize fragmentary details to construct stories that recuperate entrenched stereotypes, mystify certain powerful and oppressive actors or forces, and ultimately avoid transformative messages and discourses (2020, 3–5). Jane O'Boyle and Queenie Jo-Yun Li's (2019) account of media reporting on US campuses illustrate that it is far easier to identify the framing of victim-blaming and conservative coverage than of liberal reports. Yet such reporting can be characterized by a marked "support of feminism alongside a concurrent de-politicization" (De Benedictus, Orgad, and Rottenberg 2019, 718–19). In the two subsections that follow, I deal with the specific forms and effects of this depoliticization in the "empathetic" framing of selected stories.

Silence Breakers as Victims in Empathetic Coverage

Various feminists have drawn attention to the significance of whistleblowing in holding powerful men accountable through the #MeToo movement and in asserting accusers' agencies and voices (see Gill and

Orgad 2018; Starkey et al. 2019). Showing how certain media coverage conveys this significance, Jesse Starkey, Amy Koerber, Miglena Stenadori, and Bethany Pitchford argue that a media focus on the agency of silence breakers creates a frame "corresponding with . . . social norms that applaud brave individuals who risk their own security to fight an unjust system" (2019, 445). Yet while a focus on patriarchal and entitlement is clearly crucial to any critique of sexual violence, a fixation on perpetrators' actions vis-à-vis their victims' bodies can reinforce the status of violated subjects only as mute and passive bodies.

In some ways, therefore, agency is defined only with reference to the moment of silence breaking. The identity of the silence breaker may continue to be framed in terms of tropes of passivity, helplessness, and victimization. Such framing can encourage pro-victim sentiment at the same time that it perpetuates a view of accusers simply as fragile and anonymous cyphers of suffering or as vulnerable beings whom others need to protect. In other words, this framing can entrench gendered assumptions and hierarchies in which certain subjects seem innately less capable, visible, and able than others to function in ways that are defined as normatively "human." These "lesser" subjects are seen to be in need of guardianship rather than to deserve support or solidarity. Dealing with the way that these messages are sometimes conveyed in narratives that have driven #MeToo mobilization, Atwood argues that they are "feeding into the very old narrative that holds women to be incapable of fairness or of considered judgment[,] . . . giving the opponents of women yet another reason to deny them positions of decision-making in the world" (2018).

This projection of accusers as subjects who are deeply affected by social worlds yet are unable to participate fully in them is evidenced in the following extract from the *Canadian Press* report dealing with the charges laid against Galloway:

> The former University of British Columbia student who accused Steven Galloway of sexual assault says her complaint against the acclaimed author was not about a "consensual affair." The woman, identified only as MC or main complainant, has released a statement through her lawyer, speaking publicly for the first time since Galloway was suspended over what the university described as "serious allegations" last November. MC has stayed silent since Galloway was

suspended, out of respect for the process and the confidentiality of everyone involved. "The so-called 'secrecy' of the investigation process has protected Galloway, perhaps more than anyone else," the statement said. (Kane 2016)

In this extract, the anonymous accuser is referred to as "MC" or "the woman," her opaqueness underscored by the way that "she says" in the first sentence later shifts to "the statement said." Despite being embedded in layers created by namelessness and indirect speech, the accuser is simultaneously defined as agential. She therefore acquires agency within the context of "the statement," and it is through disembodied enunciation that she is foregrounded as a protagonist instigating action. Significant, too, is the way this representation of passive subjectivity encourages what Rodino-Colocino terms "passive empathy," which is predicated on an "irreducible difference—a recognition that I am not you. . . . [and] empathy is possible only by virtue of this distinction" (2018, 96).

In the reports of the two other newspapers discussed here, the *Mail and Guardian* and the *New York Times*, the passivity of complainants is conveyed through the characterization of them, especially of their reported speech. Possibly to convey authenticity, the accuser's voice is rendered in language conveying remarkable naivete and hesitancy. For example, Ronell's accuser, a mature graduate student, is quoted in the *New York Times* in the following way: "The day he arrived, she asked him to read poetry to her in her bedroom while she took an afternoon nap, he said. 'That was already a red flag to me,' said Mr. Reitman. 'But I also thought, O.K., you're here. Better not make a scene'" (Greenberg 2018).[2]

In a similar vein, the South African complainant in the *Mail and Guardian* report is quoted as follows: "It's a big thing. People know who Doron is. Doron is Equal Education. He is celebrated. . . . So how you respond to him, we all fear how it will affect your job or whatever" (quoted in Allison and Collison 2018). The language of this statement contrasts diametrically with the language of the accused, whose speech, as indicated in the following extract, is generally thoughtful, brief, and legalistic. "I deny in the strongest possible terms the outrageous claim that I 'attempted to remove her pants and force [myself] on her sexually.' It feels ridiculous to be saying this but I am congenitally cautious in the bedroom to the point where women have often told me to stop asking them if they are okay and just enjoy the experience" (quoted in Allison and Collison 2018).

From the point of view of the writers and the newspaper, the purpose of this contrast may have been to demonstrate the social power of the accused. Yet the effect is also to infantilize accusers, who come across as needy, vague, or inconsistent. The authority of the accused's voice of masculinized reason is contrasted with the feminized uncertainty, emotionalism, and naivete of the "truth teller." Innocence is therefore constructed with reference to conventional binaries between reason and emotion, masculinity in relation to femininity, and erudition as opposed to ignorance.

In explaining the complexity of understanding sexism, Peter Glick and Susan Fiske (2001) distinguish between hostile sexism and benevolent sexism. Hostile sexism is explicitly disparaging of women. It would therefore generate the misogynistic framing of women who accuse men of sexual assault as liars, sexual manipulators, and so on. Benevolent sexism condemns the sexual violation of women yet patronizingly casts women affected by it as victims in need of help and support rather than as agents and actors with the capacity to drive their own struggles and envisage their own freedoms. Developing their earlier conclusions about the conflictual nature of these forms of sexism, Glick and Fiske, in more recent work, argue that "BS [benevolent sexism] was the carrot aimed at enticing women to enact traditional roles and HS [hostile sexism] was the stick used to punish them when they resisted. One emphasizes reward and the other emphasizes punishment (hence their differing valences) but both work toward a common aim: maintaining a gender-traditional status quo" (2011, 532).

Although this explanation suggests that sexism is conscious, it is significant that media representations draw on such entrenched and hegemonic frames. Stories therefore end up othering subjects who seem to be unrepresentable in new or different ways. In constructing representations that have "public resonance," journalists turn to "familiar story patterns [that] have the power to give order and meaning to the social world" (Askanius and Møller Hartley 2019).

The othering evident in the representation of women as voiceless or inarticulate frames women's silence breaking in patronizing ways. Rather than critiquing the gender hierarchy and stereotypes that rationalize and promote certain subjects' sense of entitlement, this othering confirms them. The sentimental response to others' pain in a way that reinforces their "othering" has become prominent in liberal media representations of the others' pain (see Razack 2007). As illustrated in the next section, liberal news media coverage of #MeToo can also run the risk of resorting to stock formulae (with extremely troubling political overtones) in order to generate emotional responses from audiences.

Villains, Scandals, and Tabloid Coverage

Stock formulae can be conveyed in certain #MeToo coverage through the representation of the accused through tropes of absolute villainy. Lisa Duggan (2018) has commented on this in North American academic institutions, where elaborate legal and administrative procedures seem to support rational assessment, although the pretense of rationality is belied by contradictory, messy, and often Kafkaesque administrative and legal logics that generate a climate of fear and suspicion. According to Duggan, the binaristic logic of pitting accusers' victimhood against accused's villainy in the academy is exemplified in Title IX of the Education Amendments Act of 1972 regarding sexual assault and harassment cases. Laura Kipnis (2017) develops Duggan's argument by claiming that the paranoid focus on sexual danger on campuses can reinforce a sense of the absolute vulnerability of women as potential victims of omnipotent and ever-present predators.

The Cartesian logic in the representation of the accused is very pronounced in media coverage, where guilt is imagined only as the antithesis of innocence and through exaggerated representation. The dualism of guilt and innocence may be necessary within legal discourse, but it is noteworthy how both verbal and visual description in media reporting sustains this dualism by inflating certain figures' palpable guilt. The image of the white man accused of harassment in the *Mail and Guardian* coverage of the Legal Resources Centre case in South Africa provides an example of this dualism. One photo in the *Mail and Guardian* represents a white man, talking volubly and using elaborate hand gestures, seated next to a Black woman, who appears—in the instant of the taking of the photo—to be overawed and even frightened.[3] This photo appears to have been randomly sourced from a digital archive, but when appended to this story, it creates the impression of a hectoring white patriarch silencing an anxious young Black woman. The image, taken years before the accusation, has nothing to do with the content of the story covered; it is a randomly selected image, one easily acquired by journalists who can now access large stores of images on the internet. But it serves to quicken the text in ways that an earlier tradition of media critics did not begin to imagine; the image in this report anchors the text rather than the text anchoring the image. Unlike cases where journalists select images among photographs of an event they cover, in the present journalists can often easily find images to illustrate and amplify their stories. The text is therefore verified by the unmistakable "proof" of photographic representation. Even though most readers are aware of this "sleight of hand," digital storytelling and modes of storytelling facilitated by digitized archives and image access have a logic that we all collude with and acquiesce to.

As each of these reports reveals, narratives of women's victimization by predatory villains are framed as plots of melodrama and sensationalism. Central here are details reminiscent of the reporting of sexual intrigues in the tabloid press. As Rosalind Gill and Shani Orgad have observed, this framing raises the question of whether the visibility of #MeToo results from its calls for justice or from the salacious content that it brings to the surface: "To put it somewhat crudely, is it sexism or sex that sells?" (2018, 1323). The following extract from the *Mail and Guardian* reveals the conventions of tabloid coverage of sex scandals. Meticulous details about sexual actions, references to specific places that encourage voyeuristic participation, and plots that pace eroticized behavior jointly work to titillate readers:

> The most serious allegation came from Jane—not her real name, although her identity is known to the M&G [*Mail and Guardian*]— who alleged that Isaacs "made a lot of untoward remarks to me and sent me sexually suggestive texts, asking what I was wearing and if I touch myself." She was working on a project in the activism space at the time. This behavior culminated in Isaacs attempting to force himself on her, she claimed. "After dinner one night, he took me to a historical stone house on the top of Kalk Bay where he started to kiss me forcefully and tried to take my pants off.
>
> "He is not a big guy but I still had to fight him off. He did persist for a bit, then was offended because I rejected him," she said.

> Jane said after she confided in someone about the incident, Isaacs
> came to her house and threatened her. "He said if I dare tell anybody
> else I would never work in activism again in South Africa. I told him
> I was not scared of his threats and it seemed like I was the first per-
> son to stand up to him," she said. (Allison and Collison 2018)

The tone, subject matter, and style of writing here are similar to features of the report on Ronell's case in the *New York Times,* where the accuser recounts his version of her overtures: "Then, he said, she pulled him into her bed. 'She put my hands onto her breasts, and was pressing herself—her buttocks—onto my crotch,' he said. 'She was kissing me, kissing my hands, kissing my torso.' That evening, a similar scene played out again, he said" (Greenberg 2018).

The salacious detail as well as the style of reporting are reminiscent of tabloid sex scandal coverage. As a consequence, sexual violence ends up being eroticized, so such stories ultimately become about sex, not about violence. It is as though media interest in sensationalizing stories about publicly known figures was taking precedence over any politically motivated or principled attention to the key subject at hand: sexual violence. Media representation can thus transform the political subject of sexual violence into a familiar, titillating tabloid narrative: the sexual intrigues and scandalous behavior that lead to the fall of prominent public figures. It may be that because commentators have very few legacies to draw on to describe sexual assault, they fall back on a titillating media genre that has long been in place but that does not challenge the indignities and violence that accusers actually experience.

Certain media reports, in legitimating the accusations of particular victims or survivors, seem to advance the goals of the #MeToo movement as one focused on radically unsettling the gendered hierarchies and myths that support normalized violence. This essay has shown that these stories, by avoiding traditional media rape myths and victim blaming, do seem to serve the goals of the movement defined in this way. This is especially true if we consider the movement's focus on victim-centeredness and silence breaking. Both principles have been pivotal to #MeToo's efforts to surface hidden stories and generate collaboration with a view to effecting change. Yet the affective responses that are galvanized by this framing can be totally out of synch with a transformative agenda.

Such an agenda would challenge the gendered stereotypes and hegemonic images or narratives that have long naturalized, popularized, or mystified disempowering and reactionary norms about social subjects and power relationships.

De Benedictus, Orgad, and Rottenberg (2019) argue that the media's publicizing of the movement is often in line with a neoliberal feminist agenda that focuses on redress for particular individuals (who are often privileged in terms of race, professional status, or class). I have sought to show that, apart from privileging the struggles of relatively privileged individuals, even seemingly positive coverage can promote hegemonic storytelling about sex, violence, and gendered identities. Familiar and dominant frames may certainly galvanize readers' attention and emotional responses, but the goals of political transformation require us to pay critical attention to what Sara Ahmed (2004) describes as the cultural politics of emotion. Invoking Ahmed, Carolyn Pedwell and Anne Whitehead remind us that "one of the reasons that social transformation is so difficult to achieve, that relations of power are 'so intractable and enduring, even in the face of collective forms of resistance,' is the strength of our affective attachments to social norms. Feminist engagement with affective politics thus requires attention to the ways in which feelings can (re)produce dominant social and geopolitical hierarchies and exclusions" (2012, 120).

References

Ahmed, S. 2004. *The Cultural Politics of Emotion*. London: Routledge.

Allison, S., and C. Collison. 2018. "NGO's Sexual Harassment Woes Grow." *Mail and Guardian*, May 18. At https://mg.co.za/article/2018-05-18-00-ngos-sexual-harassment-woes-grow/.

Askanius, T., and J. Møller Hartley. 2019. "Framing Gender Justice: A Comparative Analysis of the Media Coverage of #MeToo in Denmark and Sweden." *Nordicom Review* 40 (2): 19–36.

Atwood, M. 2018. "Am I a Bad Feminist?" *Globe and Mail*, January 13. At https://www.theglobeandmail.com/opinion/am-i-a-bad-feminist/article37591823/.

Cuklanz, L. 2020. "Problematic News Framing of #MeToo." *Communication Review* 18 (4): 1–21.

De Benedictis, S., S. Orgad, and C. Rottenberg. 2019. "#MeToo, Popular Feminism, and the News: A Content Analysis of UK Newspaper Coverage." *European Journal of Cultural Studies* 22 (5–6): 718–38.

Duggan, L. 2018. "The Full Catastrophe." *Bullybloggers,* August 18. At https://bullybloggers.wordpress.com/2018/08/18/the-full-catastrophe/.

Evans, A. 2018. "#MeToo: A Study on Sexual Assault as Reported in the *New York Times.*" *Occam's Razor* 8:11–16.

Gill, R., and S. Orgad. 2018. "The Shifting Terrain of Sex and Power: From the 'Sexualization of Culture' to #MeToo." *Sexualities* 21 (8): 1313–324.

Glick, P., and S. Fiske. 2001. "Ambivalent Sexism." *Advances in Experimental Psychology* 33:115–88.

———. 2011. "Ambivalent Sexism Revisited." *Psychology of Women Quarterly* 35 (3): 530–35.

Greenberg, Z. 2018. "What Happens to #MeToo When a Feminist Is the Accused?" *New York Times,* August 13. At https://www.nytimes.com/2018/08/13/nyregion/sexual-harassment-nyu-female-professor.html.

Harris, K. L. 2019. *Beyond the Rapist: Title IX and Sexual Violence on US College Campuses.* Oxford: Oxford University Press.

Hartocollis, A. 2019. "New Wave of Student Activism Presses Colleges on Sexual Assault." *New York Times,* June 8. At https://www.nytimes.com/2019/06/08/us/college-protests-dobetter.html.

Kane, L. 2016. "Woman Who Accused Writer Steven Galloway of Sexual Assault Issues Statement." *Canadian Press,* November 24. At https://www.google.com/search?client=safari&rls=en&q=Kane,+L.+2016.+%E2%80%9CWoman+Who+Accused+Writer+Steven+Galloway+of+Sexual+Assault+Issues+Statement.%E2%80%9D+Canadian+Press,&ie=UTF-8&oe=UTF-8.

Kipnis, L. 2017. *Unwanted Advances: Sexual Parancia Comes to Campus.* New York: Harper.

Lewis, D. 2018. "Violence against Women and the Politics of Feminism." *Amandla* 60 (November 1). At https://aidc.org.za/violence-against-women-and-the-politics-of-feminism/.

Naylor, N. 2018. "'The Only Black Woman at the Social Justice Philanthropy Dinner Party': Navigating Patriarchy, Power, and Racism within Social Justice Spaces." *Sur* 15 (28): 89–104.

O'Boyle, J., and Q. Li. 2019. "'#MeToo Is Different for College Students': Media Framing of Campus Sexual Assault, Its Causes, and Proposed Solutions." *Newspaper Research Journal* 40 (2): 1–19.

Pedwell, C., and A. Whitehead. 2012. "Affecting Feminism: Questions of Feeling in Feminist Theory." *Feminist Theory* 13 (2): 115–29.

Raphael, Y. 2019. "Civil Society's #MeToo Moment: When Activists Become Abusers." *Daily Maverick,* August 6. At https://www.dailymaverick.co.za /article/2019-08-06-civil-societys-metoo-moment-when-activists- become-abusers/.

Razack, S. 2007. "Stealing the Pain of Others: Reflections on Canadian Humanitarian Responses." *Review of Education, Pedagogy, and Cultural Studies* 29 (4): 375–94.

Rodino-Colocino, M. 2018. "#MeToo: Countering Cruelty with Empathy." *Communication and Critical/Cultural Studies* 15 (1): 96–100.

Starkey, J., A. Koerber, M. Stenadori, and B. Pitchford. 2019. "#MeToo Goes Global: Media Framing of Silence Breakers in Four National Settings." *Journal of Communication Inquiry* 43 (4): 394–407.

Tuerkheimer, D. 2019. "Beyond #MeToo." *New York University Law Review* 94 (5): 1146–208.

Notes

1. *Editors' note:* See also the chapter by Guadalupe-Diaz and Whalley in this volume for more analysis of the Ronell case.

2. *Editors' note:* For an analysis of the Ronell case that foregrounds the uses and misuses of queer experiences in #MeToo, see Guadalupe-Diaz and Whalley's chapter in this volume.

3. The image, with the caption "LRC Allows Harasser to Resign," is available at https://mg.co.za/article/2018-06-01-00-lrc-allows-harasser-to-resign/.

PART III

HIGHER ED AND THE DISRUPTION OF EVERYDAY VIOLENCE AND EXCLUSIONS

6

#GamAni

How #MeToo Inspired the American Jewish
Community to Look Inward . . . and Where the
Human Family Goes from Here

Keren R. McGinity

I was born and raised a Jewish American, but the journey to activist took decades—decades of studying, researching, writing . . . and decades of sexual harassment. I was hurt, I was betrayed, and now I am angry. I am angry about what I and so many other women have experienced. I am angry about what people of all genders have endured for far too long. And I am angry that toxic masculinity continues to be made light of at the highest levels in this country. Coined in the men's movements of the 1980s, *toxic masculinity* evolved into an umbrella term for misogyny, homophobia, and men's violence in the second decade of the twenty-first century (Harrington 2020). Earlier American ideals of manhood such as loyalty, productivity, and service were replaced by macho men who exhibited aggression, domination, and violence, reinforcing a gender binary that limited men and belittled women (Faludi 1999). As a feminist scholar, I see toxic masculinity as a sign of contemporary gender politics that reinforces the subjugation of women by men. A month prior to the US presidential election of 2016, then candidate Donald Trump illustrated masculinity's new low point when he shrugged off a conversation about grabbing women by the genitals as "locker-room banter" (on *Access Hollywood*, quoted in Fahrenthold 2016). This mentality contributes to a global system of oppression of women. That the man who bragged he could do whatever he wanted to women came to occupy the White House is emblematic of this American epidemic.

129

I thought "me too" from the moment I first read the words in October 2017. But I did not say them or write them or post them on social media. Why was it so hard to say "me too"? I've thought a lot about the many times men have touched me without my consent. All were evidence of the patriarchy that convinced some men they had an inalienable right to girls' and women's bodies (see, e.g., McGinity 2019). Trained as a gender historian and a social scientist, I went over each occurrence chronologically in my head. When I was in elementary school, a man rubbed his naked penis against me at the Bronx Zoo. When I was in high school, the father of children I was babysitting came up behind me and slipped his hands down the front of my blouse. When I was a twenty-year-old in downtown Boston, a group of young men walking the opposite direction passed by, and one of them grabbed my breasts. As I was teaching a night section of Ivy League athletes in Providence, a student draped his arm over my shoulder and suggested that he deserved a better grade. During my postdoctoral training in Ann Arbor, a married neighbor stroked my face over lunch, and an attorney squeezed my butt when I thanked him for helping with a negligent landlord. Then I got to the most recent incident and stopped in my mental tracks.

Before the #MeToo movement began, Steven M. Cohen, the oft-quoted sociologist of American Jewry, used the pretense of professional advice and connections to lure me to a candle-lit dinner far from the academic conference and prying eyes of our colleagues. He probed my personal life, asking me one inappropriate question after another. He strangely took my hand in his and held it across the table until I carefully withdrew it from his grasp, afraid to bruise his ego. After I rebuffed his suggestion of walking me to my hotel room and firmly said "good night," he suddenly pressed his body against mine and kissed me in a manner suitable only for lovers. I ran back to my hotel room, repulsed, horrified, confused, and in tears.

Pursuing justice and pursuing it justly constitute one of Judaism's core obligations. In the Torah, it is written: "Justice, justice you shall pursue" (Deuteronomy 16:20). Yet how does one pursue justice when the perpetrator is held up on a communal pedestal? How does one call out a sexual predator when one has been socially brainwashed to be a "nice, straight Jewish girl"? Not make waves? Make room for men?

Strong gender and Jewish dynamics contributed to my initial silence. Cohen was older, tenured, and significantly more powerful. I had just finished a research fellowship and was staring unemployment in the face. The interconnectivity of Jewish academia combined with this perpetrator's status meant that saying "me too" would draw attention to something very wrong in the Jewish community in general and in Jewish studies in particular, where men continue to earn more than women. The ideas that the Jewish people are one big family, that we are responsible for each other, and that we should not speak ill of each other kept a muzzle on me. The Hebrew phrase *Kol Yisrael arevim zeh bazeh* (All of Israel is responsible for one another) was inscribed on my brain,[1] as was the Jewish law against *lashon hora* (evil tongue or gossip). These precepts caused intense reluctance to report and concern about communal shame. The mere thought of speaking out paralyzed me with fear and questions. What would people think? How would Cohen react? Would he sue me? Would I be judged for blowing the whistle on someone considered to be a Jewish academic superstar? Would my years of hard work and scholarship be shredded? It did not occur to me *then* that speaking out is actually consistent with Jewish values and academic integrity. I did not yet realize the hypocrisy of a Jewish communal "family" that sent its own unarmed daughters into the lion's den.

Sad to say, but I also questioned the value of my voice: I thought I needed a team of women's #MeToo stories to outweigh one man's voice, a concept later reinforced by the Ford–Kavanaugh hearings. Attorney Debra Katz, who advised Christine Blasey Ford, suspected that US Supreme Court justice nominee Brett Kavanaugh had victimized other women and knew that finding them was critical.[2] It is the twenty-first century, but in a society where men's voices carry more value than women's, he said/she said can be a losing battle for any woman who has experienced sexual assault.

Cohen and some of his closest collaborators unabashedly dominated the academic discourse on intermarriage, my area of research. His notoriety in the press and his incessant emails to the Association for the Social Scientific Study of Jewry (ASSJ) listserv meant that his name appeared on my screen weekly, sometimes multiple times a day. When our physical paths crossed at academic gatherings, I darted around the room to keep him at arm's length or positioned a friend between us.

As I learned more #MeToo stories, a sense of urgency began to well up inside me. Six years after the incident with Cohen, I read an article that asked in its headline: "When Will US Jews Confront Sexual Harassment and Other Abuses of Power?" (Medoff 2017). Hmm . . . I'm a US Jew. Finally, my Jewish and feminist identities intersected, igniting my fire to speak out. I published an op-ed titled "American Jewry's #MeToo Problem: A First Person Encounter" in the *New York Jewish Week* (McGinity 2018). Since then, people have told me I was so brave, but jumping into the abyss felt like a *Thelma and Louise* moment without anyone's hand to hold.

Within hours after my story went live, I heard from women who had privately complained years earlier about being harassed and assaulted by Cohen. They were told: *he* has a family, and dragging *his* name through the mud would ruin *his* career.

What I learned when I finally spoke truth to power fills me with amazement and hope for all who have suffered, for academia, and for the Jewish community. The academic leaders in whom I confided that I had written a soon-to-be-published #MeToo piece took immediate action to protect other women by disinviting Cohen from speaking on campus and by writing a hashtag #WeToo blog expressing solidarity. Within hours after my story went live, I was inundated with an overwhelming deluge of kindness, support, and gratitude. I heard from leaders of major organizations, such as the American Jewish World Service, the Jim Joseph Foundation, Aviv, Keshet, Hillel International, and the Schusterman Foundation. In addition to hearing from women who had been abused, I also heard from bystanders who wished they had been upstanders. Their experiences ranged from recent to decades old, and the telling of their stories was triggered by learning about my story. In some cases, they had not told anyone before then. I became a keeper of dark secrets, a human vault. The volume of support and thanks meant that the days when people brushed off inappropriate behavior as "Steve being Steve" were coming to an end. As the comedian Steven Colbert quipped leading up to the Kavanaugh hearings: "People who say 'boys will be boys' . . . shouldn't be allowed to raise boys. Or girls. Maybe a plant. A cactus." If only Colbert could have voted on that Supreme

Court nomination. While the nation is experiencing unprecedented political upheaval, the American Jewish community is actively working to create safe, respectful, and equitable work environments and communal spaces in line with Jewish ethics.

The expression "timing is everything" has great resonance regarding Jewish women speaking their truths and the Jewish community holding perpetrators accountable. The response to my experience made me realize how significantly the #MeToo movement was changing attitudes that could influence multiple sectors of the Jewish community, while also exposing areas resistant to change. I heard from a wide cross-section of leaders of the Jewish community, from fellow academics and lay leaders to philanthropic foundations and clergy. The volume of support and thanks I received meant that the time when people brushed off inappropriate behavior as "Steve just being Steve"—the Jewish version of "boys will be boys"—was coming to an end. Still, a few friends and colleagues were concerned. Was I getting a lot of blowback? Did people believe me? How was I fairing? I was surprised by the questions, which reflected a pre-#MeToo mentality of victim blaming. Fortunately, in June 2018 not a single person questioned my credibility or decision to speak truth to power. It was as if the Jewish community had finally gotten the wake-up call it needed to openly discuss and address a serious problem.

The academic field of Jewish studies was the first to react, but the ripple effects went far beyond it. Once I used my voice and my words appeared on June 21, 2018, Cohen promptly ceased his near daily postings on the ASSJ listserv to which we both belonged; he has not posted since. He apparently identified himself as the person in the op-ed I wrote, even before being contacted by either the investigative reporter Hannah Dreyfus or Marviette Johnson, the Title IX officer at Hebrew Union College–Jewish Institute of Religion (HUC-JIR), where he had a tenured position. Although a reliable source informed me that Cohen had lawyered up, likely hoping that I would be the only woman to come forward and preparing for a he said/she said fight, it quickly became clear that the many women he had abused over decades had something to say. He resigned from his honorary position as director of the Berman Jewish Policy Archive, a research database housed by Stanford University; he was also removed as a board member of *New Voices,* a magazine written and edited by Jewish college students.

Two months after I went public and four weeks after Dreyfus's comprehensive exposé in July 2018 (Dreyfus 2018a), bringing to light the fact that Cohen's sexual misconduct and abuse of power were a pattern of behavior spanning decades, the Title IX investigation ended with his resignation (under duress) from HUC-JIR (Jewish Telegraphic Agency 2018). As soon as the college issued a statement announcing this news, my phone blew up. It was my half birthday, and the relief of knowing that Cohen had been effectively knocked off his communal pedestal was the best present. I was never interested in having him face criminal charges. I wanted people who thought they knew Cohen, who socialized and prayed with him, who hired him and paid him, instead to see his true colors and women to be out of harm's way. That, to my mind, was justice.

Although the profession of Jewish studies had begun to look inward at the issue of sexual harassment the fall prior to my speaking out, and a somewhat clandestine group of community activists had already been operating for two years, the second half of the year 2018 was a turning point. Responding to the larger #MeToo movement, the Association for Jewish Studies (AJS) crafted a sexual harassment policy in the fall of 2017 and required conference attendees to sign it upon registration. Under the inspiring leadership of Christine Hayes, an esteemed Yale professor and president of the AJS, the AJS organized a Sexual Misconduct Taskforce and conducted a survey of its members' experiences. Cohen's AJS membership was revoked, and he was banned from attending the annual conference in December 2018. In 2019, the AJS convened legal and organizational experts to train members of the new Committee on Sexual Misconduct on how to manage both informal and formal complaints.

Grassroots efforts had been under way as early as 2016 when Naomi Eisenberger of the Good People Fund and Jamie Allen Black of the Jewish Women's Foundation of New York partnered to convene pilot programs (an in-person seminar, a webinar, and later a workshop attended by dozens of Jewish organizations) that recognized the communal responsibility to move beyond talk about sexual harassment to change the cultural structures and systems that enabled gender discrimination of all kind. In an aptly titled article published in November 2017, "Sexual Harassment Is Not a Jewish Value," Eisenberger and Black wrote, "We in the professional Jewish community cite our deeply held values as driving our work. But we must embrace the notion that these values, such as social justice, begin at home." It was, as these authors described, "a perfect storm" that encouraged people to begin publicly sharing stories about gendered power dynamics and sexual harassment on the #GamAni (#MeToo) Facebook group to raise awareness and request change. At an event called "Revealing #MeToo as #WeToo in Jewish Communal Life," held at the United Jewish Appeal–Federation of New York's headquarters in midtown Manhattan on January 25, 2018, approximately 250 leaders heard dramatic readings about sexual harassment that illuminated the pressing need for the Jewish community to finally take action (Hanau 2018). The mission was clear: find ways to dismantle the patriarchal structures that enabled sexual misconduct and abuses of power.

Jewish clergy stepped up in solidarity and to learn. More than one hundred rabbis joined a webinar titled "#MeToo from the Pulpit: A Rabbi's Role in Creating Safe, Respectful Synagogue Communities." Human resources consultant and sexual-harassment-avoidance trainer Fran Sepler told the audience: "It's time that we begin consciously tearing down the misogynist culture that has been left untouched for far too long—and build a new, feminist culture instead" (quoted in Dubofsky 2018, 29). With the goal of changing culture within the Reform movement, the Central Conference of American Rabbis (CCAR) launched the Taskforce on the Experience of Women in the Rabbinate. To some who read the taskforce's findings, it was surprising that even forty-five years after the first woman became a Reform rabbi, women rabbis are still subjected to "gender-based bias, inappropriate comments, sexual harassment, sexual assault, lack of proper institutional support, undermining behavior and issues related to contracts, pay equity and parental leave," and to others it was an obvious part of daily life. Partnering with HUC-JIR, the Union for Reform Judaism, and members of the Women's Rabbinic Network (WRN) leadership, the CCAR declared: "It is our ethical and professional mandate to address these deeply troubling challenges. This newly created Taskforce will study the realities women face in order to identify their root causes and potential solutions." It has begun providing a slew of resources—including sermons and text study, articles and professional tools, rituals, a bibliography and research papers—and developing a program called "Excuse Me, What Did You

Say?," intended to better enable women rabbis to professionally handle situations in which people make inappropriate comments to them.[3] Rabbi Mary Zamore, executive director of the WRN, understands that creating change also requires that institutions and communities take responsibility: "It is impossible to move forward without doing the institutional and communal *teshuva,* repentance, making amends for our past failures to listen to victims and to ensure their safety in our communities. As Jews, this is an essential step [*sic*]. The community cannot move forward without reflectingand examining our past."[4]

The importance of women's stories to make visible the many experiences of inequality and abuse in the Jewish community became paramount. No better example exists than the Archiving #MeToo project launched by the Jewish Women's Archive in January 2018 in partnership with several other organizations. As executive director Judith Rosenbaum explained, "Taken together, these stories illustrate the systems and structures that shape women's experiences, as well as women's collective power to make change. In other words, they contain within them both the problem and the seeds of its solution" (2018a). The #MeToo collection, which Rosenbaum and others have begun to analyze, comprises mountains of evidence about the pervasiveness of sexual harassment of Jewish women, about Jewish women's awareness of the ways cultural expectations have shaped them, and about how their effort to minimize unwanted sexual behavior indicated, as one woman realized, "the enormity of the problem."[5] Looking inward and recording stories were a necessary beginning; fortunately, Jewish #MeToo activists were just getting started.

Once a major player in the world of Jewish academia and communal policy making was unmasked as a serial sexual abuser, professors and journalists shook the community fully awake with a slew of hard-hitting articles. The Jewish studies scholars Kate Rosenblatt, Lila Corwin Berman, and Ronit Stahl pounced on the male-dominated Jewish communal leadership who hired only other men, including Cohen, and participated in "aggressive boundary policing": "Most troubling about the data-driven mode of Jewish continuity conversations are its patriarchal, misogynistic, and anachronistic assumptions about what is good for the Jews." They minced no words: "It is time to acknowledge that a communal obsession with sex and statistics has created pernicious and damaging norms" (2018).[6] Susan Weidman Schneider, editor in chief of *Lilith* magazine, wrote that "when a flawed male with a lot of power shapes Jewish priorities" the community lost out (2018); the policies around interfaith marriage, she argued, were built on Cohen's flawed findings based on questions and hypotheses that precluded realities of other social scientists who studied the community through a gender lens. The English professor Helene Meyers described Cohen weaponizing his professional prestige and power against women and questioned: "Which of my male colleagues listened to an academic gatekeeper brag about 'sleeping with all of the smart Jewish women' and said or did nothing?" (2018). The philanthropist Barbara Dobkin, who supported advancing women in the Jewish community for many decades, articulated surprise when some leaders in the Jewish community resisted "examining the links between the personal behavior of Cohen and Steinhardt and their shared investment in Jewish continuity." The Jewish philanthropist Michael Steinhardt had similarly abused his power and sexually harassed women (Otterman and Dreyfus 2019). Dobkin asked pointedly: "How can we, as a Jewish community, fail to interrogate the relationship between actions that degrade women and a worldview in which Jewish women are valued most for their ability to give birth to Jewish babies?" (2018).[7] Indeed!

During the remainder of 2018 and in 2019, the initiatives around #MeToo in the Jewish community grew exponentially. Gone were the days when nothing happened when Jewish women told other people about Jewish men sexually harassing and assaulting them, other than that they were advised to avoid one-on-one meetings with a particular financial donor or to "grow thicker skin."[8] Once the organized Jewish community—that is, people who work as professionals in the Jewish community—understood that it was not immune from what was occurring around the #MeToo movement in the secular world, an army of women and a small but growing cadre of male allies began to respond. One of the next steps was to create a third-party organization that was dedicated to this effort. The SafetyRespectEquity (SRE) Coalition was founded in March 2018, bringing together twenty-five Jewish organizations and institutions under one umbrella. The leaders announced: "The purpose of the partnership is to ensure that safe, respectful and equitable workplaces and communal spaces become universal in Jewish life and that sexual harassment and misconduct, as well as gender and sexual orientation discrimination, and their related abuses of power, are no longer tolerated in the Jewish community" (*eJewishPhilanthropy* 2018). The SRE Coalition focused its efforts on making a commitment to address ethical workplace and communal-space behavior; raising awareness and providing education that supports culture change; developing policies and procedures to prevent and respond effectively; and offering concrete training and support. This ambitious endeavor brought together leaders working in nearly every nonprofit arena, acknowledging: "We must live up to the values within Jewish tradition that call upon us to raise our voices and lead where our community and society have fallen short" (*eJewishPhilanthropy* 2018).

A wellspring of new efforts has sprung up in the Jewish community in a relatively short amount of time, some independently started by women who experienced sexual misconduct and abuse of power first-hand and some at least partially funded by the SRE Coalition. Rachel Cohen founded Shema Koleinu (Hear Our Voices), a nonprofit based in California offering support and healing for Jewish adults abused by clergy. Shira Berkovitz founded Sacred Spaces, partnering with Jewish leaders "to build healthy and accountable institutions whose very culture and daily operations prevent opportunities for harassment for assault" across five continents.[9] The Jewish Community Centers (JCCs) Association of North America began piloting to provide training, information, and tools to help local JCCs become harassment- and discrimination-free spaces. Numerous other Jewish organizations focused on creating safe environments on college campuses, at summer camps, and within congregations. The Shalom Hartman Institute started a research and education project called "Created Equal: Men, Women, and the Ethics of Shared Leadership" to help educational leaders. Slingshot, an organization that mobilizes young philanthropists, began work on a guide to funding with a gender lens and accompanying curriculum. Organizations and individuals with a wide range of expertise—from rabbinic to legal and everything in between—were enlisted to do a groundbreaking series of webinars for the SRE on topics that are critical to creating cultural change: preventing and addressing harm; setting expectations for interpersonal conduct; establishing pay equity; reporting and responding; educating and training.[10]

Yet challenges remain for the Jewish community and likely will for years to come. Although all of the communal efforts are historical firsts, actually changing behaviors that have been engrained for generations takes considerably more time and energy. Shifra Bronznick, the founding president of Advancing Women Professionals in the Jewish Community who has been fighting for gender equality for decades, observed, "It's not like nothing's happened, but it's not like we're so woke."[11] Bronznick describes the current situation as living in "parallel universes." In one universe, women are leading and in power, as is evident in their current extensive leadership in social movements (the women's movement, the Black Lives Matter movement, the LGBTQ movement), in business, and in academia, and there are now women philanthropists.[12] In the other powerful universe, however, is "the real fight to take away women's rights to their bodily autonomy, even in the case of rape and incest"—that is, the right to choose abortion. "We have the sexual harasser in chief in the White House."[13] A community can make only as much progress as all of its schools, synagogues, nonprofits, and agencies are willing and able to do. As states have begun requiring private employers to distribute written antiharassment policies in workplaces, to require anti harassment training for employees, and to extend the statute of limitation for filing harassment complaints, the Jewish community continues struggling with how to regulate interpersonal behavior (Dreyfus 2018b).

The negative narrative on intermarriage that Cohen and his collaborators spouted for a generation is being rethought. There is now breathing room for other voices, new research questions, and analyses as well as greater potential for alternative narratives to be taken seriously by the Jewish communal world. There is also tremendous opportunity to allow people to self-identify as Jews in meaningful ways. Rather than being limited to definitions according to Jewish denomination or synagogue affiliation, American Jews are free to find their own alternative expressions of Jewishness that defy organizational definitions about authenticity and observance.

Moving forward, I want to see a true cultural shift. I want to see more women and non-gender-binary people in positions of leadership. I want to see women and non-gender-binary people being paid equally as men for the same work. I want to see men standing up to other men who engage in sexual misconduct and abuse of power. I want to see men acknowledging that the lack of gender equality is part of the system of oppression that discourages men from speaking up when they witness other men misbehaving. And I want to see men participating equally in domestic labor and childcare. Fifty years ago the Redstockings feminist Pat Mainardi wrote "The Politics of Housework" about the inequalities between men and women in domestic labor, yet making beds and play dates continue to be socially deemed "women's work": the dad who does more is called an "involved father," but there is no such thing as an "involved mother."

There is a world of educating to do as we move forward to repair the world. Scholars and activists are in this together, and there is no precedent, no clear road map. We must put one foot in front of the other. We will make mistakes, and we can learn from them and keep moving forward. There are many wonderful men out there, allies whose scholarship and activism are inspirational (see, e.g., Burrell 2019 and Slucki 2019)[14].

Feminists of all genders, ages, colors, economic statuses, religions, and nationalities must say "no" to being treated as less than equals. We must use our voices to speak out. We must persist in preventing de facto sexism and harassment across the spectrum of egregiousness from dictating our lives. Only then will the world finally know peace.

Humans categorize; it's how we operate in the world. But speaking out emboldened my belief that we can choose our own labels. People have called me a victim. Although I was victimized, I reject that label because it deprives people of agency. People have called me a survivor. Although I can write these words, I did not battle cancer, nor was I liberated from a concentration camp like my coreligionists after the Holocaust, the systematic genocide of Jews and other human beings Hitler deemed undesirable. I am a *per*sister! A "persister" is any organism that survives in spite of opposition or extreme conditions. My use of this term and the meaning I intend are social rather than microbiological, inspired by the feminist movement's employment of the expression "Nevertheless, she persisted." Senate majority leader Mitch McConnell said these words after stating, "She was warned. She was given an explanation," regarding Senator Elizabeth Warren after she was interrupted while reading the words of Coretta Scott King by presiding Senate chair Steve Daines for supposedly violating Senate Rule XIX. As the *Atlantic* culture reporter Megan Garber wrote, "It was that most classic of things:

a woman (sharing the words, no less, of another woman) told by a man to shut up" (2017). Although sexual predators and gatekeepers have influenced my career, I *per*sisted; I kept researching, publishing, teaching, and serving my community and my country. *Our country.*

I also persist in seeking the truth and in speaking truth to power. One of the most toxic flaws of our society is the focus on binaries. Binary thinking is an either/or mentality. Good *or* bad. Strong *or* weak. Democrat *or* Republican. Binary thinking encourages polarization and tribalism: us *or* them. I believe that as a society we must move from binary thinking and toward dialectic thinking. Dialectic thinking is the both/and approach. Dialectic thinking looks beyond a single element about people—the color of their skin, their heritage, or how they worship—and instead into the depth and complexity of who they are. Instead of man or woman, we are man, woman, *and* transgender. We aren't Black or white; we are dark chocolate, white chocolate, *and* every shade of milk chocolate—thank you, *Daily Show* host Trevor Noah. Not one religion or another but many different religions. We're religionists, spiritualists, and secularists. The decline in consumer popularity of the Victoria's Secret brand could not come soon enough. Its fueling of men's fantasies through the objectification of women's bodies (and the lack of body diversity) contributes to binary thinking that has encouraged some men to prove their manliness by "scoring" with women. The personal connection between the CEO of Victoria's Secret's parent brand, Leslie Wexner, and the late pedophile Jeffrey Epstein as well as the open petition from one hundred Victoria Secret models to protect them from sexual misconduct cast serious doubt on whether such a company should continue to exist (Erskine 2019; Gold 2019). Dialectic thinking makes room for the reality that women are much more than our physical bodies, that we deserve equal treatment and respect in all realms of life.

Rather than thinking of individual religious groups as separate families, I am convinced that people of all faith backgrounds belong to one family: the human family. After a terrorist slaughtered eleven of my Jewish brothers and sisters in Pittsburgh, the first text I received was from my Muslim sister Sameera Qureshi. The next was from my Greek Orthodox sister Dina Zingaro. Then I saw an image of a man of color holding a sign that read "Jewish Lives Matter." The #MeToo movement is part of the American history of social movements that have united people of diverse backgrounds for the greater good. The late reggae musician Bob Marley (1963–1981) sang the following words in 1980: "Get up. Stand up. Stand up for your rights! Get up. Stand up. Don't give up the fight!" More recently, the hip-hop artist Mona Haydar has called out and taken down the patriarchy in her song "Dog." If you have not heard the lyrics yet, the song is a must-listen. While Haydar calls out hypocrite Muslim men in particular, her poetry speaks volumes about all people of all genders and all backgrounds who think that they somehow are above their religion or the law. Conceiving of ourselves as belonging to one human family, we can work across faith communities and continents to stop sexual misconduct and abuse of power.

I implore readers of this volume to be *per*sisters and brothers who stand up for each other and fight together. *Per*sisters and brothers, siblings in solidarity who break down binaries rather than reinforce them. *Per*sisters and brothers who find solidarity across groups instead of forming battle lines between them. We are not responsible for perfecting the world, but nor should we do nothing. We must get up, stand up, and call out the international dogs. To be free from sexual misconduct and abuse of power is a human right we all deserve. Together we must persist in spreading truth and love to prevent sexism, antisemitism, ethnocentrism, racism, classism, and gender discrimination from dictating our lives and tearing apart our human family. Together, as the famous song says, "we shall overcome someday." Let us make it soon!

References

Bronznick, S. 2019. Interviewed by Robert Bank. SafetyRespectEquity Summit, Summer. Private video on VIMEO.

Burrell, S. 2019. "It's Time for Men to Take Responsibility for Ending Male Violence." Blog, December 7. At https://www.whiteribbon.org.uk/news/2019/12/6/its-high-time-men-take-on-the-onus-for-stopping-male-violence?.

Central Conference of American Rabbis. N.d. "Taskforce on the Experience of Women in the Rabbinate." At https://www.ccarnet.org/rabbinic-voice/task-force-on-the-experience-of-women-in-the-rabbinate/.

Dobkin, B. 2018. "Why the 'Jewish Continuity' Conversation Must Change in the Era of #MeToo." *eJewishPhilanthropy*, October 5. At https://ejewishphilanthropy.com/why-the-jewish-continuity-conversation-must-change-in-the-era-of-metoo/.

Dreyfus, H. 2018a. "Harassment Allegations Mount against Leading Jewish Sociologist." *New York Jewish Week,* July 19.

———. 2018b. "#MeToo in the Jewish Community: Where Are We Now?" *New York Jewish Week,* June 20. At https://jewishweek.timesofisrael.com /me-too-in-the-jewish-community-where-are-we-now/.

Dubofsky, C. 2018. "Women Who Are Rabbis Experience Their Own Brand of Harassment." *Lilith* magazine 43 (1) (Spring): 27–29.

Eisenberger, N., and J. A. Black. 2017. "Sexual Harassment Is Not a Jewish Value." *eJewishPhilanthropy,* November 12. At https://ejewishphilanthropy .com/sexual-harassment-is-not-a-jewish-value/.

Eisner, J. 2018. "Family Is a Jewish Value: Don't Let the Mistakes of a Few Rob Us of That Gift." *Forward,* September 16.

eJewishPhilanthropy. 2018. "Safe, Respectful, Equitable: Launching a New Partnership for Jewish Communal Life." March 8. At http://safetyrespectequity .org/webinars/.

Erskine, B. 2019. "The Real Reason Victoria's Secret Is Closing so Many Stores." *TheList,* May 2. At https://www.thelist.com/151899/the-real-reason-victorias-secret-is-closing-so-many-stores/.

Fahrenthold, D. A. 2016. "Trump Recorded Having Extremely Lewd Conversation about Women in 2005." *Washington Post,* October 8. At https:// www.washingtonpost.com/politics/trump-recorded-having-extremely-lewd-conversation-about-women-in-2005/2016/10/07/3b9ce776-8cb4-11e6-bf8a-3d26847eeed4_story.html.

Faludi, S. 1999. *Stiffed: The Betrayal of the American Man.* New York: Morrow.

Garber, M. 2017. "'Nevertheless, She Persisted' and the Age of the Weaponized Meme." *Atlantic,* February 8.

Gold, H. 2019. "Victoria's Secret's New Marketing Campaign Is Inspired by #MeToo." *New York Magazine,* September 11. At https://www.thecut .com/2019/09/victorias-secret-rebranding-for-women.html.

Hanau, S. 2018. "Town Hall Meeting Puts Spotlight on Harassment." *New York Jewish Week,* January 30.

Harrington, C. 2020. "What Is 'Toxic Masculinity' and Why Does It Matter?" *Men and Masculinities,* July 17, 1–8.

Jewish Telegraphic Agency. 2018. "Steven Cohen Resigns from HUC Following Sexual Misconduct Investigation." *Jewish Week/Times of Israel,* August 22. At https://jewishweek.timesofisrael.com/steven-cohen-resigns-from-huc-following-sexual-misconduct-investigation/.

Kantor, J., and M. Twohey. 2019. *She Said: Breaking the Sexual Harassment Story That Helped Ignite a Movement.* New York: Penguin.

McGinity, K. R. 2018. "American Jewry's #MeToo Problem: A First Person Encounter." *New York Jewish Week,* June 21.

———. 2019. "Why It Was So Hard to Say #MeToo and What I Learned When I Finally Did." Special issue on patriarchy, *AJS Perspectives*, Spring, 20–22.

———. 2020. "The Unfinished Business of the Sexual Revolution." Special issue on women and gender, *Journal of American Jewish History* 104 (2–3) (April–July): 207–13.

Medoff, R. 2017. "When Will US Jews Confront Sexual Harassment and Other Abuses of Power?" *Jerusalem Post*, December 23.

Meyers, H. 2018. "When an Accused Sexual Harasser Is an Academic Super-star."*Lilith*blog,August7.Athttps://www.lilith.org/blog/2018/08/when-an-accused-sexual-harasser-is-an-academic-superstar/.

Otterman, S., and H. Dreyfus. 2019. "Michael Steinhardt, a Leader in Jewish Philanthropy, Is Accused of a Pattern of Sexual Harassment." *New York Times*, March 21. At https://www.nytimes.com/2019/03/21/nyregion/michael-steinhardt-sexual-harassment.html.

Pogrebin, L. C. 2018. "The Many Gradations of #MeToo." *Moment*, November 8.

Ravblog. 2018. "A #MeToo/#GamAni Confession for the High Holy Days." Central Conference of American Rabbis blog, August 31. At http://ravblog.ccarnet.org/2018/08/metoo-gamani-confession-high-holy-days/.

Rosenbaum, J. 2018a. "Archiving #MeToo." *eJewishPhilanthropy*, January 21.

———. 2018b. "#MeToo: The Shaping of Gender and Jewish Identity." Presentation for the Association for Jewish Studies Conference, Boston, December 16–19.

Rosenblatt, K., L. Corwin Berman, and R. Stahl. 2018. "How Jewish Academia Created a #MeToo Disaster." *Jewish Daily Forward*, July 19.

———. 2020. "Continuity Crisis: The History and Sexual Politics of an American Jewish Communal Project." Special issue on women and gender, *American Jewish History* 104 (2–3) (April–July): 167–94.

Schneider, S. W. 2018. "From the Editor." *Lilith* magazine, Summer, 3.

Shain, M. 2018. "Don't Dismiss Steven Cohen's Research." *New York Jewish Week*, July 25.

Slucki, D. 2019. "I'm a Jewish Dad. Here's How I'm Raising My Son to Be a Feminist." *Kveller*, October 25. At https://www.kveller.com/im-a-jewish-dad-heres-how-im-raising-my-son-to-be-a-feminist/.

Zamore, Mary L. 2018. "Jewish Institutions, Not #MeToo Victims, Must Change the Status Quo." *Forward* blog, Scribe network, February 14. At https://forward.com/scribe/394371/jewish-institutions-not-metoo-victims-must-change-the-status-quo/.

Notes

1. Shavuot 39a in the Talmud. The Talmud is the Jewish oral tradition that accompanies the Tanakh (the Torah, or Hebrew Bible), a record of rabbinic teachings that interprets and explains how the commandments are to carried out, and the primary source of Jewish religious law and theology that interprets the scriptures.

2. Even after another woman (Deborah Ramirez) came forward about Kavanaugh's behavior, he was still confirmed (see Kantor and Twohey 2019, 205, 225).

3. Rabbi Amy Schwartzman, co-chair of the CCAR Taskforce on the Experience of Women in the Rabbinate, interviewed by the author, November 8, 2019; Central Conference of American Rabbis n.d.

4. Mary Zamore, email to the author, November 20, 2019. See also *Ravblog* 2018 and Zamore 2018.

5. These stories came from individuals in the Jewish community and beyond it; therefore, I defer to Judith Rosenbaum's (2018b) analysis (with the exception of this brief quote) rather than the stories themselves.

6. See also Rosenblatt, Corwin Berman, and Stahl's expanded article "Continuity Crisis: The History and Sexual Politics of an American Jewish Communal Project" (2020) and my response, "The Unfinished Business of the Sexual Revolution" (McGinity 2020).

7. Dobkin was writing against pieces that separated abusive men's misconduct from their communal and scholarly endeavors. The latter type of articles merits only a footnote to illustrate that not all Jewish women could immediately see the inherent conflict of interest between some men's claim to care deeply about the Jewish community through their research and philanthropy and their abuse of women. See, for example, Eisner 2018; Pogrebin 2018; and Shain 2018.

8. Former Hillel International staff member, confidential interview by the author, September 2, 2018.

9. See the Sacred Spaces website at https://www.jewishsacredspaces.org/.

10. See the SRE website at http://safetyrespectequity.org/webinars/.

11. Shifra Bronznick, interviewed by the author, November 8, 2019.

12. For example, Barbara B. Dobkin is a visionary philanthropist. See https://jwa.org/aboutjwa/whoweare/board.

13. Bronznick 2019, quoting Donald Trump saying, "I grope women's pussies because I can."

14. *Editors' note:* See also Burrell's chapter in this volume.

7

Intimacy, Transgression, Ethics

Scripts and Silences in Gendered Academia

Rukmini Sen

To engage with the dynamics and responses to #MeToo in higher education in India, as this chapter does, we must first examine the increasing presence of women students and a rhetoric of gender equality promoted within institutions of higher learning. The higher-education landscape in India is rapidly and vastly transforming. In postcolonial societies such as India, education and law are two major sites through which social emancipation is expected and possible, if one is able to access them. According to the sociologist Satish Deshpande, formal access to higher education has expanded exponentially (Deshpande 2011). Between 1991 and 2013–2014, total enrollment in higher education increased 6.5 times (from 49 million to 323 million); the number of universities nearly quadrupled (184 to 723); and the gross enrollment ratio for the 18–23 age group almost tripled (from 8.1 percent to 23.9 percent). Women now account for almost 42 percent of total enrollment but still comprise only around 18 percent in the technical-professional fields (Kapur and Mehta 2017). The lower castes are also increasing their share in enrollment but are still below their share with respect to their percentage of the overall population. There are also important differences by gender, field of study, and region. Yet by all indications Hindu upper-caste males, who comprised more than two-thirds of all graduates in the not-too-distant past, are now a minority among currently enrolled students even as they are still overrepresented relative to their share of the overall population (Kapur and Mehta 2017). It is significant to underline that although higher-education institutions (HEIs) in India have always been extremely gendered spaces, the portion of women in higher education went up from 39 percent to 46 percent from 2007 to 2014 (International Monetary Fund 2015). Girls outscore boys in Class X performance, yet enrollment of women in professional courses and PhD programs is still much smaller than enrollment of men. The Indian Institutes of Technology (IIT) decided to create at least 550 extra seats exclusively for women in the class starting July 2018 as the nation's premier engineering colleges seek to strike a better gender balance. In 2017, when IIT admitted nearly 11,000 students, the percentage of women at some of the institutes fell below 10 percent (P. Verma 2018).

Interestingly, although women's access to higher education has widened, female participation in India's labor force declined to a low of 27 percent in 2014 from 34 percent in 1999, according to a study by the International Monetary Fund in 2015. If women's labor-force participation has decreased, the other factor to look into is marriage. Here we see that although the median age of marriage has increased, it continues to be low: 19.2 years for women in 2011 (up from 18.2 in 2001), according to 2011 census data. Men married on average at the age of 23.5 in 2011, up from 22.6 in 2001 (*Sample Registration System* 2014, table 4.1). This connection among women's increased access to higher education, lower labor-force participation, and a minor increase in the average age of women marrying suggests a dual narrative of opportunity and stagnation.

The past two decades have simultaneously been about increasing the presence of women in HEIs and initiating various gender-based initiatives in these spaces. It is necessary to locate women students' expressions of anger, vulnerability, discomfort, and anxiety around sexual relations and transgressions at the current moment as both the result of feminist politics outside HEIs and the institutional responses to gender-based violence and discrimination inside HEIs. The promise and the discomforts around this contemporary moment are connected to broader feminist politics, particularly to interactions inside and outside of university spaces. In the past two decades, more than eighty women's studies centers were funded by the University Grants Commission, which is the apex of social science and humanities education in India, controlling, monitoring, and evaluating its organization. These centers were set up with a mandate to engender disciplines as well as to implement various outreach initiatives related to gender sensitization (Sen and Menon 2020). Women's Development Cells were also established to take care of awareness and quasi-legal activities on violence and oppression in different women's colleges across the country (e.g., Lady Shri Ram College n.d.). Many of these institutions came into being as early as the mid-1980s. After 1997, to implement the *Vishaka* judgment (an Indian Supreme Court judgment that pronounced for the first time the definition of sexual harassment in the workplace), the need for having anti–sexual harassment bodies on campuses was felt. From 2013 and due to a statutory mandate, the Sexual Harassment of Women at the Workplace (Prevention, Prohibition, and Redressal) Act of 2013,[1] anti-sexual harassment committees have become mandatory in HEIs. Together with these cells and committees, there are also emerging queer collectives, *dalit-bahujan* study circles, and courses on gender, sexualities, and masculinities being introduced through English, sociology, law, political science, and development studies programs in addition to women studies centers or women's/gender studies programs.

In examining #MeToo in India, it is essential to keep in mind that this overall political, pedagogical, and policy transformation has made it possible for the millennial student to talk gender, talk equality, talk feminism(s), especially within social science and liberal arts HEIs in various parts of India. The articulation may not always have been easy and has been met with resistance by authorities, yet there is no denying that there is a pattern of mainstreaming in the language and rhetoric of gender in HEIs within the past decade.

It is against this backdrop of, on the one hand, the increasing presence of women students and, on the other hand, a rhetoric of gender equality being promoted within institutions of higher learning that #MeToo in universities in India has to be contextualized. The current moment is a 2017 moment, yet the ripples of it can be traced further back through a blog post written by an Indian law student in 2013. In that post, she hesitantly disclosed the experience of sexual assault she experienced as an intern by a judge of repute. In the blog titled *Through My Looking Glass,* the law student, without disclosing the judge's name, reflected on the practices of feminism itself (James 2013). This was important especially at a euphoric juncture after the nationwide protests in December 2012 against the gruesome sexual violence that occurred in Delhi. She wrote,

> I am not trying to say that anger at the violence that women face is not a just or true response, but the polarization of women's rights debates in India along with their intense emotionality, left me feeling that my only options were to either strongly condemn the judge or to betray my feminist principles. Perhaps this confusion came out of an inadequate understanding of feminist literature, but if so, isn't then my skewed perception a failing of feminism itself? If the shared experiences of women cannot be easily understood through a feminist lens, then clearly there is a cognitive vacuum that feminism fails to fill. Feminists talk of the guilt a woman faces when sexually harassed, like it is her fault. I felt a similar guilt, except, my guilt wasn't at being assaulted, but at not reacting more strongly than I did. . . . Despite the heated public debates, despite a vast army of feminist vigilantes, despite new criminal laws and sexual harassment laws, I have not found closure. The lack of such an alternative led to my facing a crippling sense of intellectual and moral helplessness. (James 2013)

This chapter engages with what issue this current #MeToo moment more collectively raises. It engages with questions about ambivalences in both feminism and law, echoing what this law student expressed in the blog post in 2013. It brings in questions of what is the *right* feminist response when faced with sexual violation. It is also important to confront what happens when emotions do not have a name or voice or meaning within the existing feminist repertoire and there is an absence of closure. Through her blog, the reflexive millennial student interrogates years of feminist politics and law reform.

In 2015, another law student wrote "Confessions of a Slut" in *Glasnost,* an independent online student magazine of a Delhi law school. She wrote a long essay on the everyday sexism in a law school campus, ending with a few questions:

> We feel entitled to know what happened, what the victim feels, why she isn't speaking up, if she did speak up: why did she speak up like

that, why did she file a complaint, why did she not, and of course . . .
why hasn't she let it go? We have no idea of what is going on in anyone's mind or life, and have no right to go around inquiring or commenting about the same. We as a campus not only have been
insensitive and have openly condemned victims; we have created a
culture of harassment wherein girls are being shut up and policed.
Perhaps we have created a hierarchy in our mind wherein certain
forms of harassment merit a response from the victim and other
forms need a toned down response. (Mahajan 2015)

This student questions the HEI, which is assumed to be a more democratic space and yet one that may not allow everyday gendered practices
to be spoken about openly. The two law students—both of whom name
themselves and use online mechanisms, such as the blog, to articulate
their painful experiences—raise questions on gendered campus cultures,
feminist praxis, and structures of law. As if with some continuity but
through very different modes of action, the #MeToo moment also
brought us to the crossroads of sexual transgressions/harassment within
campuses and an everyday culture of misogyny permeating many forms
of interpersonal behavior.

Millennial university-going students across various Indian cities
are protesting in a new language since the Delhi gang rape of 2012.
Moving away from notions of protection, this language reclaims freedom: freedom from both *baap* (father) and *khap* (community policing)
and freedom to claim city roads and transport at any time day or night.
It makes proclamations over one's own body and sexual autonomy while
also screaming "Pinjra tod!" (Break the hostel chains!). It is important to
recognize that these chains are not just of or about the campus hostels
for women being locked up at night—the night curfew that all halls of
residence practice, especially for women—but a metaphor for defining
much of women's experiences, their being chained by casteist heteropa-
triarchy. These feminist voices—aloud and abound—are democratizing
public and private spaces as well as spaces at the cusp of both (e.g., student accommodations such as hostels), marking women's entry to the
broader political environment of HEIs, and making use of not just
the streets and posters but also blogs, Facebook pages, Instagram, and
Twitter to make themselves heard.

Evolution of the Law on Sexual Harassment in India, 1997–2013: From a Hostile Work Environment to a Criminal Work Space

In India, the legal discourse on sexual harassment has been tied up with rape. A gang rape of a lower-caste woman employee during work hours in 1992 led to multiple protests by women's groups across the country, a writ petition filed in the Supreme Court, and the subsequent judgment (*Vishaka and Others v. State of Union of India*) that cited the United Nations Convention on the Elimination of All Forms of Discrimination against Women (CEDAW) of 1979 and established fundamental rights of the Indian Constitution to defining sexual harassment for women at the workplace for the first time in 1997.[2] Bhanwari Devi, the woman who was gang-raped, had confided to two of her coworkers about the *anyaya* (injustice) meted out to her. Kanchan Mathur wrote, "It is noteworthy that in common village parlance, rape is usually referred to as *anyaya* or *burakaam* (wrong deed) rather than as '*balatkaar*' (rape)" (1992, 2223). This is an important issue for consideration in the current moment because how women talk about rape or any form of sexual violation to their trusted ones or even in a court of law can be affected by a limited vocabulary or by taboo or by unfamiliarity with certain words or even the hesitation to say a word. In the case of Bhanwari, *balatkar* (rape) could have been the taboo word. However, what does it mean when a woman says she has been wronged? And what are the ways in which she may be wronged? It is much more disconcerting to confront the wrong here than to think immediately of how it can be righted. Without going into the details of the Bhanwari Devi gang-rape case history, it is necessary to remember that the Supreme Court judgment led to a definition of sexual harassment, which included such unwelcome sexually determined behavior (whether directly or by implication) as *(a)* physical contact and advances; *(b)* a demand or request for sexual favors; *(c)* sexually colored remarks; *(d)* the showing of pornography; *(e)* any other unwelcome physical verbal or nonverbal conduct of a sexual nature.

Subsequent to this judgment, due to political initiatives by students and faculty a university-specific prevention-and-grievance redressal body in Jawaharlal Nehru University, New Delhi, was created in 1999 and called the Gender Sensitization and Committee against Sexual

Harassment. In other HEIs in Delhi, to redress matters of sexual harassment, the Delhi University Apex Committee against Sexual Harassment was formed in 2007; Indira Gandhi National Open University formed a similar committee in 2008, Jamia Milia Islamia in 2011, Dr. B. R. Ambedkar University Delhi in 2014, and National Law University Delhi in 2015. Using Articles 14, 15, 19 (1(g)), and 21 of the Indian Constitution as well as Articles 11 and 24 of CEDAW, the *Vishaka* judgment stated that such conduct can be humiliating and may constitute a health-and-safety problem. Such conduct is discriminatory when the woman has reasonable grounds to believe that her objection to it would disadvantage her in connection with her employment, including in recruitment or promotion, or when it creates a hostile working environment. An extremely significant aspect of this judgment was in the pronouncement that "all employers or persons in charge of [a] work place whether in the public or private sector should take appropriate steps to prevent sexual harassment." The importance placed on prevention could not be more appreciated because most legal provisions are usually aimed at punishment after an act of violation rather than at ways of preventing it. Specific affirmation of raising the issue of sexual harassment in workers' meetings and of making explicit the rights of any female employer needed to be prominently communicated to everyone in the workplace. Effective complaints procedures through complaints committees and remedies including compensation must be provided for, according to the judgment.

After this 1997 moment, the subsequent legal moment that substantively addressed sexual harassment was after the Delhi gang rape and the Justice Verma Committee report in 2013 (J. Verma 2013). The chapter "Sexual Harassment at the Workplace" in this report suggested adding an explanation after the definition of sexual harassment. The recommended explanation read: "In determining whether the behavior or act complained of is unwelcome, one of the factors to be given due weight shall be the subjective perception of the complainant." The committee added that women in the armed forces and police, female agricultural workers, and women students and staff of all schools and educational institutions should be among the set of people covered under the legislation. The committee recommended reconsidering the provisions that only written complaints would be acceptable as well as that a complaint would need to be made within a three-month period after the harassment, both of which, ironically, were retained in the legislation regarding sexual harassment. Although the Verma Committee very pragmatically suggested the need to set up Employment Tribunals (not Internal Complaints Committees), where complaints would be reported, it also suggested certain proactive steps that the employer could take—such as affirmatively raising the subject of harassment, expressing strong disapproval of harassment, developing appropriate sanctions internally for when an instance of sexual harassment is brought to the employer's notice, informing employees of their right to raise complaints and of how to raise the issue of harassment, and developing methods to sensitize all those concerned. Finally and very significantly, in order to create a more conducive environment for lodging complaints, the committee suggested deleting the provision that an aggrieved woman be punished if she made false complaints. It is important to note that the Verma Committee's suggestions did not see the light of the day. The legislation that was eventually enacted in 2013 was far removed from the feminist spirit of the *Vishaka* judgment despite foregrounding sexual harassment as a violation of Articles 14, 15, and 21 of the Indian Constitution.

Specific legislation, the Sexual Harassment of Women at the Workplace (Prevention, Prohibition, and Redressal) Act, enacted by the Parliament in 2013 had the same definition of sexual harassment as the 1997 judgment, however. According to this legislation, the workplace was widely defined to include public-sector offices, private-sector enterprises, hospitals, sports institutes, any place visited by an employee in relation to employment, or even a private dwelling. Implied or explicit promise of preferential or detrimental treatment, interference with work, an intimidating or offensive work environment, and humiliating treatment have all been affirmed to amount to sexual harassment. The legislation defined the duties of the employer to include providing workplace "safety," organizing sensitization programs on the legislation for employees, and treating sexual harassment as misconduct under service rules. At the same time, however, this legislation for women was among the first in India to add a provision for taking action against a woman for lodging what are determined to be false/malicious complaints or providing what are determined to be misleading documents.

Another major limitation of the legislation is the proposal that an aggrieved woman can take steps to settle matters through conciliation. This provision contradicts both the spirit of the *Vishaka* judgment as well as the main point of the legislation to create a nonhostile work environment. The proposal posed that compensation be determined on the basis of mental trauma or suffering caused to the aggrieved woman, loss in career opportunity, or medical expenses incurred by her for any kind of treatment. A simultaneous process that occurred in 2013 was the inclusion of Section 354A in the Indian Penal Code, defining sexual harassment and punishment for this criminal offense.[3] The term *sexual harassment* entered criminal law for the first time in the history of India under the provision of assault or criminal force toward a woman with intent to "outrage her modesty," a broad provision existing since colonial times. The latter criminal law provision in fact was the basis of the terms *eve-teasing* and *molestation,* more popular before *sexual harassment* became socially accepted not just as a legal term but as a commonsensical term. Punishment for sexual harassment in the Indian Penal Code has been pronounced as up to three years of imprisonment or a fine or both.

Certain legal questions can be raised before moving on to the next section. First, the two legal homes of sexual harassment in India have been rape and the "outraging of modesty." One cannot forget that even during the time of the *Vishaka* ruling, the case originated in an incidence of gang rape and that this incident did not vanish from the legal imagination. From the gang rape in Rajasthan to the one in Delhi in 2012, powerful and gruesome incidents of rape remained at the backdrop of legal pronouncements of sexual harassment of women in the workplace. It is in this overcriminalization as well as criminalization through the perspective of rape that we find the (im)possibility to come to legal resolutions or closure of incidents of sexual violations within higher-education institutions. In this sense, the nature of the HEI as a workplace needs to be understood differently from that of many other workplaces.

Second, according to Catherine MacKinnon (2003), if (non)consent is the basis of any rape trial, then proving unwelcome conduct is crucial for identifying any act of sexual harassment. This suggests that in both workplace and university settings it is the absence of affirming to a sexual relation or intimacy or intercourse that is the basis of proving that the violation actually occurred. In contrast, Drucilla Cornell (1993) believes that power and unilateral imposition are another way to understand any act of sexual violence. If we go with the latter understanding, then we can at least start with a determination of believability—believing the complainant and her testimony and then trying to get the respondent to prove that it was otherwise if the complainant decides to take the legal route.

Third, is it possible to understand sexual harm or harassment as a civil rights violation or a violation of self-respect and/or honor? This question, in turn, is in one sense a continuation of the gendered power-hierarchy perspective and a way to eliminate the sexual from the harassment and understand the violation as an act of humiliation and civil harm.

The final question to ask is: What does it legally mean to engage with sexual harassment speech? Under most situations of complaints, committees in India, having quasi-legal status since 1997 and legal status since 2013, there is a gap between the originating context/intentions of the speaker in testimony and the kind of effects that speech (unintentionally) produces. Moving closer to criminality from testimony makes it more difficult legally to attain justice from the process of a legal encounter.

Toward a Reimagination: Speech and Silence around Intimacy and Transgression

The trouble of intimacy in HEIs is the final topic we turn to in this chapter. The law evolved in the manner it did so that the focus would remain on nonconsent and unwelcome behavior and speech. Although not explicitly addressed until the #MeToo moment, the trouble remained in speech: the expression of an experience and the manner in which the telling of that experience would find a resonance in law. Connected with questions of sexual surveillance and the suppression of love talk among students, does talking about sexual harassment affect the talking of intimacy or erotics in HEIs? If one does a review of the sociology of intimacy literature through Anthony Giddens (1992), Neil Gross (2005), and Lynn Jameison (2011), one might propose that intimate relations are those with emotional and cognitive closeness and/or with subjective experiences—feeling mutual love, being of like mind, and being special to each other. In these transforming times, with the demands of being more empathetic, more democratic, and "friendlier" teachers in HEIs, are flows of power disrupted? How do gender and caste relations play out through these flows? Does instilling feminist consciousness as teachers involve intimate play in classrooms? The use of the self/experience and empathy as a form of pedagogy, which are the bedrock of feminist teaching, enables making connection with bell hooks's proposition that "we could bring a quality of care and even love to our students" (1994, n.p.). Do faculty judge students' being (and being expected to be) obedient as submitting, and is the inability to resist interpreted as consent or willingness?

What kind of feminist discussions are happening around the multiple relationships and roles that are inhabited by faculty and students in HEIs—as classmates, friends, lovers, teachers, supervisors, colleagues? And how then are obedience, respect, awe, and submission, on the one hand, and supporting indulgence, being friends, or being close, on the other hand, practiced, breached, talked about, or kept in the dark? Even before the certainty of a complaint is arrived at, cultures of transgressions are ignored, tolerated, negotiated, even (reluctantly) allowed within campuses, as the blog post of 2015 mentioned in the first section reveals.

In this context, it is relevant to engage with two kinds of impossibilities that feminists refer to in two different cultural contexts, both of which suggest the limits of speech and of speaking to the law. As V. Geetha has written, "It is intelligible speech that challenges the stubborn indifference to sexual hurt which impunity cultivates and feeds on. Yet, the conditions that make speech possible are uneven and varied, and the act of speaking is almost always fraught. In this event, those who speak out, whether victim-survivors, witnesses or those who act on their behest, find themselves having to not only make words mean, but to ensure that they stay in place, and do not break under pressure" (2016, 5). The process of going through with a legal complaint is usually about being consistent, and yet the experience of sexual violation is troubling; memory can be patchlike, and the testimony can be tentative. Such hesitation and self-doubt are highlighted in the following statement:

> A complaint biography would include those times we decide not to make complaints—not to say something or not to do something—despite an experience or even because of an experience. A complaint

can mean being prepared to talk about difficult and painful experiences over and over again, often to those with whom you have not built up a relationship of trust and those who represent an organization that is implicated in some way in what you are complaining about. You might decide not to complain because of your attachments; to a person, a group, a department, an institution: you might take seriously the warnings that a complaint would be damaging; you might worry about causing damage. And you might make a decision not to complain because you cannot risk the consequences of complaint. A decision not to complain can be influenced by past experiences; you might not be confident your complaint would be taken seriously because you have not been taken seriously. (Ahmed 2017)

Both Geetha and Ahmed in the contemporary moment raise questions around the impossibility of speech and the realities of hesitation. Speaking out against everyday forms of unwelcome or unwanted behavior by men in the workplace was commonly seen in posters that various women's groups in India started creating and circulating after the *Vishaka* judgment in 1997: "Is Your Flirting Hurting?" (Murthy and Dasgupta 2013, 69), "Eve teasing/sexual harassment is not an expression of masculinity, no more silence" (Murthy and Dasgupta 2013, 70), and "Any action which makes a woman uncomfortable amounts to sexual harassment, Beware" (*Poster Women* 2006, 30). The underlining intention of all of these posters was to ensure that there be talk on sexual harassment. The notion that speech be used to bring (nonconsensual) experiences into the public realm has been encouraged and emphasized in feminist politics.

Breaking the silence, or *chuppi toro,* has been part of posters and campaign slogans in India since the 1980s, when rape and domestic violence were discussed publicly in ways that it had not been earlier. At the same time, there is a need to believe as well as to confront the fact that one is not alone in these (unwanted) experiences: some may have spoken about the unacceptable behavior to a friend, some may have complained about it formally to a committee, some could be waiting for the right moment to express themselves, and others may never speak about their experiences. Not speaking, however, does not erase the experience of the experience. Speaking and speaking within law are different. Law expects speech and also that which can be articulated well within its definitions and explanations. Speaking can entail hesitation and not always promptness or accuracy. Speaking to the law usually means for the legal apparatus to endorse or give legitimacy to speech or to reach certainty around evidence from the speech. If, as it has been repeatedly said and felt in the women's movement, incidents of sexual violence are greater in number than those reported, then it is obvious that there are multiple spaces and stages between the experience of sexual transgressions and the lodging of a complaint of sexual harassment. One way of making sense of the #MeToo moment is to locate it in this position in between (real) experience and (hesitant) complaint.

As Linda Alcoff (2009) asks, Is the act of speaking out about transforming power relations and subjectivities, or, rather, does the discourse of confession enhance the power of its administering subjects? Survivors' speech can be silenced directly, or survivors can be labeled mad, hysterical, or helpless—victims who need protection—thus questioning the authenticity and believability of both the act of speaking and who is speaking. Are there spaces in institutions of higher learning in India to have conversations on the ordinariness and everydayness of (sexual) transgression? Cultures of conversation (between students, between faculty, between faculty and students, between administrative staff) need to be crafted, moving beyond the complaints culture. This involves not merely training in and awareness of the provisions of laws on sexual harassment but also the inculcation of a democratic space that is able to acknowledge the complex life-worlds (and therefore words) that students inhabit in institutions of higher learning in contemporary times. It is necessary to think about the chances of enabling conversations on the reality of the unwelcome within intimate yet powered relations between teacher and student as well as of a different discourse on the ethics of keeping distance. For instance, the Harvard University website informs faculty about professional conduct, within which maintaining a certain form of distance is intrinsic to such conduct. A section on interpersonal relations within professional conduct suggests: "The power teachers exercise over students to penalize or reward in the form of grades and recommendations requires caution in interpersonal interactions, and the need to avoid the kind of familiarity that compromises objective and fair evaluation of a student's work. In particular, sexual advances towards or liaisons with one's students are inappropriate. Within these limits, however, intellectual mentoring and friendly interaction are important elements of the learning and teaching process" (Harvard University n.d.; see also Harvard University 2020).

There is no such provision on professional conduct that faculty in HEIs in India are expected to adhere to. In fact, there is no code of conduct or of ethics that faculty must sign in public-university systems in India. If, on the one hand, we are to start a discussion around professional ethics, on the other hand very little reflection exists on defining the limits of interpersonal dynamics in the classroom. The university classroom is yet to be a site of inquiry or reflection, although much interrogation has interestingly happened around the school classroom. It seems relevant to ask whether the power hierarchies in a classroom can be a common experience that students may want to converse about. Is there any way that experiences of being supervised be another common chord among research scholars because it involves a more interpersonal, close encounter between students and faculty that does not always take place in the classroom but at various sites—from the faculty office room to maybe even a bar or the faculty member's residence? Clearly, there are no feminist resolutions regarding these kinds of complex questions around classroom dynamics and gendered student–faculty relations and regarding ways of creating spaces to talk about them.

The Millennial Student and Feminist Futures

It is important to note that within a transforming landscape of young, aspiring, freedom-seeking students of plural genders in institutions of higher learning across Indian cities, there will constantly be a desire to talk about, discuss, and debate sexual politics, thereby challenging cultures of silence around these topics. This observation by no means suggests that these conversations have not happened in the past or even that they can now easily transpire between students—the diversity and the hierarchy of locations that students themselves occupy sometimes obscure or make it very difficult for these conversations to take place. Moreover, enabling democratic spaces for dialogues to happen between faculty and students is difficult, yet it is not impossible, and #MeToo has shown that there is an urgent need to make those efforts in HEIs.

Creating these conversations to tease out nuanced meanings around consent and transgression may be more crucial than trying to understand what it is that those who have articulated their experiences in social media "really want."

Since 2013, where this chapter began as the prehistory to the current #MeToo movement, the attempt by students in HEIs has constantly been to alert their institutions about their concerns—about the kinds of misogyny rampant on campus—rather than to lodge complaints against specific individuals or to take the prescribed legal route. However, various aggrieved women within this period have used the complaints mechanisms within their institutions to reach some form of (legal) conclusion. The #MeToo narratives can thus be assessed as serving various purposes: as catharsis, as warnings, as forms of disclosure, as ways to build support, and as means for creating connections. At the same time, none of these purposes may lead to punishment, forgiveness, consolation, or reconciliation. Closure may not be the immediate desire at this moment; unwrapping and colistening may instead be what this new feminist moment signals. Feminist politics has never been a static discourse in India. Dissent and fissures have only enriched that politics, and at this moment of disagreements and differences there is still the promise of constituting a relational prism: an alliance or camaraderie of new languages and methods of feminist praxis. How does feminist politics engage with adult (bruised) intimacies in HEIs—some of which are consensual, some of which are at that cusp of passive rather than affirmative consent and mired in gendered power equations, and others are coercive and silenced? The importance of this moment lies in the future of taking forward these messy conversations and creating a politics that doesn't necessarily involve the criminalization of sexual violence that was focused on the 1980s and 1990s.

As much as there is a constant need to strengthen the autonomous and independent functioning of the anti–sexual harassment committees in HEIs and in all workplaces, there is also an equal if not greater need to co-constitute cultures of (informal/collective) conversations, even if fractured. The complaint-evidence-committee mechanism is not the only method of doing feminist politics, especially when it comes to questions of sexual transgressions in HEIs. The future feminist journey in India includes care as pedagogy and care as practice, creating physical and virtual spaces of cathartic conversations and understanding the pillars of the feminist past on which the millennial student stands while at the same time not undermining that student's language and politics.

References

Ahmed, S. 2017. "A Complaint Biography." Feminist Killjoys, August 9. At https://feministkilljoys.com/2017/08/09/a-complaint-biography/.

Alcoff, L. 2009. "Discourses of Sexual Violence." *Global Framework Philosophical Topics* 37 (2): 123–39.

Cornell, D. 1993. *Transformations: Recollective Imagination and Sexual Difference.* New York: Routledge.

Deshpande, S. 2011. "Revisiting the Basics." Seminar paper. At https://www.india-seminar.com/2011/624/624_satish_deshpande.htm.

Geetha, V. 2016. *Undoing Impunity: Speech after Sexual Violence.* New Delhi: Zubaan Books.

Giddens, A. 1993. *The Transformations of Intimacy: Sexuality, Love, and Eroticism in Modern Societies.* Stanford, CA: Stanford University Press.

Gross, N. 2005. "The Detraditionalization of Intimacy Reconsidered." *Sociological Theory* 23 (3): 286–311.

Harvard University. 2000. "Interpersonal Relations. Professional Conduct." In Preceptor Group, *Preceptor Handbook.* At http://abel.harvard.edu/calculus/preceptorbook.html#AEN9.

———. n.d. "Professional Conduct." At https://www.seas.harvard.edu/sites/default/files/files/Student%20Affairs/Professional-Conduct.pdf.

hooks, b. 1994. *Teaching to Transgress: Education as the Practice of Freedom.* New York: Routledge.

International Monetary Fund. 2015. *Tackling Challenges Together.* Annual report. Washington, DC: International Monetary Fund.

Jameison, L. 2011. "Intimacy as a Concept: Explaining Social Change in the Context of Globalisation or Another Form of Ethnocentrism." *Sociological Research Online,* December 2.

James, S. 2013. "*Through My Looking Glass* blog." *Journal of Indian Law and Society,* November 6. JILSBLOGNUJS. At https://jils.co.in/through-my-looking-glass/.

Kapur, D., and P. B. Mehta. 2017. *Navigating the Labyrinth: Perspectives on India's Higher Education.* Hyderabad, India: Orient Black-swan.

Lady Shri Ram College. N.d. "Women's Development Cell." At https://lsr.edu.in/students/societies/womens-development-cell/.

MacKinnon, C. 2003. *Towards a Feminist Theory of the State.* Cambridge, MA: Harvard University Press.

Mahajan, A. 2015. "Confessions of a Slut." *Glasnost,* June 4. At https:// glasnostnludelhi.wordpress.com/2015/06/04/confessions-of-a-slut/.

Mathur, K. 1992. "Bhateri Rape Case: Backlash and Protest." *Economic and Political Weekly* 27 (41): 2221–224.

Murthy, L., and R. Dasgupta. 2011. *Our Pictures, Our Words: A Visual Journey through the Women's Movement.* New Delhi: Zubaan Books.

Poster Women: A Visual Archive of the Women's Movement in India. 2006. New Delhi: Zubaan Books.

Sample Registration System: Baseline Survey 2014. 2014. At https://www .censusindia.gov.in/vital_statistics/BASELINE%20TABLES07062016 .pdf.

Sen, R., and K. Menon. 2020. "From Perspective to Discipline: Mapping Forty Years in Women's/Gender Studies in India." *Doing Feminisms in the Academy: Identity, Institutional Pedagogy, and Critical Classrooms in India and the UK,* R. Govinda, F. Mackay, K. Menon, and R. Sen, 85–121. New Delhi: Zubaan Books.

Verma, Justice J. S., chairman. 2013. *Report of the Committee on Amendments to Criminal Law.* New Delhi: Government of India, January 23. At https:// www.thehindu.com/multimedia/archive/01340/Justice_Verma_Comm_ 1340438a.pdf.

Verma, P. 2018. "IITs Creating Extra Seats for Women to Lift Gender Ratio." *Economic Times,* January 18. At https://economictimes.indiatimes.com /industry/services/education/page-1-iits-creating-seats-to-lift-gender- ratio-_-industry-welcomes-move-to-lift-gender-ratio/articleshow /62547957.cms.

Notes

1. Parliament of India, Sexual Harassment of Women at the Workplace (Prevention, Prohibition, and Redressal) Act, Act No. 14, April 22, 2013.

2. *Vishaka and Others v. State of Union of India,* AIR 1997 SC 3011, at https://indiankanoon.org/doc/1031794/.

3. Criminal Law (Amendment) Bill, 2013, at https://www.prsindia.org /sites/default/files/bill_files/Criminal_Law_%28A%29%2C_2013.pdf.

8

Queering #MeToo

Working toward Queer and Trans Inclusion

Xavier L. Guadalupe-Diaz and Elizabeth Whalley

During the midst of the #MeToo movement in 2018, news broke that Avital Ronell, an esteemed professor at New York University (NYU), had been found culpable during a Title IX investigation of sexual harassment. Nimrod Reitman,[1] Ronell's graduate advisee, reported experiencing extensive sexualized electronic communications and coercive sexual contact by Ronell as well as professional retaliation when he resisted her advances. Ronell received a year's suspension from the school (Greenberg 2018).

Zoe Greenberg broke the story in her *New York Times* article "What Happens to #MeToo When a Feminist Is the Accused?" (2018), which launched the case into the national spotlight. The situation became a salacious media story due primarily to three factors: the identification of Ronell as a feminist scholar, the reversal of the traditional gender roles within sexual harassment, and the contrasting sexualities of those involved. Although Ronell and Reitman's relationship was heterogender in composition, their sexualities were not heterosexual per se: Ronell identifies as a queer woman and lesbian, and Reitman as a gay man.

Ronell defended her relationship dynamic with Reitman as existing within a context of queer culture, where, allegedly, such interactions are normalized. In public statements released in her defense, she asserted: "Our communications—which Reitman now claims constituted sexual harassment—were between two adults, a gay man and a queer woman"

163

(quoted in Greenberg 2018). Ronell also referenced conversations with Reitman as "campy[2] communication" (quoted in Greenberg 2018) and "gay-coded" (de Silva 2017). Such a response raised important questions between the use of the queer community as an explanation or a shield from the power and control within sexual harassment. Can sexual harassment exist between queer and trans people, or does the inherent sexualization of queer relationships negate this possibility?

Many prominent gender scholars came to Ronell's defense. A group of international academics, which most notably included the gender theorist Judith Butler, penned a letter to NYU that defended Ronell and defamed Reitman. Fellow NYU professor Lisa Duggan published a widely shared blog piece discussing the case in which she referenced the mainstream misunderstanding of queer friendship as a "culture clash." She elaborated: "The nature of the email exchange resonates with many queer academics, whose practices of queer intimacy are often baffling to outsiders. . . . Forms of intimacy well outside the parameters of heterosexual (and, homosexual) courtship and marriage are commonplace among queers who [do] not clearly separate friendship and romance, partnership and romantic friendship" (2018).

Where some saw the contextualizing of the case within sexual and gender fluidity as an explanation, still others saw this contextualization as excusing sexual violence. Does queer lexicon negate the adviser/advisee power dynamic and the expectation of the professional workplace?

Ronell's behavior and Reitman's victimization fell beyond the scope of the modern #MeToo movement, which has worked largely to address the heteronormative gendered power dynamics that foster hostile social environments for cisgender women. The marginalization of queer and transgender people from the movement is way off the platform from which Tarana Burke founded the #MeToo movement. Her initial project explicitly addressed the need to center "the most marginalized of us"—namely, survivors of color as well as queer and transgender survivors of sexual violence (Warfield 2018). She has asserted that #MeToo is not a women's movement: it is a survivors' movement for all genders. Yet #MeToo has become cis- and heteronormative. Less has been done to complicate the realities of gender outside of white cis- and heteronormative binaries (man/woman), an omission that Burke has addressed as occurring "because we are conditioned to respond to the vulnerability of White women" (quoted in Warfield 2018).

Ronell complained that Reitman was "comparing me to the most egregious examples of predatory behaviors ascribable to Hollywood moguls who habitually go after starlets" (quoted in Greenberg 2018). Ronell's distinguishing of herself from the mainstream #MeToo story is another iteration of the issue, according to Burke: "Women of color, transwomen, queer people—our stories get pushed aside and our pain is never prioritized. . . . People are okay when you're talking about the big, scary bad guy. Let's talk about Harvey Weinstein and R. Kelly and Les Moonves, all of these big boogeymen. . . . [W]e have to examine all of our behavior . . . and it's gonna be uncomfortable" (quoted in Vagianos 2019). Ronell relied upon the rigidly gendered public discourse around #MeToo to neutralize her behavior, which in turn serves to marginalize and normalize queer and transgender sexual violence.

Despite the queerness evident in the inception of the #MeToo movement, queerness is also being used to erase queer and trans survivors from the mainstream movement.[3] This limited frame causes queer and trans sexual violence, such as faced by Reitman, to be labeled a normal interpersonal relationship taken in queer context (Ison 2018). Such erasure of violence highlights the need for an advancement of the discourse regarding the #MeToo movement as it relates to queer and trans communities. Thus, we argue the #MeToo movement needs to be queer(ed) in two ways: (1) by building a structural understanding of power as untethered from static binary sex and gender categories and (2) by addressing the complexities of the liminal spaces of queer sex positivity. In this chapter, we extend cases of queer sexual violence further: What happens to #MeToo when a queer or transgender person is the accused? What happens to #MeToo when a transgender or queer person is the victim?

We aim in part to address Duggan's "culture clash" to understand where the #MeToo movement and queer contexts overlap. We have structured this discussion in three parts. First, we survey contemporary research on the prevalence and forms of sexual violence (harassment and assault) within queer and trans communities. Second, the traditional cis–het understandings of gender and power are disrupted, and we propose how contexts of power can be queered to situate queer and transgender people's experiences of sexual violence. Finally, we conclude by proposing ways that the #MeToo movement can return to its roots while moving forward toward trans- and queer inclusivity.

Transgender and Queer Sexual Violence Victimization

The issues surrounding the measurement of sexual violence in the queer and transgender communities have been documented throughout the literature. These limitations include a lack of consistent metrics, heterosexist and phallocentric definitions of sexual violence, and hesitancy among LGBTq victims to contribute to data that might be used to perpetuate stereotypes of queer people as sexually violent predators.[4] The limited studies of sexual assault victimization in LGBTq populations do reveal that queer and transgender people report higher levels of sexual assault than cisgender or heterosexual populations. National studies find disproportionately high rates of sexual victimization among bisexual and lesbian women. Emily Rothman, Deinera Exner, and Allyson Baughman's (2011) metastudy of seventy-five studies of LGB sexual assault victimization concluded that although research consistently documents lesbian and bisexual women as having the highest rates of lifetime sexual assault within the LGB community, gay and bisexual men are more likely to experience sexual violence related to a hate crime.

The few intersectional large-scale quantitative studies of sexual abuse, race, and sexual identity have not found significant racial differences in victimization rates among white, Black, Latinx, and Asian American queer and transgender people (Balsam et al. 2015; Coulter et al. 2017). However, one study of lesbian, bisexual, and two-spirit American Indian and Alaskan Native women found a lifetime sexual assault rate of 85 percent, compared to a rate of 35 percent for all Native women (Lehavot, Walters, and Simoni 2010; Tjaden and Thoennes 2000).

Studies of sexual assault of transgender people show a significantly higher rate of sexual victimization compared to the rate in cisgender populations. The United States Transgender Survey (USTS) of 2015, a nationwide study, determined that 47 percent of transgender respondents had experienced sexual assault in their lifetime. These rates were higher for transgender people of color, with the highest rates of victimization reported by American Indian (65 percent), multiracial (59 percent), Middle Eastern (58 percent), and Black (53 percent) transpeople. Transgender men (51 percent) and nonbinary people with "female" on their original birth certificate (58 percent) had higher rates of sexual victimization than transgender women (37 percent) and nonbinary people with "male" on their original birth certificate (41 percent) (James et al. 2016). Elevated levels of victimization for people of color remained true among transgender men and nonbinary people with "female" on their original birth certificate.

Workplace Sexual Harassment of Queer and Transgender People

Expanding the conceptualization of what sexual harassment encompasses allows for the decentering of the hegemonic narrative and therefore for the inclusion of transgender and queer experiences. In his article on queering sexual harassment law, Brian Soucek (2018) describes the case *Franchina v. City of Providence* (881 F.3d 32), wherein a lesbian firefighter was sexually harassed by her coworkers. To drive Franchina out of the workplace, the firemen in her crew made comments that denigrated her sexual identity but were not based in their desire to have sex with her. Using the judicial precedent set in this case, Soucek describes how sexual harassment is not limited to unrequited sexual desire; it can also be based on the treatment of an individual's sexual or gender identity. This definition places more transgender and queer people's experiences of harassment squarely within the #MeToo movement.

In one of the few studies of workplace sexual harassment faced by LGB people, 76 percent of respondents reported having experienced sexual or gender harassment at work at some point in their lives (Rabelo and Cortina 2014). The USTS reported that, overall, 46 percent of transpeople had experienced sexual harassment in the past year, and 15 percent of respondents had been physically, verbally, or sexually harassed at work because of their transgender status. The survey also documented higher rates of workplace sexual harassment for American Indian and Middle Eastern transpeople.

Scholarship on queer sexual harassment highlights the frequency of heterosexual comments about converting queer employees to heterosexuality and of boundary crossing in professional relationships after sexual identity disclosure by heterosexual and queer coworkers alike. For queer women, their queer sexual identity contributes another dimension to sexual harassment in addition to the unwanted sexual attention many women experience in the workplace. This dimension can be in part attributed to the portrayal of lesbian sex in pornography and the larger culture, which compounds the experiences of harassment faced by queer women. Lesbian sex in heterosexual pornography typically includes a heterosexual man within a threesome, suggesting that lesbian sexuality is inherently still within the heterosexual masculine purview. Heterosexual pornography rarely includes male-on-male sexual interaction, leaving the impression that lesbian and queer women remain in the heterosexual domain and may be sexually receptive to heterosexual men ("convertible") and that lesbian sex serves the purpose of men's sexual gratification (Giuffre, Dellinger, and Williams 2008). In the workplace, the sexualization of queer, trans, and women's bodies as well as the heterosexist belief in masculine sexual privilege leave queer and transgender people, especially queer and transgender women and those assigned female at birth, vulnerable to multiplicative sexual harassment.

The tokenization, fetishization, and hypersexualization of transgender and queer people creates further vulnerability to sexual abuse and harassment. Transgender people are understood in hegemonic culture as hypersexualized figures. Such hypersexualization renders transpeople to be viewed as inherently "unrapable" and unable to be sexually harassed. This helps explain why the highest rates of sexual abuse and harassment are reported by transpeople of color, who face interlocking systems of oppression that hypersexualize their bodies in the public sphere. Robert Coulter and colleagues (2017) speculate that the racial discrimination faced by transpeople of color combine with interpersonal and structural transphobia to create increased vulnerability to sexual violence. This argument can also be applied to understanding the increased vulnerability faced by queer people of color. The historical and contemporary hypersexualization of people of color as well as queerness together warp the social understanding of their sexual victimization. An example of this can be seen in the case of Jerry Sandusky, who was convicted of committing forty-five counts of sexual abuse over a span of decades while his abuse was concealed by Penn State. Carine Mardorossian points to the fact that most of Sandusky's victims were African

American boys to explain the cultural struggle to categorize and understand Sandusky's abuse. The media, for example, used myriad words and euphemisms to discuss the crimes, revealing the journalists' racialized and heterosexist reluctance to "call rape, rape" (2014, 3).

Structural Barriers within LGBTq Sexual Harassment

For transgender and queer-identified people, sexual harassment and assault are interpersonal violences enabled by structural violences. Survivors of workplace sexual violence must navigate the legalization of discrimination in addition to the power entrenched in employment structures. Workplace discrimination against LGBTq people is legal in twenty-six states and the US military. In 2017, the former attorney general Jeff Sessions published a memorandum explicitly defining sex discrimination as something that occurs to biological males and females, thus specifically excluding transgender people from this definition. One study of transgender discrimination in Texas found that although 79 percent of transpeople surveyed experienced harassment at work, only 14 percent of the workforce in Texas is covered by local nondiscrimination laws (Mallory and Sears 2015).

The USTS determined that 30 percent of transgender respondents employed in 2014 had been fired, denied a promotion, or experienced another form of workplace harassment because of their gender identity or expression (James et al. 2016). The rate of transgender unemployment is three times that of the general US population, and the unemployment rate for transgender people of color is four times that of the general population. These quasi-legal forms of discrimination expose transpeople to heightened levels of economic vulnerability. The barriers to locating new employment could place a transgender victim of sexual harassment in a coercive position with respect to decisions about sexual activity and disclosure of harassment. The threat to out a victim professionally or personally is emboldened by the legalization of discrimination against transgender and queer people alike. Taken together, the legalized discrimination and cultural biases against LGBTq people can entrap them in a precarious and abusive situation without recourse and in ways that warrant their centralization in the #MeToo movement.

The (De)Sexualization of Sexual Violence Perpetration

Several studies of sexual assault perpetration limit questions regarding perpetration to men, thus reconstructing the heteronormative perceptions of sexual assault. Such an oversight erases the possibility of women perpetrating sexual violence against any gender and has particular implications within transgender and queer communities. The simultaneous fetishization of lesbian sex and invalidation of nonpenetrative sex contributes to the social invalidation of sex that does not include a cisman. Along this logic, if lesbian sex is not "real" sex, sexual violence between women, genderqueer, or gender-nonconforming people is invalidated. Sexism also frames stereotypical understandings of sexual assault as "forcible," which continues to be used in much legislation and academic research on sexual assault. If sexual assault is (falsely) understood as exclusively violent, and women are understood as nonviolent and lacking physical strength, the possibility of a sexually violent woman is again invalidated.

Understanding the perpetration of sexual violence in LGBTq communities is further complicated by the "culture clash" referenced by Duggan in her defense of Ronell. The pro-sex ethos within queer culture as a result of hegemonic oppression of queer sexuality and transgender identities can sometimes obscure the line between sexual openness/sexual freedom, on the one hand, and sexual harassment/sexual assault, on the other. Complicating this issue, Ian Barnard (2018) describes how heterosexism and homophobia have also curated a need for sexual discretion and subtlety, which are antithetical to affirmative consent. According to William Simon and John Gagnon's sexual script theory, sexual scripts provide blueprints that guide sexual conduct and rules that promote normative sexual behavior. Studies have connected heterosexual sexual scripting to heterosexual sexual assault, but heterosexual sexual scripting can also create gender performances of sexuality that are connected to sexual assault and harassment of people within the LGBTq community. Having been sexually socialized in a compulsively heterosexual cisnormative society, those raised masculine are not often offered a social script that they can use to refuse sexual advances. Those brought up in more traditionally feminine socializations are not socialized to recognize signs of sexual disinterest or to be concerned about establishing the consent of their partner. Given the lack of queer or transgender sexual scripting in heterosexist socializations, LGBTq people often build scripts from this heterosexual blueprint. When engaging in queer flirting and sexual encounters, those socialized as feminine may be more accustomed to making choices about their own consent but may be less familiar with the need to receive consent from others. Those socialized into masculine scripts may ideally be aware they are expected to establish consent from women but not practiced in the ability to understand the importance of affirmative consent for other genders.

Queering Gender and Power

Given the aforementioned history and development of the #MeToo movement, it is critical to recenter the theoretical underpinnings that Burke envisioned would focus on some of the most marginalized populations (i.e., Black and brown girls and women, queer and transgender people). Although Burke sparked a movement that was meant to be queer and intersectional, the mainstreaming of #MeToo has seemingly marginalized queer and trans voices. The call to queer gender and power in the #MeToo movement is more of a call to recenter this critical angle that was a significant part of Burke's intent. As previously reviewed, what queering means is, by definition, complex and hotly debated. In addition to the inclusion of LGBTq and nonnormative sexualities and genders as subjects, queering involves deconstructing power and challenging assumptions behind language, culture, institutions, and more (Ball 2014). Queering is particularly relevant to the critique of the mainstream #MeToo movement because it questions the often taken-for-granted language that genders all sexual violence victims as ciswomen and all perpetrators as cismen. Beyond simply queering the subjects (i.e., including LGBTq perspectives in #MeToo), queering should also queer "our understandings of violence itself" (Ball 2016, 9). To that end, queering the language on gender and power will both critique the lack of queer and trans inclusion and challenge some assumptions behind how we understand why and how sexual violence exists.

How gender and power are conceptualized within a social change movement such as #MeToo provides its own explanation for the origins of sexual harassment and assault and therefore defines victimization and informs subsequent solutions. The mainstreaming of the #MeToo movement has resulted in a predominantly heterosexist and cisnormative view of gender as binaristic while also addressing power within a patriarchal power structure. Similarly, throughout the social scientific literature on gender violence (i.e., sexual harassment, sex trafficking, intimate-partner and sexual violence), gender has almost exclusively been treated as a binary characteristic that individuals either hold, interact with, and/or organize society around.

To adequately contextualize the queer critique to gender and power, it is important first to briefly trace mainstream feminist thought and how it has explained the existence of sexual violence. In the United States, the most dominant forms of feminist theorization in both sexual and intimate-partner violence literatures emerged from the white feminist movements of the 1970s. Broadly speaking, the dominant power critique of the time centered on the role of the patriarchal power structure in marginalizing white ciswomen in public life. This power structure fostered hostile social contexts that made ciswomen victims of rape, sexual harassment, and intimate-partner violence. Power was conceptualized largely from a macrostructural perspective that isolated patriarchy as the root cause of violence against all ciswomen. As a result, sexual violence was framed as a rigidly gendered form of patriarchal control in which ciswomen were the sole victims of solely cismen perpetrators. Further, the singular focus on gender did not adequately capture how race, class, and sexuality created divergent experiences with violence (Whalley and Hackett 2017).

The exclusive centering of ciswomen's structural marginalization in society resulted in a rather limited view of sexual violence as strictly a ciswoman's problem. The cisnormative ideology behind these early antiviolence movements was further codified within the organized response to sexual harassment as well as sexual and intimate-partner violence. Resources, organizations, and public policy utilized rigidly gendered language in codifying victim/perpetrator as a female/male binary into law. The #MeToo movement of today requires a more complex understanding of sexual violence that maintains its structural-power critique of patriarchy while also highlighting how power manifests intersectionally through interaction, language, and meaning. Black feminists had long argued that gender is complicated by race, class, sexuality, and various other identities that create distinct realties and inequalities across and within groups. The binaristic language that white feminists used to understand sexual violence often slipped into the creation of a theoretical wedge between men and women. Black feminists argued that these false binaries pitted them against the Black men with whom they collectively experienced white-supremacist marginalization. Extending these points, queer perspectives offer the theoretical language needed to highlight the cisnormative assumptions behind much of the #MeToo discourse; this is a version of queering that "aligns most closely with the poststructuralist foundations of queer scholarship" (Ball 2016, 10). More specifically, one way in which queering gender and power highlights queer and trans struggles with sexual violence is through a poststructuralist critique of language. Kath Browne and Catherine Nash state that queering is a form of thought that is "positioned within conceptual frameworks that highlight the instability of taken-for-granted meanings and resulting power relations" (2010, 4). Applying this form of queer critique shows that much of the mainstream #MeToo movement takes for granted the binaristic language that almost exclusively centers ciswomen as the only victims of sexual violence at the hands of cismen.

Queering challenges the power behind assumptions of heterosexuality and cisnormativity while also interrogating power beyond the organization of society by connecting the interactional reality of daily life to structurally engrained inequalities. Power has been conceptualized in a variety of ways, but here power "can be understood as the ability to project one's own desires onto another. With less power, there is a diminished (but not eliminated) capacity to enact negative consequences against a potential perpetrator" (Guadalupe-Diaz 2019, 13). Power is structured in the organization of society in how it distributes resources but can also be leveraged through interpersonal interaction. Power is innately racialized, classed, and gendered in ways that may lend more opportunities for privileged groups to abuse and harass those who are more marginalized. This conceptualization of power can explain why ciswomen are disproportionately harassed by cismen, but it can also explain harassment beyond this cisnormative binary. For example, Mardorossian notes that "rape is an issue that primarily affects women not because they are women but because they often—although not necessarily—occupy the positions of the structurally subordinate in relations of domination" (2014, 8).

Given that gender has long organized the economy, labor, and schools in ways that have marginalized those who are assigned "female" at birth, the structural order of society places many ciswomen in positions that are often less powerful than those that cismen occupy. However, power can also be situationally deployed between individuals of any identity. For example, although ciswomen are uniquely vulnerable to sexual and intimate-partner violence, this conceptualization of power can also be used to explain the higher rates of sexual violence within queer and transgender communities (Guadalupe-Diaz 2015; Messinger 2017). Further, studies on transgender and queer sexual and intimate-partner violence have shown that some perpetrators are themselves also transgender or queer (Guadalupe-Diaz 2019). Regardless of identities and their relationship to structural hierarchy, individuals can leverage situational power and structural vulnerability against their target. Clare Cannon, Kate Lauve-Moon, and Fred Buttell note that "people, based on their social location, use tactics and strategies available to them to negotiate dynamics of power" (2015, 670). This helps, in part, to explain how sexual violence is deployed between members of the same gender, by ciswomen against cismen, between transgender individuals, or even between a lesbian professor and her gay graduate student.

Queer and transgender people also contend with the stereotype of their sexuality or gender as a sexual danger. In a heterosexist and transphobic society, deviance from heterosexuality and cisnormativity is socially constructed as a predatory threat. As is true with many moral panics, this fear also translates to the need to protect children. The need to disentangle unwanted sexual advances by LGBTq people from stereotypes of child predation should be central to the #MeToo movement's deconstruction of sexual violence, gender, and power. Transgender children and adults alike have been cast as sexual threats, which can be seen in the discourse around transgender bathroom-use politics (e.g., the hypersexualization of transgender people). Trans bodies, especially trans bodies of color, are framed in political discourse as sexual threats, even though it's more likely that trans bodies are victimized in public accommodations. The way in which transphobia and cisnormativity have coded transwomen as sexually predacious "men" renders the sexual assault of transwomen as outside of the mainstream social understanding of sexual violence victimization.

Where some in the #MeToo movement may avoid discussing LGBTq sexual assault perpetration in order to dodge confirming these homophobic or transphobic stereotypes, this avoidance has contributed to the systematic erasure of LGBTq sexual victimization. As Barnard delineates, a less idealized understanding of queer sexuality is needed within the #MeToo movement to create a space for "quotidian gayness that doesn't have to be good gayness" (2018, 109). Examining sexual violence using a gendered structural-power framework allows the #MeToo movement to have a more nuanced and inclusive understanding of sexual victimization.

Moving toward Queer and Trans Inclusion in the #MeToo Movement

In this concluding section, we propose ways that the #MeToo movement can return to its roots while moving forward to trans and queer inclusivity. #MeToo's current rigid structural-power analysis does not always capture a full understanding of how violence manifests across varying identities. The sexualization of people of color and LGBTq people creates an overlapping hypersexualization of queer and transgender bodies that renders the sexual violence they face invisible, while embedding such harassment in a subculture that normalizes sexual boundary crossing. Given the high rates of both sexual assault and harassment in LGBTq communities, Burke's founding guidance to structure the #MeToo movement around queer and trans people of color was warranted and necessary. By centering the compounding oppressions that queer and transgender people face when experiencing or speaking out about sexual violence, we can dismantle the interlocking nature of the structures of sexual abuse.

To queer #MeToo is then, in part, to open up the language that erroneously "essentializes maleness with violence and femaleness with victimization" (Mardorossian 2014, 9). The language of #MeToo must recognize how gender and power are contextualized by situation and intersecting identities that inform how sexual violence is experienced, perceived, and responded to. Steven Boughton emphasizes that although "gender can be a form of power," the underlying issue in sexual violence is not solely gender but the interpersonal consequence of power, control, and coercion (2018). The Ronell case not only exemplifies the complexities of how queer identities jar the mainstream collective idea of what constitutes sexual violence but also shows how queerness has been leveraged to normalize coercive sexual actions. For example, Jess Ison argues that "what was significant (and problematic) was the way Ronell used queerness to justify her actions, calling on the deviance narrative that has been used to oppress queers who transgress homonormativity. Here, the claiming of queerness that is pathologized and criminalized as a justification for sexual assault appears to be a tactic of the queer abuser" (2019, 160). Yet another famous instance of this leveraging of "deviant" queerness can be seen within the pattern of those who respond to allegations of sexual abuse by coming out as LGB, as was seen in Kevin Spacey's response to multiple charges of sexual assault during the beginning of the mainstream #MeToo movement. Queering #MeToo therefore also involves challenging the ways in which queer sex positivity can and has been used to mask sexual coercion. When queer and trans experiences are centered within the #MeToo movement, queer sex positivity can be called upon to incorporate consent-focused culture that prioritizes mutual respect and affirmation.

In moving toward queer and trans inclusion, the #MeToo movement must also contend with the institutions of accountability (e.g., reporting systems) that marginalize LGBTq survivors of sexual violence. Despite the fact that the #MeToo movement has inspired many survivors to come forward, less has been done to challenge the ways in which institutions foster coercive power structures that create opportunities for sexual assault and empower few to disclose their victimization. Hannah McCann (2018) argues that the #MeToo movement should interrogate the structures in place that cultivate coercive interpersonal relationships and that systemically marginalize the lived realities of those with less power, whether it be in the Hollywood setting or in the adviser/advisee relationship in academia. Importantly, the legality of the aforementioned employment discrimination on the basis of sexual orientation and/or gender identity and expression further exacerbates the coercive dynamics within institutions that may lead to sexual assaults.

Queering #MeToo involves the cultivation of new systems of accountability that not only challenge the institutionalized nature of power that contextualizes sexual violence but also seek to offer alternatives for disclosure and healing. Mainstream #MeToo responses have often involved a racist, queerphobic criminal-legal system that deters disclosure from queer and trans survivors or results in traumatic, unhelpful responses to them when they do speak out. In one example, Neesha Powell (2018) offers an alternative response that includes a focus on the promotion of healthy relationships at work and school that seek to normalize discussions of sexual coercion and assault, which often thrive in secrecy. Finally, queer and trans intersectional frameworks have informed applications of transformative justice that can provide an accountability structure that does not involve the criminal-legal system. Transformative justice involves facilitating a structured process of dialogue between offender, survivor, and community in a way that offers an opportunity to center survivor experiences, establish offender and community accountability, and work toward the healing of harm. Several existing initiatives, such as the Anti-Oppression Resource and Training Alliance (AORTA) and Creative Interventions, offer frameworks that are trauma informed and involve the centering of survivor needs while empowering communities to respond and ask, "What do we need to have justice"? (AORTA n.d.; Creative Interventions n.d.). These resources highlight the role of community in both creating and resolving harm. "We usually think of the person doing harm as the one to be accountable for violence. Communities must also recognize, end and take responsibility for violence by becoming more knowledgeable, skillful and willing to take action to intervene in violence and to support social norms and conditions that prevent violence from happening in the first place" (Creative Interventions 2019). Such an intervention calls on institutions to hold not just offenders but also themselves accountable to their coercive own power. Simultaneously, the community accountability within transformative justice also names the need for queer communities to recognize their participation in the cultural normalization of sexual violence.

Ultimately, the recentering of queer and trans voices requires that #MeToo challenge the cisnormative and heterosexist language that marginalizes many survivors. This change involves a recalibration of how gender and power are understood intersectionally, with an emphasis on how power is both structural but also enacted and leveraged through interaction across *all* gender identities and expressions. Creative and imagined futures should interrogate existing accountability structures and pave the way for transformative approaches that seek redress and reparation over punishment.

References

AORTA. N.d. "Destabilizing Rape Culture through Transformative Justice." Anti-Oppression Resource and Training Alliance. At https://aorta.coop /portfolio_page/destabilizing-rape-culture-through-transformative-justice/. Accessed October 14, 2019.

Ball, M. 2014. "Queer Criminology, Critique, and the 'Art of Not Being Governed.'" *Critical Criminology* 22 (1): 21–34.

———. 2016. *Criminology and Queer Theory: Dangerous Bedfellows?* New York: Springer.

Balsam, K. F., Y. Molina, J. A. Blayney, T. Dillworth, L. Zimmerman, and D. Kaysen. 2015. "Racial/Ethnic Differences in Identity and Mental Health Outcomes among Young Sexual Minority Women." *Cultural Diversity and Ethnic Minority Psychology* 21 (3): 380–90.

Barnard, I. 2018. "Queer: Good Gay, Bad Gay, Black Gay, White Gay?" *QED* 5 (2): 105–11.

Boughton, S. 2018. "#UsToo: A Queer Perspective on #MeToo." *Medium,* January 19. At https://medium.com/@stevenboughton/ustoo-a-queer-perspective-on-metoo-7298042a28b5.

Browne, Kath, and Catherine J. Nash. 2010. *Queer Methods and Methodologies: Intersecting Queer Theories and Social Science Research.* London: Routledge.

Cannon, C., K. Lauve-Moon, and F. Buttell. 2015. "Re-theorizing Intimate Partner Violence through Post-structural Feminism, Queer Theory, and the Sociology of Gender." *Social Sciences* 4 (3): 668–87.

Coulter, R. W., C. Mair, E. Miller, J. R. Blosnich, D. D. Matthews, and H. L. McCauley. 2017. "Prevalence of Past-Year Sexual Assault Victimization among Undergraduate Students: Exploring Differences by and Intersections of Gender Identity, Sexual Identity, and Race/Ethnicity." *Prevention Science* 18 (6): 726–36.

Creative Interventions. 2019. *Creative Interventions Toolkit: A Practical Guide to Stop Interpersonal Violence.* Oakland, CA: Creative Interventions.

———. N.d. Website. http://www.creative-interventions.org/. Accessed October 14, 2019.

De Silva, Mangalika. 2017. "Press Release on Behalf of Professor Avital Ronell." At https://theoryilluminati.com/texts-and-contexts/f/an-eleven-month-denial-of-all-nimrod-reitman-allegations.

Duggan, L. 2018. "The Full Catastrophe." *Bully Bloggers,* August 18. At https://bullybloggers.wordpress.com/2018/08/18/the-full-catastrophe/.

Giuffre, P., K. Dellinger, and C. L. Williams. 2008. "'No Retribution for Being Gay?': Inequality in Gay-Friendly Workplaces." *Sociological Spectrum* 28 (3): 254–77.

Greenberg, Z. 2018. "What Happens to #MeToo When a Feminist Is the Accused?" *New York Times,* August 13. At https://www.nytimes.com/2018/08/13/nyregion/sexual-harassment-nyu-female-professor.html.

Guadalupe-Diaz, X. 2015. "Same-Sex Victimization and the LGBTQ Community." In *Sexual Victimization: Then and Now,* edited by T. N. Richards and C. D. Marcum, 173–92. Thousand Oaks, CA: Sage.

———. 2019. *Transgressed: Intimate Partner Violence in Transgender Lives.* New York: New York University Press.

Ison, J. 2019. "'It's Not Just Men and Women': LGBTQIA People and #MeToo." In *#MeToo and the Politics of Social Change,* edited by B. Fileborn and R. Loney-Howes, 151–67. Cham, Switzerland: Palgrave Macmillan.

James, S. E., J. L. Herman, S. Rankin, M. Keisling, L. Mottet, and M. Anafi. 2016. *The Report of the 2015 US Transgender Survey: National Center for Transgender Equality.* Washington, DC: National Center for Transgender Equality.

Lehavot, K., K. L. Walters, and J. M. Simoni. 2010. "Abuse, Mastery, and Health among Lesbian, Bisexual, and Two-Spirit American Indian and Alaska Native Women." *Psychology of Violence* 1 (S): 53–67.

Mallory, C., and B. Sears. 2015. "Employment Discrimination Based on Sexual Orientation and Gender Identity in Texas." Williams Institute, University of California at Los Angeles.

Mardorossian, C. M. 2014. *Framing the Rape Victim.* New Brunswick, NJ: Rutgers University Press.

McCann, H. 2018. "Big Reputations: Who Has the Power to Speak# MeToo?" *Australian Humanities Review* 63:185–89.

Messinger, A. M. 2017. *LGBTQ Intimate Partner Violence.* Berkeley: University of California Press.

Meyer, M. 2005. *The Politics and Poetics of Camp.* London: Routledge.

Powell, N. 2017. "Here's How We Can Center Queer & Trans Survivors in the #MeToo Movement." *Everyday Feminism,* December 11. At https://everydayfeminism.com/2017/11/lets-center-queer-trans-survivors/.

Rabelo, V. C., and L. M. Cortina. 2014. "Two Sides of the Same Coin: Gender Harassment and Heterosexist Harassment in LGBQ Work Lives." *Law and Human Behavior* 38 (4): 378–91.

Rothman, E. F., D. Exner, and A. L. Baughman. 2011. "The Prevalence of Sexual Assault against People Who Identify as Gay, Lesbian, or Bisexual in the United States: A Systematic Review." *Trauma, Violence, & Abuse* 12 (2): 55–66.

Simon, W., and J. H. Gagnon. 1987. "A Sexual Scripts Approach." In *Theories of Human Sexuality,* edited by J. Geer and W. O'Donoghue, 363–83. New York: Springer.

Soucek, B. 2018. "Queering Sexual Harassment Law." *Yale Law Journal Forum* 128:67–85.

Tjaden, P. G., and N. Thoennes. 2000. *Full Report of the Prevalence, Incidence, and Consequences of Violence against Women: Findings from the National Violence against Women Survey.* Washington, DC: National Institute of Justice.

Vagianos, A. 2019. "Tarana Burke: '#MeToo Is Not a Women's Movement.'" *Huffington Post,* April 24. At https://www.huffpost.com/entry/tarana-burke-me-too-not-womens-movement_n_5cc06af3e4b0764d31db5d88.

Warfield, Z. 2018. "Me Too Creator Tarana Burke Reminds Us This Is about Black and Brown Survivors." *Yes Magazine,* January. At https://www.yes-magazine.org/people-power/me-too-creator-tarana-burke-reminds-us-this-is-about-black-and-brown-survivors-20180104.

Whalley, E., and C. Hackett. 2017. "Carceral Feminisms: The Abolitionist Project and Undoing Dominant Feminisms." *Contemporary Justice Review* 20 (4): 456–73.

Notes

1. We have included Reitman's name here because of his choice to speak out publicly as the victim in this case.

2. The term *camp* is used to connote an over-the-top, effeminate style of parody historically connected to queer culture of the 1960s, often termed *gay parody.* For more on the queer history of camp, see Meyer 2005.

3. Although there is much debate about what constitutes "queer(ing)," we use the word *queer* as both an umbrella term for nonheterosexual, noncisgender identities (e.g., lesbian, gay, bisexual, transgender and queer [LGBTq], queer, and transfolks) and as an operational concept that seeks to destabilize taken-for-granted assumptions behind normative language.

4. For a more complete review of the methodological limitations in research on sexual violence perpetrated against members of the LGBTq community, see Guadalupe-Diaz 2015.

TENSIONS AND CONFLICTS WITHIN #MeToo

9

On Being Public

Feminism, Sexual Harassment, and
the Question of Palestine

Ruth Preser

> This essay has a public. If you are reading (or hearing) this, you are
> part of its public. So first let me say: Welcome.
> —*Michael Warner, "Publics and Counterpublics"*

> These four questions about truth-telling as an activity—who is able
> to tell the truth, about what, with what consequences, and with what
> relation to power.
> —*Michel Foucault, Fearless Speech*

Voice, visibility, and recognition are paradigmatic to feminist politics,
which assumes that a successful penetration into the public sphere is the
condition for negotiating and acquiring equal rights and civic belonging
(e.g., Fraser 1990; Halpern 2013; Herzog 1999). The optimistic version
assumes that the transformation in women's lives results from empowerment and agency, emphasized in politicizing the personal, voicing
one's stories, and presenting them in public. In other words, emancipa-
tory potential resides in compelling the public to witness the effects of
oppression and eventually, after sustained discursive contestation, in
succeeding in making these effects a common concern (Fraser 1990).

But what happens when a public or, better yet, a feminist counterpublic is reluctant to witness the realities disclosed by its members?
Current critique of the #MeToo movement asserts that although the

183

public outcry over sexual harassment and sexual violence promotes awareness, a few concerns have been raised regarding the movement's whiteness, which reflects colonial power relations by primarily centering the experiences of White Western women, celebrity culture, and the erasure of male and LGBT victims (Corrigan 2019; Mack and Na'puti 2019; Phipps 2019).[1] This chapter addresses the feminist script of being public in cases of sexual violence and explores refusals to publicly address questions concerning women's lives by looking at one of the most divisive debates in Israeli feminism: the occupation of Palestine. My analysis is based on a heated debate that took place in 2010 in an online email list comprising a few hundred Israeli feminist activists, scholars, and organizations. One of the list members, a prominent feminist activist, was dismissed from her job upon publicly exposing a case of sexual harassment and applied to her feminist sisters for their public support in her struggle against the persecution she experienced. Here the plot thickened because the college that dismissed her is located in the West Bank on confiscated Palestinian land. The "thickening" of the debate—namely, the intersection of sexual and colonial violence—serves me in complicating the prescriptive discourse of #MeToo. As Ashley Noel Mack and Tiara Na'puti argue, a decolonial perspective is necessary when addressing gendered violence within settler-colonial nation-states and within the context of disenfranchisement. They maintain that colonial unknowing actively works to produce ignorance and that the rhetoric of the #MeToo movement reflects colonial epistemology by reaffirming white Western female subjectivity (2019, 348).[2]

A feminist commitment to decolonization within analytical practice requires actively understanding gendered violence, such as sexual assault, as part of colonial violence and attends to the combined processes of racialization, gender dichotomization, and heterosexism (Mack and Na'puti 2019, 348). Following Mack and Na'puti's analytical framework, this chapter seeks to contribute to current decolonial feminist critique of the #MeToo discourses. By asking "Who is served by feminist convictions of voice, visibility, and publicness that underline current struggles against sexual violence?," I explore the intersection of sexual assault, colonial violence, and feminist efforts to speak in public.

Although this chapter does not suggest that there is a coherent feminist discourse or a unified movement in Israel, the online platform that I discuss did represent many feminist groups and causes in Israeli society, and its debates emphasize Israeli feminism(s) as a contested field of action. Employing Eve Sedgwick's (2003) concept of periperformativity and Michel Foucault's (2001) notion of parrhesia, I ask the following questions: What it is that we desire when we desire being public? What does it entail to be a feminist in public and to be public as a feminist? And what happens once we come together as a public? The first section in the chapter, "Feminist Counterpublics," elaborates on the concept and its localization in the Israeli context. The second section, "Sexual Harassment and the Question of Palestine," discusses the intersection of gender-based violence and settler colonialism in the context of Israel-Palestine. The third section, "The Contract," concludes the chapter.

Feminist Counterpublics

Coined by Nancy Fraser (1990) as "subaltern counterpublics," alternative publics are constituted by subordinate social groups (such as women, workers, peoples of color, and LGBTs) to serve as parallel discursive arenas in which members invent and circulate counterdiscourses. These counterdiscourses voice oppositional interpretations of identities, interests, and needs. Subaltern counterpublics emerge in stratified societies in response to exclusions within dominant publics. They help expand discursive space through contestation insofar as they assume an orientation that is publicist and aim to disseminate their discourses into ever-widening arenas (Fraser 1990, 67). Feminist counterpublics bear a dual character, being both spaces of withdrawal and regroupment and spaces for agitational activities directed toward the wider public (Fraser 1990, 68). Such is the case of a feminist subaltern counterpublic that invests in disseminating a view of domestic violence as a widespread systemic feature of male-dominated societies and that eventually, after sustained discursive contestation, succeeds in making this view a common concern (Fraser 1990, 71). Indeed, "speaking out" is central to feminist politics, which associates speech with freedom and equal citizenship. In the case of struggles against sexual violence, a discursive contestation is frequently shaped by acts of telling sexual stories in public as a means to change hegemonic language, generate communities, and create spaces for these stories to be heard (Plummer 1995, 9). As stories construct a moral self, a domain of intimate desires and intimate being that bears a concern regarding the public sphere, and as no account takes place outside the structure of address, sexual violence narratives allow us to investigate the social boundaries of what can be said about the intimate and how it should be narrated and represented in public (Butler 2001, 26; Plummer 1995, 152, 155).

A counterpublic relies on addressable objects that are conjured into being to enable the oppositional discourse and that give the public its existence—for example, terms invented by feminists to describe social reality, including *sexism, the double shift, sexual harassment,* and *marital, date, and acquaintance rape* (Fraser 1995, 67; Warner 2002, 51). However, as Fraser (1990) points out, not all subaltern counterpublics are always necessarily virtuous; some may practice their own modes of informal exclusion and marginalization. Many women do not enjoy the recognition and advancement that have been achieved by a small group of white, middle-class women, a point of contestation within #MeToo (Arruzza, Bhattacharya, and Fraser 2019; Gieseler 2019). And although digital technology creates platforms for sharing experiences and visibility for people who fight for recognition, minorities within the feminist movement may find themselves ignored and displaced from dialogues even on those platforms (Gieseler 2019, 64). Thus, sites of recognition and visibility, such as the #MeToo campaign, work in two ways: they serve as a platform for publicly speaking against sexual violence, and they serve as a reminder of the possibility that a minority's voice might be hijacked or whitewashed for the "greater good" or "larger cause" (Gieseler 2019, 64).

Moreover, a public discourse is generated by a performance that outlines its participants as belonging to the world that is condensed in the public discourse (Warner 2002, 82). A counterpublic not only maintains awareness of its subordinate status in regard to a dominant public but might also be regarded by this public with hostility. Hence, a counterpublic socially marks and stigmatizes its participants distinctively as those who belong to this counterpublic. However, occasionally, the participants of a counterpublic might not to want to be mistaken for the kind of person who would participate in this kind of contestation or be present in this kind of scene (Warner 2002, 86, 88). This complicates the business of freedom and belonging as the danger of stigmatization and its consequences hover over those struggling to belong through oppositional performance.

In Israel, the presence of women in public discourse is strongly connected to their perceived roles as wives and mothers or potential mothers. Motherhood is constructed not as a private role but as a public one, a discourse that maintains women as neither altogether excluded nor merely marginalized (Herzog 1996, 5). It is not uncommon to see women's activity in the public sphere constrained to "feminine" niches (Herzog 1996, 9). For example, when feminists infiltrate a national discourse on the traditionally perceived male issues of war and security, the public discourse is gender biased and frames these feminists as mothers and daughters (see, e.g., Amir and Kotef 2007; Lemish and Barzel 2000).

The Israeli feminist movement is built upon a network of nongovernmental organizations (NGOs) and groups and comprises activists who frequently are involved simultaneously in more than one organization. Although always fragmented, the movement has maintained an active presence in the public sphere through continuously redefining social issues and pointing out the intersectionality of gender, class, ethnic, and national oppression (Herzog 2008, 273). This effort to introduce diverse views of society and definitions of the social order has produced contested fields of action (Herzog 2008, 275), one of which is the occupation of Palestine.

As an ethnocracy, or a regime that facilitates nondemocratic seizure of the country and polity by one ethnic group, Israel does not incorporate fundamental democratic tenets, such as equal citizenship and protection against the tyranny of the majority (Yiftachel 1998). It pushes to maintain an ethnic Jewish majority, determines the hierarchical relations between various Jewish and non-Jewish ethnoclasses, and has a wide-ranging impact (Yiftachel 1998, 364–65). In Israel's militaristic society, women are considered to be lesser political beings to men; their status as political actors within the discourse of national security is that of caregivers and family agents. Accordingly, the public ear is attuned only to political statements that women make in their capacity as mothers and wives (Amir and Kotef 2007, 987). In this sense, security and militarism shape gender roles and identities, affect women's activism, breach and suspend potential cooperation and solidarity between

Jewish and Palestinian women, sustain gender inequalities, and sabotage the struggle for women's equality (Sasson-Levy and Misgav 2017).

One of the earliest documents emphasizing this schism in the young feminist movement in Israel occurred in 1980 when a fierce dispute abruptly terminated a feminist conference. This premature ending was followed by a press release clarifying the occurrences that led to the sudden dissolution of the event:

> Following a workshop on the topic "The Arab Woman's World," which also hosted Palestinian women, we proposed [the following] statement . . .
>
> "We express our solidarity with our Palestinian sisters in the Occupied Territories, with their struggle for social equality as women, and with their struggle against the occupation, as Palestinians. The end of the occupation is a crucial condition for a shared struggle and the liberation of both Palestinian and Israeli women."
>
> During the discussion, another articulation was brought to the table:
>
> "We, feminists in the State of Israel, express our identification with Palestinian women in particular, and with Arab women throughout the Middle East in general, in our shared struggle for self-determination and liberation."
>
> In response, a new motion was proposed, intended to remove both proposals from the agenda. However, this motion was dismissed[,] . . . [a] step which put an end to the conference.
>
> We would like to stress that this dismaying closure will not terminate the struggle and solidarity of feminists in Israel.[3]

A feminist proposition that included sisterhood, Palestine, Occupied Territories, and liberation was denounced and replaced by a softened articulation: "sisterhood" was converted into "identification," and the "Occupied Territories" gave way to the "State of Israel" and the "Middle East." At least "women" and "liberation" were still there, until the consensus crashed altogether, leaving us with an ambiguous conclusion that includes "feminist struggle," though unclear to what end; "solidarity," though we're not sure with whom; and "feminists" and "Israel," but without "Arabs," "Palestine," or even "Middle East."

This was not the first time that the Israeli feminist movement was divided by the question of Palestine. In her memoir, Marcia Freedman (1990), a veteran feminist activist and a former member of the Israeli

Parliament, reflected on the line drawn by Israeli feminists in the 1970s, demarcating issues of women's oppression from issues of the oppression of Palestinians.

Sexual Harassment and the Question of Palestine

On March 19, 1998, the Israeli Prevention of Sexual Harassment Act came into effect. The act was the outcome of a rare, combined effort of the Israeli Justice Department, Israeli feminist legal academics, and the legal department of the Israeli Women's Network, a feminist NGO that studied the vast international material on sexual harassment and presented the Israeli Parliament with an informed and comprehensive draft statute law (Kamir 2005). The act defines requests for sexual favors, including in a quid pro quo context; unwanted sexual advances; any sexual, verbal, or physical conduct; repeated references directed toward a person that focus on the person's sexuality; an intimidating or humiliating reference directed toward a person concerning the person's sex or sexuality; the creation of a "hostile environment"; and other conducts of a sexual nature (e.g., staring at someone's body or giving a compliment that refers to bodily parts) as a criminal offense (Yanisky-Ravid 2019). Furthermore, the act adopts the subordinate rule; namely, it assumes that in a context of power relations, sexual harassment exists without the prior condition to refuse the advances, with or without consent (Yanisky-Ravid 2019). Within the first weeks of the law coming into effect, dozens of sexual harassment complaints were filed. In the following months, media reports of sexual harassment attracted much public attention (Kamir 2005). Although it is difficult to measure the mitigating effect of the act, there are growing numbers of sexual harassment cases. Known public figures, such as national and local leaders, commanders in the Israeli Defense Forces, and police force personnel, have become subject to legal procedures, which may reflect rising public awareness (Yanisky-Ravid 2019).

It is in this feminist spirit and public atmosphere that Hannah Kehat, a prominent Orthodox-religious feminist, turned to an online Israeli feminist network of NGOs, academics, and activists pleading for solidarity. Kehat had been dismissed from her teaching position at Orot College, located in Elkana, a settlement in the West Bank. She claimed that she was fired for leading a successful struggle against sexual assault within the Jewish National Religious community, in which she publicly exposed a sexual harassment scandal that brought about the dismissal of a prominent rabbi and educator. Kehat's appeal to the feminist digital network as well as the solidarity this appeal invoked should not come as a surprise.[4] Issues concerning sexual violence and the persecution of those who fight publicly against perpetrators are the bread and butter of feminist activism to this very day. This is so especially in regard to women's employment and freedom of occupation, which is threatened in so many cases in which a woman ventures to go public.

The feminist network at large was in favor of engaging in public acts of solidarity, such as issuing a petition in support of Kehat's struggle against her college. However, some questioned the ethics of such an intervention, which they felt disregarded the ongoing violation of Palestinians' human rights. The latter argued that Palestinians cannot enjoy the freedom of employment and of consciousness that Kehat struggled to maintain. Fearing that supporting such a case might contribute to the normalization of the occupation, the opponents pointed out that the college where Kehat taught stood on confiscated Palestinian land in violation of international law. Moreover, many Palestinians were deprived of basic freedom of movement, which prevented them from attending universities and schools or going to work. If solidarity were to be professed by Israeli feminists, some interlocutors argued, it should be solidarity with Palestinian women under military occupation; and if a petition were to be issued, it should call for the mass resignation of all who taught in the debated college.

Some women pointed out that the settler-colonial regime was maintained on the backs of Mizrahi Jews and migrants from the former Soviet Union—those subordinate within the ethnic Jewish divide in Israeli society, who lived wherever they were sent by state authorities or wherever they could afford, within either the 1948 or the 1967 colonial project.[5] As maintained by one of the interlocutors, a migrant from the former Soviet Union, many migrants had no notion of what or where the "Green Line" is,[6] and most immigrants would have preferred living in the center of Tel Aviv if only they could afford it. Another interlocutor pointed to the Israeli immigrant-absorption and dispersal policy since 1948, which channeled Mizrahi immigrants to peripheral development towns.[7] She reminded the email-list members that many women do not have the privilege of being fired from academia because they do not have the chance of being employed by it in the first place. Solidarity, she claimed, does not exist—not along the national divide or along the ethnic divide; and feminist solidarity is not equally distributed at the intersection of nation, ethnicity, or class. On top of that, she added, Mizrahi women's struggles hardly ever achieve the level of reinforcement, engagement, and resonance that Kehat's case had gained. Hence, it was precisely due to the fact that class is a powerful category that Kehat should not be apologetic about her livelihood. In response, Kehat, who at that time also resided in the West Bank, argued that she too opposed the occupation; however, as a mother of six she could not simply uproot her kids from their home and schools because it was incongruent with her ideology. "Life," she concluded, "is complicated" (quoted in Friedman 2010).[8]

Feminist life continued to be complicated. In the summer of 2014, the Women Wage Peace (WWP) movement was established as a response to the Protective Edge military assault in Gaza.[9] It declares itself "nonpolitical," its members asserting that they wish to be inclusive of all women in Israeli society, their political position notwithstanding. The mission statement in Hebrew asserts that the movement is not ideological but *pragmatic*.[10] Although the WWP does not identify as a feminist movement, it incorporates ideological and discursive traits that may be identified as feminist, including solidarity among women as the foundation for activism and social change with the explicit aim of uniting women throughout the country; recognition of gender bias in negotiations for peace and hence the need for increased women's representation and endorsement of United Nations Security Resolution 1325; the fostering of a nonhierarchical organizational structure and the sharing of leadership ("leaderful," in their language); and the training of women to take their "mandate seat at the table."[11]

Joining the movement's communal fast outside the prime minister's residence in 2015, held by WWP in commemoration of the Protective Edge military assault, Shoshana London Sappir (2015) described how the organizers repeatedly emphasized that the movement was "not leftist," thus adopting the same rhetoric that had fueled a delegitimization campaign against leftist activists:

In an attempt to appeal to the broadest audience possible, they refused to take a stand on any of the core issues that define the struggle for peace as I understand it, and which is what drove me to join them: social justice, human rights, occupation, racism, equality, democracy. The most they would commit to was demanding the government "return to negotiations," the slogan writ large on our banners, under the title of the fast. It should come as no surprise that many a passerby shouted out, "with whom?" even from moving cars. As for the war we had gathered to commemorate, the discourse was limited to our desire as Israelis to keep our loved ones out of harm's way, but stopped at recognition of the destruction we had wrought on the Palestinian side.

When visitors from the public or the press asked about the group, I was dismayed to hear WWP people repeatedly describe it as an apolitical women's movement and emphasize that it was "not leftist." . . . I was shocked by how casually they distanced themselves from the Left and adopted a rhetoric that has fueled a campaign of delegitimization and jeopardized the safety of leftist activists.

The low point for me was when the organizers invited the wife of one of the heads of Elad, an organization dedicated to evicting Palestinians from their homes and replacing them with Jews, to join us for a dialogue.[12] Their line of thinking, they explained to me, was that we can find common ground with other women in the desire for peace even if we do not agree on the details.

Although at times the investment in creating or maintaining a public and penetrating the public sphere may reach some strange conclusions, I do not wish to ridicule it. Rather, I would like to look at the process whereby these exchanges underscore the negotiations over what determines a feminist public, who (and what) is fit to go public, and what happens once we come together as a public. In particular, I wish to reflect on the poignant efforts and failures to demarcate feminism as a site of witnessing and witnessing as inherently feminist.

I focus on witnessing for two reasons. First, feminist investment in telling stories in public and in compelling the public to see, recognize, and know the realities these stories portray assumes that the public sphere is a site of witnessing and accountability. To paraphrase Foucault's (2001) discussion of truth telling, feminism is invested in a public verbal activity that involves criticism, risk to the speaker, and a sense of duty to improve society, other people, and oneself. Second, feminist publics, which maintain a shared awareness of their subordinate status in a dominant order, strive to expand discursive space (Fraser 1990; Warner 2002). In other words, a feminist reproach or criticism is made in the context of inferiority in power and vulnerability and therefore may manifest reluctance to say everything (Foucault 2001, 52–57).

In his analysis of truth telling in ancient Greece, Foucault differentiated a male-born citizen of the polis, who had the right to use fearless speech (parrhesia) that took the form of truthful political criticism, from a female-born citizen, whose parrhesia took the form of a confession about herself and a truthful accusation against another person (or deity) more powerful than she. A gender bias in truthful political criticism is evident in the Israeli public debate as well. For example, the Israeli antioccupation organization Breaking the Silence, which focuses on soldiers' testimonies of their military service in the Occupied Palestinian Territories, constructs its public appeal by invoking valorized cultural symbols and meanings, first and foremost by inhabiting war experience as a privileged source of knowledge (Katriel and Shavit 2013). This symbolic capital is inherently masculinist and militarist in the localized Israeli version of fearless speech and public condemnation of the occupation (Katriel and Shavit 2013, 99).[13] However, Jewish women do exercise fearless speech, as Merav Amir has demonstrated in her study of Checkpoint Watch, an organization of Israeli women opposing the Israeli occupation, who witness, monitor, and document the detrimental effects of checkpoints on the lives of West Bank Palestinians (2014, 364). Amir suggests that this form of reporting to the Israeli citizenry is parrhesian talk—namely, a form of knowledge transference that bestows on its target audience accountability and a moral duty to act (2014, 376).

As we have seen, feminist publics embed moments and acts of disengagement or disinterpellation (Sedgwick 2003)—namely, a failure or momentary collapse in the consensus that such a space of a "we" of witness is expected to invoke. Sedgwick notes that these collapses or refusals to engage in the act of witnessing are not manifested through a powerful formulaic negative response but through a renunciation, a "count me out," and the refusal to be interpellated as a witness (2003, 70).[14] Demonstrating an act of refusal to witness, Sedgwick contends that any queer who has struggled to articulate to friends or family why he or she loves them but just does not want to be at their wedding knows from the inside the dynamic of compulsory witness generated by a public that comes together (72).

Kehat's appeal to the Israeli feminist public to support her struggle and to go public with this support rested on her assumption of a preexisting consensus on what may or may not be witnessed and addressed by a feminist public. The interpellation of the members of the digital network as witnesses to her suffering was based on Kehat's guaranteed agency—namely, that she had a pretty good idea of how to be public and what was considered legitimate to call for in a feminist public and as a feminist public. Indeed, the response was overwhelmingly supportive: the petition was issued and endorsed by many feminist NGOs and prominent academics and activists, though some shunned this compulsory witnessing. [15]

It is important to note that those refusing or deflecting the logic of automatic solidarity with Kehat are precisely those whom the discourse of WWP defines itself by excluding: "lefties." It seems that simply invoking the state of settler-colonial occupation is taken as a move that counters the normalization and obfuscation of the Israeli occupation regime (Katriel and Shavit 2013, 89, 101). Of course, the exclusion of leftists is not entirely shocking; Foucault noted that truth telling is a public activity that involves certain privileges and duties but also risks and dangers. Thus, going public involves awareness of the consequences and is intended to limit the risk one takes (2001, 32–33). So, we could assume that feminist truth telling, courageous as it may be, might regretfully result in a forgetting: in the case of Israel, it might involve a ("*pragmatic*") forgetting of Palestine as a strategic means or simply as part of the truth-telling contract.[16]

The Contract

Mack and Na'puti (2019) argue that practices of colonial unknowing actively work to produce ignorance about relations of colonialism. Colonial unknowing renders unintelligible the effects of colonial relations of power. In the Israeli context, the contract of truth telling in cases of sexual violence consists of a sort of "deal" between the one lacking the power (feminist discourses) and the one who has the power (hegemonic discourses). This "deal" delineates the conditions whereby one may exercise fearless speech without being punished. Of course, this contract has its limits; women have been punished for speaking of sexual assault in public, as in Kehat's case. Thus, going public does not involve reckless courage because the contract of fearless speech involves awareness of the consequences and is intended to limit the risk one takes in going public (Foucault 2001, 32–33). We might argue that forgetting, or the process by which a people fails to be visible from the perspective of the colonizer (Hochberg 2015), predetermines the conditions of speaking in public in the Israeli society. In other words, recruiting legitimacy to be feminist in public as well as invoking a consensus and engaging witnesses, either against sexism (Kehat) or for peace (Women Wage Peace), prescribe a forgetting.[17]

As Gil Hochberg (2015) and Adi Kuntsman and Rebecca Stein (2015) maintain, the conditions of seeing and knowing the Israeli–Palestinian conflict do not organize along the dichotomous lines of exposure versus concealment of colonial violence. Indeed, various normalizing mechanisms such as public secrets and exceptionalism come into play in justifying this learned myopia. By "myopia," I do not suggest that feminists fail to see. Rather, the reading I suggest points to the mechanisms of public secrets, or pseudosecrets (Sedgwick 1990, 67–68), which determine how, who, and what should and can be verbalized, witnessed, and validated in public.

The crucial moments when a "feminist killjoy," to use Sara Ahmed's (2017) articulation of the person who performs the costly act of refusal and disengagement, insists on pointing to these secrets might not overcome the dominant sphere of witnessing and knowing, but they may nevertheless render visible a certain public's reluctance to see and know (Hochberg 2015). Such moments may underline the "deal": the acts of dissent and disengagement by both the killjoys and their pragmatic sisters unveil the public contract or the contract on how to be feminist in public and issue a call to problematize the feminist investment in the public sphere as a source for legitimacy and a utopian horizon. They demonstrate our poignant fantasy about the public sphere: if only we could decipher the best way to speak truth, then power, finally, would listen. As Hannah Kehat contends, life is complicated, and reading feminist negotiation with, in, and through the public sphere may provide an analytical road map of contemporary "deals" of how to be public. These negotiations animate the violence that continuously puts us at risk of exclusion or worse, no matter how "pragmatic" we may be. This risk makes us vulnerable to symbolic and material violence and leaves traces that we should and indeed must read to understand what it means these days to be an activist, a scholar, or a movement that is invested in going public.

References

Aharoni, S. 2011. "Gender and 'Peace Work': An Unofficial History of Israeli–Palestinian Peace Negotiations." *Politics & Gender* 7:391–416.

Ahmed, S. 2017. *Living a Feminist Life.* Durham, NC: Duke University Press.

Alterman, R. 1995. "Can Planning Help in Times of Crisis: Planners' Response to Israel's Recent Wave of Mass Immigration." *Journal of the American Planning Association* 61 (2): 156–77.

Amir, M. 2014. "Women Speaking of National Security: The Case of Checkpoint Watch." *International Political Sociology* 8:363–78.

Amir, M., and H. Kotef. 2007. "(En)Gendering Checkpoints: Checkpoint Watch and the Repercussions of Intervention." *Signs* 32 (4): 973–96.

Arruzza, C., T. Bhattacharya, and N. Fraser. 2019. *Feminism for the 99%: A Manifesto.* London : Verso.

Butler, J. 2001. "Giving an Account of Oneself." *Diacritics* 31:22–40.

Corrigan, L. M. 2019. "The #MeToo Moment: A Rhetorical Zeitgeist." *Women's Studies in Communication* 42 (3): 264–68.

Foucault, M. 2001. *Fearless Speech.* Edited by J. Pearson. Los Angeles: Semiotext(e).

Fraser, N. 1990. "Rethinking the Public Sphere: A Contribution to the Critique of Actually Existing Democracy." *Social Text* 25–26:56–80.

Freedman, M. 1990. *Exile in the Promised Land: A Memoir.* Ithaca, NY: Firebrand Books.

Friedman, Y. 2010. "Hannah Kehat: I Was Sexually Harassed as a Child." *Srugim News,* May 27.

Gieseler, C. 2019. *The Voices of #MeToo: From Grassroots Activism to a Viral Roar.* Lanham, MD: Rowman & Littlefield.

Gillis, R. 2016. "Ethnic Identity in the Israeli Settlements." *Theory and Criticism* 47:41–63.

Gordon, A. 2008. *Ghostly Matters: Haunting and the Sociological Imagination.* Minneapolis: University of Minnesota Press.

Halpern, R. 2013. *Where Am I Situated? Gender Perspectives on Space.* Tel Aviv: Beit Berl College and Friedrich Ebert Foundation.

Hasson, Nir. 2014. "Hidden Links Unearthed between State, Settler Group at Israel's Most Controversial Dig." *Haaretz,* November 17.

Herzog, H. 1996. "Why so Few? The Political Culture of Gender in Israel." *International Review of Women and Leadership* 2 (1): 1–18.

———. 1999. *Gendering Politics: Women in Israel.* Ann Arbor: University of Michigan Press.

———. 2008. "Re/visioning the Women's Movement in Israel." *Citizenship Studies* 12 (3): 265–82.

Hochberg, G. Z. 2015. *Visual Occupations: Violence and Visibility in a Conflict Zone.* Durham, NC: Duke University Press.

Kamir, O. 2005. "Sexual Harassment Law in Israel." *International Journal of Discrimination and Law* 7:315–35.

Katriel, T., and N. Shavit. 2013. "Speaking Out: Testimonial Rhetoric in Israeli Soldiers' Dissent." *Versus* 116:81–105.

Khazzoum, A. 2003. "The Great Chain of Orientalism: Jewish Identity, Stigma Management, and Ethnic Exclusion in Israel." *American Sociological Review* 68 (4): 481–510.

Kot, V., M. Yemini, and M. Chankseliani. 2020. "Triple Exclusion: Life Stories of Jewish Migrant Academics from the Former Soviet Union at a Contested University under Siege." *International Journal of Educational Development* 76. At https://doi.org/10.1016/j.ijedudev.2020.102191.

Kuntsman, A. 2009. *Figurations of Violence and Belonging: Queerness, Migranthood, and Nationalism in Cyberspace and Beyond.* Berlin: Peter Lang.

Kuntsman, A., and R. L. Stein. 2015. *Digital Militarism: Israel's Occupation in the Social Media Age.* Berkeley: University of California Press.

Lavie, S. 2014. *Wrapped in the Flag of Israel: Mizrahi Single Mothers and Bureaucratic Torture.* New York: Berghahn.

Lemish, D., and I. Barzel. 2000. "'Four Mothers': The Womb in the Public Sphere." *European Journal of Communication* 15 (2): 147–69.

London Sappir, S. 2015. "Why I Joined Israeli Women Fasting for Peace, and Why I Almost Quit." *+972 Magazine,* July 25. At https://972mag.com/why-i-joined-israeli-women-fasting-for-peace-and-why-i-almost-quit/109240/.

Mack, A. N., and T. R. Na'puti. 2019. "'Our Bodies Are Not Terra Nullius': Building a Decolonial Feminist Resistance to Gendered Violence." *Women's Studies in Communication* 42 (3): 347–70.

Phipps, A. 2019. "'Every Woman Knows a Weinstein': Political Whiteness and White Woundedness in #MeToo and Public Feminisms around Sexual Violence." *Feminist Formations* 31 (2): 1–25.

Plummer, K. 1995. *Telling Sexual Stories: Power, Change, and Social Worlds.* London: Routledge.

Sasson-Levy, O., and C. Misgav. 2017. "Gender Studies in Israel in the Early 21st Century: Between Neo-liberalism and Neo-colonialism." *Megamot* 41 (2): 165–206.

Sedgwick, E. K. 1990. *Epistemology of the Closet.* Berkeley: University of California Press.

———. 2003. *Touching Feeling: Affect, Pedagogy, Performativity.* Durham, NC: Duke University Press.

Shalhoub-Kevorkian, N. 2012. "The Grammar of Rights in Colonial Contexts: The Case of Palestinian Women in Israel." *Middle East Law and Governance* 4:106–51.

Tzfadia, E. 2000. "Immigrant Dispersal in Settler Societies: Mizrahim and Russians in Israel under the Press of Hegemony." *Geography Research Forum* 20:52–69.

Warner, M. 2002. "Publics and Counterpublics." *Public Culture* 14 (1): 49–90.

Weiss, H. 2011. "Immigration and West Bank Settlement Normalization." *Political and Legal Anthropology Review* 34 (1): 112–30.

Yanisky-Ravid, S. 2019. "#MeToo Movement and the Four Steps of 'Naming, Blaming, Shaming, and Amending'—Lessons from the Israeli Prevention of Sexual Harassment Act, within Physical and Virtual Spheres." February 12. NYU LAW, Labor, & Employment Law: Proceedings of the 71st NYU Law Annual Conference on Labor, 2018. At https://ssrn.com/abstract=3345712 or http://dx.doi.org/10.2139/ssrn.3345712.

Yiftachel, O. 1998. "'Ethnocracy': The Politics of Judaising Israel/Palestine." *Constellations* 6 (3): 364–90.

Notes

Parts of this article were presented at the Gender Studies Program Seminar at Ben Gurion University (2017); the Reconfiguring Cultural Inquiry conference at the ICI Berlin (2017); the Sophie Davis Forum on Gender, International Conflict Resolution, and Peace, Hebrew University (2018); the Eighth International Conference of Critical Geography, Athens (2019); the Gender Studies Programs' Annual Conference, Tel Hai, Israel (2019); and the International Symposium: Comparative Perspectives on #MeToo, University of Kentucky (2019). Parts were published in the essay "How to Be Feminist in Public," *Feministiqa* (2018). I am grateful to Paula-Irene Villa and Cristina Alcalde, the editors of this collection, for their thoughtful and instructive comments.

1. *Editors' note:* See also Guadalupe-Diaz and Whalley's chapter in this volume.

2. For example: emphasizing publicity through self-disclosure as the primary means of rhetorical agency and celebrating increased state violence through calls for harsher carceral punishments for sexual violence.

3. Jerusalem, May 26, 1980, Feminist Archives, Haifa Feminist Institute, Haifa, Israel.

4. The debate reported relates to discussions on an email list (in which the author was included) on May 5, 2010.

Israeli society is stratified by race/ethnicity, where Ashkenazi (European Jews) are the dominant group and are considered fully "Western," and Mizrahi (Middle Eastern and North African Jews) are subordinate and are considered fully "Eastern." The "orientalization" of Mizrahi is based on a binary construction that shapes and justifies unequal distribution of resources and leads to the entrenchment of a binary ethnic division. See Khazzoum 2003. Also in Israeli society, Russian-speaking migrants are considered "white but not quite" because they do not conform to Israeli models of class and ethnic distinction and categorization. See Kuntsman 2009.

5. Rachelle Alterman (1995) maintains that despite the fact that the ideological agenda of Likud (right-wing) governments to build up Jewish settlement in the West Bank was backed by budget allocations from planning policy and units, only 0.8 percent (East Jerusalem excluded) of immigrants chose to live in this region. Yet, as other scholars point out, immigrants from the former Soviet Union who had the means to do so settled in the center of the country, while others were channeled to the periphery and the West Bank because of the lower housing prices there (see Kot, Yemini, and Chankseliani 2020; Weiss 2011). For a discussion on the ethnic-class composition of Jewish settlement, see Gillis 2016.

6. The Green Line is the border between the West Bank and Israel.

7. For a discussion on immigrant-absorption policy and the geographical distribution of power and wealth along ethnic and class divides, see Tzfadia 2000.

8. See Lavie 2014 for a discussion on the Ashkenazi domination of the Israeli women's movement.

9. See the WWP mission statement in English at http://womenwagepeace .org.il/en/mission-statement/.

10. See the WWP mission statement in Hebrew at https://womenwagepeace .org.il/en/mission-statement/.

11. See the WWP mission statement in English at http://womenwagepeace .org.il/en/mission-statement/.

12. Ir David Foundation, or the City of David, is an archaeological site in the center of Silwan, a Palestinian neighborhood in East Jerusalem. It is managed by the Elad settlers' organization, which is engaged in Judaizing the adjacent Silwan. See Hassan 2014 and the Ir Amin website at http://www.ir-amim.org.il/en/tags /al-bustan.

13. On gender bias in public debates concerning national security in Israel, see also Aharoni 2011.

14. Pushing on with the Althusserian concept of interpellation, Sedgwick defines these acts as periperformatives—namely, utterances that do not fulfill the conditions of explicit performative utterances, as in "We hereby consecrate," but instead allude to explicit performative utterances, as in "We cannot consecrate" (2003, 68).

15. See the website for the Israeli Association for Feminist and Gender Studies at www.gendersite.org.il/2010/05/10/1152/ (in Hebrew).

16. See, for example, Shalhoub-Kevorkian 2012, which demonstrates that the existing Israeli human rights (and feminist) framework cannot be an emancipating force because it operates in a colonial context.

17. This is not to say that feminist groups that openly oppose the occupation do not exist. They do: for example, Isha L'Isha Haifa Feminist Center, the Coalition of Women for Peace, New Profile, Women in Black, Black Laundry, Bat Shalom, and Checkpoint Watch.

10

NiUnaMenos

Beyond the Rally, a Field in Dispute

Fanni Muñoz Cabrejo

On August 13, 2016, the NiUnaMenos (Not One [Woman] Less) movement in Peru gathered one of the most massive demonstrations in the history of the country. Little more than two years later, the feminist collectives that once assembled under the unifying demand of stopping violence against women had fragmented into separate and, in some cases, contending groups. This chapter examines the NiUnaMenos Perú movement to identify and analyze the tensions and negotiations present among the diversity of feminist collectives that participated in the first demonstration. The critical analysis I present underscores that these new collectives and the institutionalized feminist movements have different ways of doing politics in the context of globalization, the emergence of internet-based social movements, and an authoritarian society such as Peru.

My analysis pays particular attention to how gender intersects with race, class, and ethnicity. I suggest some reasons to explain how the NiUnaMenos movement is innovative and distinct from traditional forms of political organization, following Alberto Melucci's (1994) point that contemporary movements assume that they are autonomous from political systems. Likewise, contemporary movements articulate personal needs and the urge for political innovation; thus, collective claims become massive if political actors do not translate these claims into democratic guarantees (Melucci 1994, 121). I examine the fragmentation of a movement that in its origins offered a platform through which thousands of women dared to narrate the violent situations to which they were routinely subjected. Based on seven in-depth interviews with representatives[1] of the most active and diverse collectives within the movement, I provide a preliminary feminist analysis of the movement. I draw on existing scholarship on this movement in Peru as well as in other parts of Latin America. Last, the Facebook fan pages[2] of the groups and several newspapers constitute an important part of this analysis.

The Emergence of NiUnaMenos

On July 14, 2016, a ruling by the Supreme Court of Justice of Ayacucho—a region in southern Peru—gave Adriano Pozo a suspended sentence of one year in prison. By that point, a video featuring Pozo violently dragging his girlfriend, Arlette Contreras, by the hair through a hotel reception had been viewed by millions in and outside of Peru. The Court did not find that the video constituted proof of a degree of violence that would warrant Pozo go to prison. On the next day, July 15, a courtroom in Lima gave another man, Rony García, a suspended sentence of four years after his brutal aggression against another woman, Lady Guillén (née Lizeth Rosario Socla Guillén). These two acts of impunity by the Peruvian judiciary system when confronting blatant acts of men's violence against women provoked collective indignation throughout the country. This indignation, in turn, prompted the NiUnaMenos demonstration. The demonstration became the most massive protest concerning women's rights in Peru's history. According to media calculations, about 150,000 people rallied on the streets on August 13, 2016 (Chinchay and Cortijo 2016).

The NiUnaMenos movement in Peru can be explained by different factors, some of which are addressed in the testimonies of feminists of different backgrounds in this chapter. More broadly, according to feminist activists linked to political parties, one such factor is the background of continuous political demonstrations in the country, in particular those that emerged between 2015 and 2016 in response to the government's new labor laws and to the presidential aspirations of former dictator Alberto Fujimori's (1992–2000) daughter, Keiko Fujimori.[3] Moreover, the momentum of feminist collectives and the expansion of the LGBT movement created the necessary conditions for the emergence of NiUnaMenos.[4]

Throughout the region and beyond, the past decade has witnessed a wave of demonstrations denouncing violence against women across Latin American, European, and North American countries. Some of these demonstrations and movements include NiUnaMenos in Argentina (2015) and Mexico (2016) and the #MeToo movement in the United States (2018). Argentina can be understood as the first country to carry out a NiUnaMenos rally as a reaction to the femicides of María Eugenia Lancetti and Chiara Páez. According to Ana Natalucci and Julieta Rey, the Argentinian NiUnaMenos is simultaneously a demonstration, a slogan, and a collective of women that articulates "professional organizations, activists and women without previous trajectories in organized groups who get involved with the cycle" (2018, 4).[5]

In Peru, the event that triggered NiUnaMenos was the indignation felt by Peruvians in reaction to the image of Adriano Pozo dragging Arlette Contreras by her hair. This image provoked a reaction and demonstration by feminists and feminist activists from various collectives. M, a feminist and philosophy graduate from the Pontifical Catholic University of Peru (PUCP), with a Lima middle-high-class background, channeled the indignant feeling toward this image, the violence, and the impunity promoted by the judiciary system. She posted a call to action on Facebook: "When will we take the streets, sisters? When will we say 'not one woman more'?" (quoted in Caballero 2018, 103); thus, collective claims become massive if political actors do not translate these claims into democratic guarantees. Her post went viral, and within a few days more people and groups, on social media and elsewhere, joined the call for action to rally in response to the state's refusal to sanction violence against women as a crime. At the same time, different social actors began to self-organize, leading to expressions of reciprocity, exchange, and collaboration: the public domain of the demonstration's logo, donations of merchandising, free publicity panels and spots, performances, fund-raisers, the scheduling of specialists to hear testimonies, and posts in support of the rally.

NiUnaMenos thus progressed from a face-to-face group to a vast network of diverse voices connected through smartphones. It unified traditional movements, parties, syndicates, collectives, religious groups, informal friend networks, individuals, the media, and others with one common objective: to protest and end gender violence against women. To be clear, no specific organization summoned the NiUnaMenos rally, so the movement cannot be thought of as a homogeneous feminist actor. On the contrary, the women who initially promoted the demonstration on social networks were feminists and feminist activists from various contrasting backgrounds. The Peruvian rally, like the Argentinian NiUnaMenos, "did not signify the development of a generalized feminist identity, but rather an identity with many voices, diverse repertoires and political agendas" (Natalucci and Rey 2018, 17).

The feminism(s) associated with NiUnaMenos drew on a diverse group of very young women and independent activists as well as on collectives from the capital, Lima, and the country's provinces. The women from the provinces in particular were conscious of their oppression and need to fight against a system of male domination and sought to do so from their spaces, the streets and the internet, as a way to combine cyberactivism and activism. It is essential to notice that institutionalized feminism, associated with feminist nongovernmental organizations, was not a protagonist in this demonstration. It should also be noted that the struggle against gender violence has been one of the main themes of the national feminist agenda since its origins more than thirty years ago. Thus, institutionalized feminism had already made some progress within the state through the establishment of norms and the creation of public policies.

In reviewing the NiUnaMenos rallies, Bernardo Gutiérrez (2016) and Gerardo Caballero (2018) agree in pointing out that these rallies do not constitute a social movement. In Caballero's view, they are a form of collective action, but Gutiérrez considers them to have made evident a shift in the political and social paradigm throughout Latin America, where digital technology has acquired a prominent role by building a new prototype of political participation, creation, and imagination that operates with new, specific goals and with new actors moving in hybrid spaces (2016, 38). However, Gutiérrez concedes that "the most appropriate term would be the concept of 'web movement,' coined by Arnau Monterde, which refers to new social ecosystems based on 'new forms of cooperation' and not in 'great ideological dogmas.' A web, according to Doménico di Siena, is represented by 'a social structure composed by groups of people who are connected by one or several types of relations' and who share 'common interests or knowledge'" (7).

According to Manuel Castells's conceptualization, these rallies can be considered a networked social movement because the internet was one of the primary means of communication for the process. Castells identifies the social movement as a networked society, which must be analyzed based on "what [it] claims to be" (2004, 92)—in other words, based on its individual participants' discursive practices and the processes in which they are immersed. Castells defines these processes by "the social actors who aspire to a cultural change (change in values)" (2009, 394) and by beliefs that imply a transformation of mentalities and affect society as a whole. This kind of movement is emotional, formed "by process of self-governing communication, free of the control of institutional power" (Castells 2012, 27). Likewise, in movements like NiUnaMenos, digital social media "offer the possibility to deliberate and to freely coordinate actions" (Castells 2012, 27) as well as to form a relation with society.

NiUnaMenos, as a platform that denied being a collective or organization, had neither official spokeswomen nor national or international coordinators and did not pretend to be an authorized voice for the thousands of women who suffer violence every day in the country. This platform, however, prompted the emergence of two fronts from within movement: one group oriented toward self-organization and self-mobilization and another group that adopted hierarchical organization practices. According to the testimonies gathered for this study, this contradiction points to a hierarchical relationship between the frontrunners of NiUnaMenos and the feminist collectives that were not a part of the core group of the demonstration. This verticality was exposed at the assemblies and denounced in the virtual coordination spaces (for example, in Facebook Messenger chats, fan pages, and Facebook groups) during and after the rally. It especially became a point of contention when the academic feminist J, a member of the initial core group, attempted to inscribe the name "NiUnaMenos" as a trademark at the Peruvian National Institute for the Defense of Competition and the Protection of Intellectual Property (Indecopi, for its acronym in Spanish). As K explained what happened,

I think [NiUnaMenos] got out of control. It was intense; it was very emotionally charged learning, and we stop romanticizing ourselves as feminists too. Because entering into the process of NiUnaMenos, with all the ideals, and the effervescence of the moment and everything else about the construction of that space was beautiful. However, after seeing the power disputes, those things about who it includes, about who represents [it] . . . . It was all-encompassing in representativeness, who was the worthy representative of Peruvian women, of women's struggles. (ellipses indicate omission)

Confronted with these complaints and attacks, the members of the core group decided not to respond and instead avoided dialogue, insisting that NiUnaMenos was a platform for making visible the violence that women experience and for demanding that the state carry out its duty to eradicate such violence. The movement was said to be based on self-organization and self-mobilization, not on individual leaders, as in the NiUnaMenos rallies in Argentina, Chile, and Mexico. Nevertheless, many activists and collectives abandoned NiUnaMenos after the trademark incident, operating solely within their own groups.

A Field of Tension among Diverse Feminist Collectives

In Peru, more than eighty feminist collectives have emerged in the past decade. Luna Follegati (2018) points out that in the Chilean case the feminist movement must be read in a new light that reveals its apogee in the twenty-first century. The new feminist collectives represent a generational break with the so-called institutionalized feminists. The latter are focused on combating inequality, protecting sexual and reproductive rights, and supporting policies that eradicate gender violence. Because they are tied to the state, their struggle is framed as a process of state democratization. In Peru, however, as a consequence of NiUnaMenos, new collectives and groups were formed in the areas of Lima Norte and working-class neighborhoods such as San Juan de Lurigancho, Comas, and Los Olivos.

The new collectives have disrupted the feminist landscape with diverse discourses, including those linked to how women represent themselves; the freedom to control their own bodies; the importance of neighborhood community; sexual diversity and care; the struggle against violence (especially lethal violence such as femicide); the transformation of women as political subjects; performativity as bodily expression; and distance from the state. Nevertheless, some continuities exist, especially in discourses concerning gender violence and sexual and reproductive rights. Maruja Barrig (2019) calls the feminist collectives focused on these discourses "counterculture feminists." As Nancy Fraser pointed out during a recent interview in Madrid, Spain, this is a "special moment, a new wave in the formation of feminism with an enormous potential for change in regards to the two previous decades" (Fraser 2019).

The history of the feminist movements in Peru has been characterized by alternating moments of activation, silence, and even decline, particularly in the 1990s. The process developed during the past few years, however, brings a new, emerging context to light and demonstrates the configuration of different collectives that, although based primarily on student participation, are also formed by other groups linked to working-class sectors. Like the feminist movements in general in Peru, these collectives have been scattered and diverse. Virginia Vargas (2008) has identified three currents in the history of Peruvian feminism: the feminist current, the working-class current, and the political current.[6] However, unlike in Vargas's characterization of the past, today's movement reveals two main currents: institutional feminists of the twentieth century and feminists made up of several heterogeneous groups in the twenty-first century.[7]

In the latter case, these groups or comprehensive collectives consist of people from widely different backgrounds, including the new middle classes that emerged as a result of Peru's economic growth[8] and the upward mobility of those from humbler origins. The age of women participating in these collectives generally varies between nineteen and forty years old, yet the collectives also include older women. Most of these women have completed high school and are or once were university students. The collectives are usually small groups created with particular purposes. However, according to testimonies, they were built from bigger spaces where women were working, as in the Déjala Decidir (Let Her Decide) campaign in 2014.[9] Others have developed within universities and in counterculture and neighborhood areas, such as the collectives Insurgentes (Insurgents) and Poco Floro (which refers to acting instead of speaking) (interview with U, March 1, 2019), integrated by women from the metropolitan areas of Lima Norte and Lima Sur.

The groups mentioned here exhibit different ways of being feminist. The generational meaning of feminism sheds light on the plurality of the concept. One definition affirms feminists' belonging to a social class and to ethnic, racial, and sexual identities that are manifested in the language that they use. For example, a thirty-one-year-old female feminist identifies as "hybrid" because she can move between the more affluent and more deprived classes. She was born of professionals who migrated to Lima from the provinces, so, for her, being a feminist "is super cool. For me, being a feminist implies that I do not only want feminism outside the house and on the streets, but also in my personal life, in my bed, in my food, in how I see life, right? Being a feminist is very important for me, and also understanding the inequalities among women, and trying to abolish the patriarchal system, right? For me, it is a life project!" (interview with U, March 1, 2019). For another young woman of working-class origins, feminism relates to life experience but not necessarily to passing through academia:

> I think I was a bit ashamed of the idea of being linked to the old feminists, like . . . I had the idea that feminists were those institutional women, from university, and they could not be otherwise, that they were buried in books, writing big texts for thought, and I did not think that was . . . that type of feminism did not identify me, but I did not know anything else about feminism; then, with the NiUna-Menos movement, I began to understand that some platforms of articulation among women could be generated, that there was not only one feminism but different ways of being feminists. (Interview with W, February 18, 2019, ellipses indicate pauses)

Furthermore, for a fifty-year-old middle-high-class scholar who in the past participated in institutional feminism and now belongs to NiUna-Menos, "Feminism is still a possibility, maybe not on a personal level, because now I can give myself the freedom and since transnationalization and the possibility of activating in other groups, groups of other countries, et cetera, is no more. The hope that I could have in feminism in Peru is that the feminist spirit of Peruvian women finally wakes up" (interview with C, February 27, 2019).[10]

One commonality among these activists and the collectives from which they come is their life experience in a society within the global web, which, as Castells points out, "is the opposition between the logic of the global web and the affirmation of a multiplicity of local identities. . . . It may be observed that the main tendency is toward historical and cultural diversity: fragmentation rather than convergence" (2009, 66–67).

Not all collectives have physical spaces. They communicate through Facebook, Twitter, and other social media platforms. They use the street as a necessary vehicle through which to demand rights and engage in a new form of politics characterized by calling on others to assemble. Popular language representing the resolve to take to the streets in "female terms" can be found in the names chosen by the collectives: "Manada Feminista" (Feminist Herd), "Las Respondonas" (The Insolents). Another common characteristic is the use of shock strategies—for example, nudity in protests and performances—in contrast with the "rationality" heralded by the feminists of the previous century, who "must dress as civil servants" if they want to interact with the state (Barrientos and Muñoz 2018, 291). The idea behind working in smaller groups is that, according to the testimonies, more things can get done and more impact can be achieved by small groups in the struggle to end gender violence, lesbophobia, and transphobia (interview with U, March 1, 2019).

Another common characteristic of these new collectives is that just as they emerge, they disappear again: they have short lifespans. Members of one collective may form a new one with a specific goal, which leads to the disintegration of the previous collective. The goals of each group are not necessarily clear because most of them have no central organizing idea for work schedules. There is always a dynamic for activism, however, for responding to any deeds of violence against women or LGBTQ groups, and social networks are a useful tool in organizing such responses. According to the testimonies, the creation of several collectives may be explained by some group members' need for acknowledgment, including those who are dissatisfied with small actions and "would like to be the queen bee in the group" (interview with C, February 27, 2019). Similarly, the need for acknowledgment, the desire for recognition of groups that have had no access to power, and the democratization of social networks also make the proliferation of groups possible.

The collectives are strongly connected, either virtually or physically, to collectives in other countries in Latin America and Europe, specifically in Spain. C, a representative of NiUnaMenos and long-term feminist activist, for example, has connections in Madrid with Casa de América, the Women's Foreign Policy Network, and La Caja de Pandora (Pandora's Box). U keeps in touch with Argentine feminists Marian Lacono and Marta Dillon, among others. Moreover, although some collective members maintain alliances with institutional feminists, most of them consider that this is not a road to follow. According to one activist feminist in NiUnaMenos, her initial interest in participating in the collective was to build bridges between the institutional feminism of the twentieth century and these new groups. However, after observing that the two positions are not compatible due to their incapacity for dialogue and understanding, she has "confirmed that the union between the feminism of the twentieth [century] and [the feminism of] the twenty-first century is not happening" (interview with C, February 27, 2019).

Points of Tension and Conflict: Ethnicity, Race, Class, Gender

As mentioned earlier, the NiUnaMenos demonstration's organization and the actions that followed the demonstration produced a series of conflicts within the core driving group and the different participating collectives. This crisis and rupture shed light on deep problems that Peru has yet to solve, such as racism, authoritarianism, and a lack of democratic participation. These problems are linked to the history of feminism in Peru, which has been characterized by polarization among different groups, in particular a division between bourgeois women and working-class women.

Thus, the present fragmentation between the many collectives and NiUnaMenos is evident. NiUnaMenos has not had the capacity to call the collectives to action and to articulate their various goals because of this division. The core group that promoted the rally in 2016 has been labeled "the group of white women" by the other collectives. Moreover, several of the testimonies gathered for this study mention that the NiUnaMenos core group is not carrying out feminist activism, and so they delegitimize that group through the use of a "feministometer" that shows the group's opposition to dialogue and its authoritarian tendencies: "The process was quite painful. . . . We, women, were fighting for power. I found it terrible. So, I left and started activism in my district. . . . They did not realize that they were aggressive during this whole process. That aggressiveness was nonconstructive. When someone is aggressive, you cannot communicate with that person" (interview with K, March 13, 2019, ellipses indicate omission). According to the narrative of the testimonies and the reviewed information, the conflict between the collectives and the NiUnaMenos core group is linked to ethnicity, race, and class, as one of the interviewed women states: "I believe that a pretty serious problem is the division of the group of women based on issues of intersectionality, class, and race. This is a big fracture that I think is at the bottom of the first rupture in the core of NiUnaMenos" (interview with C, March 1, 2019).

Other testimonies also narrate the impossibility of "accepting differences" (interview with MT, March 1, 2019). It is no coincidence that labels such as "the white ones"[11] and the "brown" and "hybrid" feminists emerge in this context. The women with a working-class origin feel that the white feminists reject them, that the white feminists are authoritarian, privileged, and nonegalitarian. "For them, the structural violence that patriarchy exercises over us is not the most important thing. For example, they did not want to include the workers' labor or economic agenda. Even though they believe this structural violence exists, they just wanted to focus on the issue of violence, just because they are from a social class different from ours" (interview with S, February 27, 2019). In response, a member of "the white ones" states that they have never challenged the NiUnaMenos assembly (where all members of the collectives and various feminist activists attend to make joint and democratic decisions) and its leading role in the decision-making process. Yet they also argue that they had to assume the coordination of the rally because feminist activists wanted the assembly to decide on every single action, no matter how simple it was. Moreover, she is convinced that the assembly lost its democratic character and became a battlefield where consensus was not reached or responsibilities assumed for the organization of the rally. "The assembly was so frustrating . . . and very violent. . . . Someone had to take over the logistics required for the rally. If we would have waited for the assembly [to make decisions], the rally would have never occurred" (interview with N, February 12, 2020, ellipses indicate pauses).

The tension reached its climax when a decision had to be taken on which route the rally should take. Many activists rejected the route proposed by "the white ones," arguing that it had not been approved by the assembly. Tension and disagreement were blatantly obvious even during the press conference with the government representatives. "The white ones" argue, however, that the activists' insistence on changing the route was based on the commitments and decisions they had previously taken with their own political parties, who before the NiUnaMenos rally had already organized the Keiko No Va and Ley Pulpín rallies.[12]

As for the decision to register NiUnaMenos as a trademark at Indecopi, N acknowledges that "it was a mistake" due to her lack of political experience. Yet she assures that it was not a personal decision but rather a decision taken in consensus with the group to protect the name from other groups that had the intention to register it, too: "We never thought that it would be interpreted as a commercial appropriation" (interview with N, February 12, 2020). N adds that at the time she explained the reasons for that decision and offered public apologies. However, in spite of these explanations and public apologies, the feminist activists have not changed their perception of "the dome," another term coined to identify the group of "white women."

Moreover, N considers that feminist groups have used all of these disagreements to delegitimize the actions and representation of NiUnaMenos in the Peruvian feminist movement and, above all, to replicate the worldwide ideological confrontation that exists between white feminists and intersectional feminists: "We embody all of what is perceived as white feminist. It no longer matters who we are, it no longer matters if those who were present in 2016 are now absent in 2019. Nothing really matters. Neither history matters; we are already part of it" (interview with N, February 12, 2020). This rupture became explicit in the manifestation of NiUnaMenos under the banner "Women Free of Violence" on August 17, 2019, in which different collectives not only did not participate but also publicly communicated their demarcation from NiUnaMenos Perú, questioning the practices of the so-called minority group as hierarchical/tyrannical/undemocratic and noninclusive of the "collective and popular participation of workers, students, Afro-Peruvians, Indigenous women, farmers, lesbians, transpeople, and all the women and diversities that continue to organize in collectives, platforms, unions, and assemblies."[13] It is clear how these ethnic, class, and race differences may explain the hierarchy present among the groups. As Marisol de la Cadena points out, "Ethnic identities are built with interactions, according to attributes acknowledged and fixed, through conflict, in the relationship" (1992).

Final Considerations

One of the main achievements of the NiUnaMenos rally of August 13, 2016, was that gender violence against women was made visible to multiple actors, including the state, the civic consciousness, and the media. As a result, violence against women has become central to the agenda of these three actors. Another effect of the NiUnaMenos demonstration has been the creation of many diverse feminist collectives that represent a rupture from the twentieth-century feminist movement. The new collectives, whose members are mainly young people who study in urban areas, regularly regroup and rename themselves in movements without a specific physical space or organizational hierarchy. They do not seek to become institutions because their position is against the state; by shocking public opinion, they engage followers.

Another conclusion that can be made here is that among the heterogeneity of collectives formed after the NiUnaMenos rally of 2016, a sector that stands out comprises the groups within universities who question normalized behaviors such as sexual harassment. These collectives have shown an interest in linking their feminism with academia, seeking education in gender studies within an intersectional and queer lens. The collectives have characteristics in common, such as the creation of new dynamics of social action and organization in the context of a modern society experiencing its transition to postmodernity.

Yet understanding the impact of NiUnaMenos requires considering it as a movement of the twenty-first century: a social network movement that uses platforms such as Facebook. The latter, as Castells argues, "offers its users the possibility of sharing testimonies, opinions and life experiences, with a potentially gigantic number of recipients who may also express solidarity" (quoted in Caballero 2018, 229). However, this kind of network also leads to fragmentation rather than to convergence. The women who were interviewed for this study point out that social networks generate spaces of disagreement and conflict where depersonalization contributes to and escalates into denigration. "The con side of the web is that it can generate fights, distance, and political arguments on a level, like, so strong that it is impoverishing. Like for me, there are things that I have read that seem really denigrating, right? Like okay" (interview with U, March 1, 2019). This depersonalization can lead groups to turn into spaces that are unfriendly and violent for the people in them.

Although NiUnaMenos still has a strong presence in news and media, it has no significant political impact in the struggle against gender violence toward women. The movement's internal conflicts, especially those related to ethnicity, race, and class, have kept it from being a platform with a common goal for the many collectives that originally joined it. The women from the higher classes and those from the working class had significant problems communicating with each other because each delegitimized the other's experience, and their relationship was anchored in distrust and fear.

Moreover, the women of working-class origins were found to feel some social resentment toward higher-class women, which they expressed through intense stigmatization of "privileged" women. From this feeling, we can deduce some structural problems in Peruvian society as a whole, such as racism and authoritarianism. For feminist women of the working class, feminism is a left-wing struggle that corresponds to a female identity as "chola" or "brown," belonging to peripheral or working-class areas. The historian Cecilia Blondet (1995) pointed out these characteristics more than twenty years ago when she related a class dispute between "political feminists" and "bourgeois feminists."

Finally, it is crucial to say that this new wave of feminism, which remains unnamed but is characterized by its antistate and countercultural orientation, has not yet found a strategy that will allow it to act with a more powerful impact in the political field. The new feminist groups find themselves in the paradoxical position of having to decide between the transcendence of consolidating as movements vindicating their rights and the ephemeral immanence where they emerge without any continuity.

References

Arcasi Mariño, W. G. 2020. "Odebrecht Case: Judicial Branch Gives Prosecutor Office a Deadline to Accuse Keiko Fujimori." [In Spanish.] *Gestión,* January 28. At https://gestion.pe/peru/politica/keiko-fujimori-caso-odebrecht-poder-judicial-le-da-dos-meses-a-fiscalia-para-acusar-a-keiko-fujimori-noticia/.

Barrientos, V., and F. Muñoz. 2018. "The New Voices of Feminisms: Towards a Cartography of the Second Millennium's Feminism." In *Poetics of Decolonial Feminisms from the South* [in Spanish], edited by K. Bidaseca, 275–306. Buenos Aires, Argentina: Decolonial Thought Network.

Barrig, M. 1986. *Research about Employment and Female Labor.* [In Spanish.] Lima, Peru: ADEC-ATC.

———. 2019. *Interview with Maruja Barrig.* [In Spanish.] El Arriero, March 27. YouTube video. At https://www.youtube.com/watch?v=jzFibNpjTrw.

Blondet, C. 1995. "Women's Movement in Peru 1960–1990." In *Peru 1964–1994: Economy, Society, and Politics* [in Spanish], edited by J. Cotler, 103–34. Lima, Peru: IEP.

Caballero, G. 2018. "Social Networks and Feminisms in Collective Action: The Case of 'No Woman Less.'" [In Spanish.] Master's thesis, Pontifical Catholic University of Peru.

Castells, Manuel. 2004. *The Information Age: Economy, Society, and Culture.* Vol. 2: *The Power of Identity.* 5th ed. [In Spanish.] Mexico City: XXI Century Editorial.

———. 2009. *Communication and Power.* [In Spanish.] Madrid: Alianza Editorial.

———. 2012. *Networks of Outrage and Hope: Social Movements in the Internet Age.* [In Spanish.] Madrid: Free Culture.

Chinchay, M., and C. Cortijo. 2016. "The Greatest of History." [In Spanish.] *La República,* August 14. At https://larepublica.pe/sociedad/963798-la-mas-grande-de-la-historia.

De La Cadena, M. 1992. "Women Are More Indigenous: Ethnicity and Gender in a Community of Cuzco." [In Spanish.] *Journal Isis International, Women's Editorial,* no. 16: not paginated.

Follegati, L. 2018. "The Constant Appearance of the Feminist Movement: Reflections from the Contingencies." In *Feminist May, the Rebellion against Patriarchy* [in Spanish], edited by F. Zerán, 77–97. Santiago de Chile: Ciencias Sociales y Humanas LOM.

Fraser, N. 2019. "Feminism Is the Answer to Capitalism Crisis." [In Spanish.] Interview by Isabel Valdés. *El Diario.es* (Madrid), March 23.

Gutiérrez, B. 2016. *New Communication, Organization, and Collective Action Dynamics in Latin America: Technopolitic Reconfigurations.* OXFAM

research report. Nairobi, Kenya: OXFAM. At https://www-cdn.oxfam
.org/s3fs-public/file_attachments/nuevas_dinamicas_de_comunicacion_
organizacion_y_accion_social_en_americalatina._reconfiguraciones_
tecnopoliticas.pdf.

Melucci, A. 1994. "What Is New in 'Social Movements'?" In *New Social Movements: From Ideology to Identity* [in Spanish], edited by E. Laraña and
J. Gusfield, 119–49. Madrid: Sociological Research Center (CIS).

Natalucci, A., and J. Rey. 2018. "A New Feminist Wave? Gender Agendas,
Action Repertoires, and Women's Collectives (Argentina, 2015–2018)."
[In Spanish.] *Revista de estudios políticos y estratégicos* 6 (2). At https://
revistaepe.utem.cl/articulos/una-nueva-oleada-feminista-agendas-
de-genero-repertorios-de-accion-y-colectivos-de-mujeres-argentina-2015-
2018/#easy-footnote-bottom-13-836.

UNESCO, Consejo Nacional de Educación. 2017. *Revision of Educational Politics 2000–2015: Continuities on Public Policy in Education in Peru: Appren-
ticeships, Teachers, and Decentralized Management.* [In Spanish.] Lima,
Peru: UNESCO.

Vargas, Virginia. 2008. *Feminisms in Latin America: Its Contribution to Politics
and Democracy.* [In Spanish.] Lima, Peru: Flora Tristán.

Notes

Thanks to Brenda Reyna, Vanessa Laura, Claudia Medina, and Angélica
Motta for their collaborations on this chapter. Valentina Pérez Llosa translated
it from Spanish.

1. The confidentiality of the participants in the in-depth interviews has
been respected in the writing of this chapter.

2. Facebook web pages of the movements analyzed in this chapter are:
Mujer Dispara—Audiovisual Feminista (Woman Shoots—Feminist Audiovi-
sual), https://www.facebook.com/MujerDispara/; Awqa Feminista (Feminist
Awqa), https://www.facebook.com/Awqa-Feminista-1670198029945045/;
Collera Red (Collera Network), https://www.facebook.com/ColleraRed/;
Colectiva Fugitivas (Collective Fugitive), https://www.facebook.com/photo
.php?fbid=1360073374156436&set=a.101721013325018&type=3; NiUna-
Menos Carabayllo (Not One [Woman] Less Carabayllo), https://www.facebook
.com/LasCarabayllanas/; Mujeres Turbo (Turbo Women), https://www
.facebook.com/mujeresturbo/; Mujer al Volante (Woman behind the Wheel),
https://www.facebook.com/soymujeralvolante/; NiUnaMenos Los Olivos
(Not One [Woman] Less Los Olivos), https://www.facebook.com/groups
/1081408671929418/; Ruray—Colectiva Feminista Barrial en San Martín de
Porres (Ruray—Neighborhood Feminist Collective in San Martín de Porres),

https://www.facebook.com/RuraySMP/; TodasSomosMariana (WeAllAre-Mariana), https://www.facebook.com/TSomosMariana/; Bloque Universitario Feminista (Feminist University Coallition), https://www.facebook.com/bloqueuniversitariofeminista/.

3. Among notable rallies are Ley Pulpín (referring to Law No. 30288) in 2015 and Keiko no Va in 2016. Keiko Fujimori is the daughter of Alberto Fujimori, who led a dictatorship from 1992 to 2000. Keiko Fujimori defended her father's political decisions and denied the crimes committed by his regime during this period. Likewise, she became involved in judicial cases related to corruption (for example, the Odebrecht corruption scandal) and asset laundering. For more details, see Arcasi Mariño 2020.

4. These movements were not necessarily feminist, but they were spaces in which different feminist collectives converged.

5. All English versions of quotations originally in Spanish are by the translator, Valentina Pérez Llosa.

6. According to Virginia Vargas (2008), (1) the feminist current denounces the existence of a sex–gender system that subordinates women; (2) the working-class current is oriented to answering demands and necessities of women's traditional roles and is formed by women of working-class origins; and (3) the political current is that of traditional public spaces, such as parties, syndicates, and associations. The women of the latter current look to modify these spaces and open new ones in order to accomplish a greater participation, and they struggle for official and public acknowledgment of women's rights.

7. These various groups, within Lima and other Peruvian provinces, include Mujer Dispara Audiovisual (Woman Shoots—Feminist Audiovisual, 2016), Awqa Feminista (Feminist Awqa, 2017), Collera Red (Collera Network, 2017), Fugitivas (Collective Fugitive, 2016), NiUnaMenos Carabayllo (Not One [Woman] Less Carabayllo, 2017), NiUnaMenos en Los Olivos (Not One [Woman] Less Los Olivos, 2017), Ruray—Colectiva Feminista Barrial en San Martín de Porres (Ruray—Neighborhood Feminist Collective in San Martín de Porres, 2017), Mujeres Turbo (Turbo Women), Mujer al Volante (Woman behind the Wheel), Bloque Universitario Feminista (Feminist University Coallition, 2017), Manada Feminista (Feminist Herd, 2015), Colectivo Alfombra Roja (Red Carpet Collective, 2013), Semana Feminista (Feminist Week, 2013), Alfombra Roja (Red Carpet, Peru and Italy), Colectivo No Tengo Miedo (I'm Not Afraid Collective, 2014), Asociación de Mujeres Carabayllanas (Carabayllan Association of Women), Colectiva AQP Feminista (AQP Feminist Collective), Colectivo de Mujeres para el Desarrollo y la Igualdad de Género—COMUDEIG PERÚ (Collective of Women for Development and Gender Equality—COMUDEIG PERU), Colectivo Nos Están Matando (They're Killing Us Collective), Colectivo Parió Paula Percusión (Paula Gave

Birth Percussion Collective), Colectivo de Concertación por la Equidad de Género en VES (Concertation Collective for Gender Equality in VES), Comité de Vigilancia VES (Surveillance Committee VES), Colectivo por la Igualdad de Género–Piura (Collective for Gender Equality–Piura), Colectivo Réplica (Replica Collective), Colectivo Sonqo Warmi (Women's Heart Collective), Comunidad de Mujeres Positivas—Lima Este (Community of Positive Women—East Lima), Emma Jones Afrodescendientes (Emma Jones Afro-Descendants), EMPODERADXS (Empowered), Grupo de Mujeres Diversas (Diverse Women Group), La Purita Carne (The Pure Meat), Las Insurgentes (The Insurgents), Las Respondonas (The Insolents, 2016), Lesbianas Independientes Feministas Socialistas (LIFS, Socialist Independent Lesbian Feminists), Movimiento Lesbia (Lesbia Movement), NiUnaMenos (Not One [Woman] Less, 2016), Pazos Arte para la Educación (Steps Art for Education), Presencia y Palabra: Mujeres Afrodescendientes (Presence and Word: Afro-Descendant Women), RECARE, Red LGTB Arequipa (LGTB Network Arequipa), Red Peruana de Masculinidades (Peruvian Masculinities Network), Red Peruana de Mujeres Viviendo con VIH (Peruvian Network of Women Living with HIV), SEMLAC, Tamboras Resistencia (Female Drummers Resistance), Unión Popular de Mujeres Peruanas (Popular Union of Peruvian Women), Warmi Chasquis (Female Chasquis), Yemayá Batucada. See Barrientos and Muñoz 2018, 291.

8. During the period between 2000 and 2015, Peru experienced sustained economic growth of approximately 5.3 percent. During the same period, the gross domestic product per capita was 5.9 percent, one of the highest among the countries of the region. According to the National Statistics Institute, in 2015 poverty reached a low point of 21.7 percent. However, the gap between rural and urban areas has been maintained: 21.7 of all Peruvians lived in poverty in 2015, but 44.4 percent of people in rural areas were living in poverty, almost three times more than the 15.1 percent living in poverty in urban areas (UNESCO, Consejo Nacional de Educación 2017, 18).

9. The Déjala Decidir campaign is a civic effort supporting the right of thousands of women who were victims of sexual violence in Peru to decide if they want to continue a pregnancy produced by this grave attack against their lives, dignity, and fundamental rights.

10. The feminists whom the interviewees refer to include Marcela Lagarde, Rita Segato, Virginia Woolf, and Björk—the latter for her environmental activism, her creativity, and her coherence. In Peru, Rocío Muñoz, Virginia Vargas, and the women of working-class organizations are mentioned.

11. Light-skinned feminists are not necessarily white. Rather, they possess characteristics that symbolize status and economic power. They are academics, have social and symbolic capital, have class privileges and therefore power.

The "brown" feminists, in contrast, have dark skin, no social capital, and no power.

12. See note 3.

13. Please see https://www.facebook.com/notes/paro-internacional-de-mujeres-per%C3%BA/pronunciamiento-de-deslinde-con-ni-una-menos-per%C3%BA-tocan-a-una-tocan-a-todas/668535526961144/.

11

Afterword

#MeToo, Just a Hashtag?

Paula-Irene Villa and M. Cristina Alcalde

Following the momentum of 2017–2018, #MeToo was framed by part of the media as a glitzy red-carpet issue, a movement in the spotlight because it centered on highly privileged people on the global stage of stardom. The most visible protagonists within the Weinstein affair, which was perhaps the starting point of the mainstreaming of #MeToo, were prominent actresses in Hollywood. In this context, the very real issues behind #MeToo soon became associated with shallowness, artificiality, fame, and the heteronormative sexiness characterizing Hollywood. This mainstreaming, however, as many chapters have pointed to, contributed to the massive visibility of what was to become #MeToo globally (and of many other hashtags in different languages). Still today, though, some insist on reading #MeToo as a frivolous misunderstanding. Others have criticized #MeToo as faux politics, a mere hashtag in lieu of "real protest," a commodity for armchair activism instead of disruptive political action.

This volume, along with many other publications, shows—yet again—how short-sighted and misguided such framings are. From its beginning and embodied through manifestations across regional, professional, and sociocultural contexts, #MeToo has been fundamentally diverse and political and has resulted in significant repercussions across social fields. Its political scope and depth can hardly be overemphasized. It can, however, be more substantially analyzed, as contributors in this volume have done. To be clear, #MeToo has never been (merely) a VIP'ish, elitist, show-biz whim. We merely need to remind ourselves at the most basic level that before the Hollywood #MeToo, Tamara Burke articulated the realities behind #MeToo on social media in 2006. She and others have continued to generate and demand visibility for the intersectional, racialized, and class-related dimensions that fundamentally inform experiences of sexual harassment and gender-based violence across contexts. As Burke stated in 2017, and as we chose to guide our volume, "We can't afford a racialized, gendered or classist response. Ending sexual violence will require every voice from every corner of the world" (Burke 2017). This perhaps trivial but often overseen and underestimated call for nuance and plurality under the umbrella hashtag #MeToo as well as for critical intersectional analysis and political response is also one of the main insights and challenges our volume offers.

Although the #MeToo movement is often portrayed as a US American movement, our collection demonstrates how this particular social movement is in fact a global phenomenon. Again, as nearly all the case studies unequivocally demonstrate, #MeToo—plus the huge variety of corresponding slogans, such as @IndiaMeToo, #YaEsHora, #KuToo, #LetHerSpeak, #Sex4Grades, #Aufschrei, #GamAni, #ausnahmslos, #NiUnaMenos, #QuellaVoltaChe, #BalanceTonPorc, #גמאנחנו, ‏#أنا_كمان—demands to be seen as an organic part of a much longer and immensely broad and plural strand of transnational, global, and at the same time regional feminist activism against sexism and sexual and gender-based violence. #MeToo by no means came out of the blue or from Hollywood, and it will by no means disappear in the myriad trending hashtags.

Yet #MeToo, with all its achievements, is also defined by internal contradictions and conflicts. Many analyses and case studies in the previous chapters foreground the ambivalences and essential contradictions of relying on the state as an ally or on the legal system as salvation or, at minimum, as the solution. Other chapters warn us against new forms of othering, of exclusion, of new invisibilities within strands of activism (the erasure of queerness, for example, as Xavier Guadalupe-Diaz and Elizabeth Whalley point out), and among the political and legal responses (as Srimati Basu and Rukmini Sen show). Public and political visibility is a "tricky issue," and "how to be a feminist in public" is not easily achieved and has significant costs, as Ruth Preser argues. Also, #MeToo is entangled with other political and cultural discourses and dynamics in complex and sometimes disturbing ways. Within populist, often xenophobic, racist, white-supremacist, and antisemitic mobilizations, "women's rights" and even "feminisms" of sorts are used as markers of the superiority of a dominant culture and society. Although sexualized violence, sexism, and gender-based abuse are always context specific and concrete, they are by no means limited to specific religions, milieus, regions, or time periods. Despite this rather trivial fact, populist, fundamentalist, illiberal, sometimes outright racist, or xenophobic movements exploit the issue to advance their agendas, pointing fingers at the "Bad Hombres" in the United States, the Muslim/Arab male migrants in Germany, the dark Indigenous immigrants in South America—all variations of toxic stereotypes and the occidentalist trope of the "Black Man" or Other.

In the context of #MeToo, this co-optation of "women's rights" by disparate movements results in rather dubious and ambivalent situations. For example, in Germany sexualized violence and harassment have become a political issue, finally taken seriously on the political agenda in its endemic dimension, but this new recognition and visibility come infused with racist and xenophobic venom. After the "Summer of Migration" in 2015 in Germany, women's rights and the—at least rhetorical and partly legal—pushback against gender-based and sexualized violence became quite prominent but in a highly racist and nationalist framing that projected all sexism and violence onto "the migrants" (Hark and Villa 2015). In the United States, the "Make Women Great Again" conference of 2020 presented itself as an opportunity for women to regain their "natural" rights. The all-male speaker lineup promoted women's traditional roles as wives and mothers and sought to infuse "positive femininity" in women in the United States and the West. Couching this promotion in terms of supporting women, the conference co-opted "women's rights" by chastising "bad feminists" who, it argued, corrupt femininity, see sexual harassment in every "innocent" interaction, and refuse to put up with what most women consider daily forms of sexualized, gendered violence. This conference reflects the ongoing backlash against #MeToo.

As this book shows—if only in a selected variety of case studies across countries, contexts, and dimensions—the mobilization generated by #MeToo has been immensely successful, generating visibility and sustainable awareness of gender-based and sexualized violence, especially against women and other "othered" groups, such as queer or trans people, as well as of everyday sexism and the sexualization of asymmetries in the workplace and the public sphere. It has even led to specific innovative policies and legal responses. As the contributors to this book clearly demonstrate, #MeToo has already changed discourse, law, policies, cultural values, and the very concrete embodied experiences of women, queer and trans persons, and marginalized and vulnerable groups of various identities. The continued backlash underscores the necessity of ongoing efforts to make visible, engage with, and support manifestations of #MeToo. Rather than think of #MeToo's future as predetermined or as easily predictable based on its histories, we urge readers to engage with new insights gained through a deep dive into less familiar #MeToo stories and contexts. Engagement with these contexts and actions allows us to reimagine the movement's past and to make visible the global weight of myriad forms of gendered, sexualized forms of oppression. It can also allow us to imagine less familiar forms of resistance and tools for transformation. #MeToo is a success story not because of its coherence but because of the messy, rich multivocality at its center, which must guide its path forward.

References

Burke, Tarana. 2017. "#MeToo Was Started for Black and Brown Women and Girls. They're Still Being Ignored." *Washington Post*, November 9.

Hark, S., and P-I. Villa, eds. 2015. *Anti-Genderismus: Sexualität und Geschlecht als Schauplätze aktueller politischer Auseinandersetzungen*. Bielefeld, Germany: transcript.

Acknowledgments

The Comparative Perspectives on #MeToo symposium that initially brought together the contributors to this volume in 2019 was the culmination of numerous efforts and conversations and was made possible with generous funding from the University of Kentucky. In particular, we extend our thanks to Mark Kornbluh, dean of the College of Arts and Sciences at the University of Kentucky at the time of the symposium and currently provost at Wayne State University. When Cristina initially brought up the possibility of organizing and hosting a global #MeToo symposium, Dr. Kornbluh supported the idea without hesitation. Carol Jordan, executive director of the University of Kentucky Office for Policy Studies on Violence against Women, offered additional generous support toward the travel costs of many participants and was enthusiastic about the symposium and book from the beginning. At the University of Kentucky, Chelsea Cutright, graduate assistant at the time, worked tirelessly on invitations, logistics, multiple itineraries across the globe, and materials to bring us all together. Céline Lamb and Ruwen Chang also contributed to the success of the symposium through their efforts as graduate assistants at various points in this project. At Miami University, a supportive and inclusive environment allowed Cristina to complete this project. At the Ludwig Maximilian University of Munich, Rahel Zelenkowits at very short notice helped to collate the various components of the manuscript for initial submission.

At the University Press of Kentucky, Natalie O'Neal shepherded this project from initial proposal to finished manuscript. We could not have asked for a better editor. She believed in this project from the beginning and provided valuable and constructive feedback every step of the way. As we navigated different time zones, locations, and demands during a pandemic, her faith in this project helped us reach the final stage. The two anonymous reviewers for the manuscript provided incisive and detailed feedback that helped strengthen the arguments and flow of the collection. Of course, any faults remain our own.

Our biggest thanks go to the participants in the symposium. Although not all participants ultimately contributed chapters to this book, the dynamic and insightful discussions that all of us engaged in collectively informed the shape and core of this book project. As we developed this book, even as the pandemic affected each of our world locations and communities, all chapter authors dedicated significant time and effort to writing and revising their chapters. Their persistence speaks to the significance and enormity of #MeToo and to the need to continue to engage in ongoing discussions across borders, identities, and differences. Finally, and importantly, Cristina and Paula thank their families for ongoing support.

Contributors

M. Cristina Alcalde is vice president of institutional diversity and inclusion and professor of global and intercultural studies at Miami University. From 2007 to 2021, she was with the University of Kentucky, where she served as associate dean of inclusion and internationalization in the College of Arts and Sciences, as professor of gender and women's studies, and as the Marie Rich Endowed Professor. Her books include *Peruvian Lives across Borders: Power, Exclusion, and Home* (2018), *The Woman in the Violence: Gender, Poverty, and Resistance in Peru* (2010), *La mujer en la violencia* (Spanish edition, 2014), and *Provocations: A Transnational Reader in the History of Feminist Thought* (coedited with Susan Bordo and Ellen Rosenman, 2015). Her book *Dismantling Institutional Whiteness: Emerging Forms of Leadership in Higher Ed* (with Mangala Subramaniam) is forthcoming. She has also published widely in journals and edited collections on her research areas, including gender violence, migration, exclusion, and race and racialization.

Srimati Basu is professor of gender and women's studies and anthropology at the University of Kentucky. She has a bachelor's degree in English from Presidency College, Calcutta, a master's in English from Purdue University, and an interdisciplinary PhD in cultural studies, anthropology, and women's studies from Ohio State University. She is the author of the monographs *The Trouble with Marriage: Feminists Confront Law and Violence in India* (2015) and *She Comes to Take Her Rights: Indian Women, Property, and Propriety* (1999); the editor of *Dowry and Inheritance* (2005); and the coeditor (with Lucinda Ramberg) of *Conjugality Unbound: Sexual Economy and the Marital Form in India*

(2014). Some of her recent articles on masculinity, law, marriage, and violence appear in anthologies, including *50th Anniversary Commemorative Volume of Contributions to Indian Sociology* (2019), *Men and Feminism in India* (2018), *Sexuality Studies: Oxford India Studies in Contemporary Society* (2013), and *New South Asian Feminisms: Paradoxes and Possibilities* (2012), as well as in the journals *QED, Journal of Feminist Anthropology, Canadian Journal of Women and Law,* and *Economic and Political Weekly.* She is presently working on a monograph about the antifeminist men's rights movement in India.

Denise Buiten is senior lecturer in the School of Arts and Sciences and discipline coordinator for the Social Justice Program (Sydney) at the University of Notre Dame, Australia. She holds a bachelor of social sciences honors degree in gender and transformation and a PhD in sociology. Dr. Buiten began her career as a gender and development researcher in South Africa, moving into academia as lecturer in sociology and social justice in South Africa, Ireland, and now Australia. She completed a postdoctoral fellowship in gender equality and global justice at University College Dublin in 2009 and is currently a senior research associate at the University of Johannesburg, with which she engages in collaborative research. Her key research interests include gender representations in the media and gender-based violence.

Stephen R. Burrell is assistant professor (research) in the Department of Sociology at Durham University, United Kingdom, where he is a deputy director of the Centre for Research into Violence and Abuse. His research is based around critical studies on men and masculinities, and his PhD focused on work with men and boys to prevent gender-based violence in England. Dr. Burrell is currently undertaking a Leverhulme Trust Early Career Fellowship to explore connections between the climate crisis and masculine violence as well as to engage men and boys in building more caring relationships with the environment. He also cohosts the podcast *Now and Men* and has recently coauthored the book *Men's Activism to End Violence against Women: Voices from Spain, Sweden, and the UK* (2021).

Xavier L. Guadalupe-Diaz is associate professor of sociology and criminology at Framingham State University in Framingham, Massachusetts. His primary areas of research examine a range of topics related to intimate-partner and sexual violence within the LGBTQ community. His current work focuses on transgender intimate-partner violence, polyvictimization, help seeking, and queer(ing) victimology. His recent articles are featured in the *Journal of Homosexuality;* the *Journal of Interpersonal Violence; Deviant Behavior;* the *Journal of Aggression, Maltreatment, and Trauma; Sociology Compass;* and *Violence against Women.* Dr. Guadalupe-Diaz is author of *Transgressed: Intimate*

Partner Violence in Transgender Lives (2019) and coeditor (with Adam M. Messinger) of *Transgender Intimate Partner Violence: A Comprehensive Introduction* (2020).

Desiree Lewis is professor in the Women's and Gender Studies Department at the University of the Western Cape in South Africa and has interdisciplinary interests in literary, cultural, and gender studies. The author of *Living on a Horizon: Bessie Head and the Politics of Imagining* (2007) and coeditor (with Gabeba Baderoon) of *Surfacing: On Being Black and Feminist in South Africa* (2021), she has guest-edited several feminist journal special issues and has published extensively on the politics of feminism, African feminisms, and the confluence of gender, race, and sexualities. Her recent interests include neoliberal discourses, technologies, feminism, and feminist food studies. She is currently the principal researcher for an intrainstitutional Andrew Mellon–funded program titled Critical Food Studies: Transdisciplinary Humanities Approaches (see https://www.criticalfoodstudies.co.za).

Rachel Loney-Howes is a criminologist at the University of Wollongong, Australia. Her research interests are broadly concerned with the politics of voice and listening regarding sexual violence but in particular with the relationships among activism, support services, and criminal legal responses to sexual violence. She is a coinvestigator on a foundational study exploring the use and potential of alternative and informal reporting options for survivors of sexual assault. She is also collaborating on research projects that apply theories of listening to law reform on violence against women. Dr. Loney-Howes is the author of *Online Anti-rape Activism: Exploring the Politics of the Personal in the Age of Digital Media* (2020), available free via Open Access. She is also the coeditor (with Bianca Fileborn) of *#MeToo and the Politics of Social Change* (2019).

Keren R. McGinity is the interfaith specialist at the United Synagogue of Conservative Judaism and research associate at the Hadassah-Brandeis Institute at Brandeis University. She earned her PhD from Brown University, where she was appointed a visiting assistant professor of history, and was the inaugural Mandell L. Berman Postdoctoral Research Fellow in Contemporary American Jewish Life at the University of Michigan's Frankel Center for Judaic Studies. Her pioneering books *Still Jewish: A History of Women & Intermarriage in America* (2009), a National Jewish Book Award Finalist, and *Marrying Out: Jewish Men, Intermarriage, and Fatherhood* (2014) changed the narrative about Jewish continuity by focusing on gender and change over time. She was a Forward 50 honoree in 2018 for her clarion call for a Jewish response to the #MeToo movement. She is also named on *Lilith* magazine's "7 Jewish

Feminist Highlights of 2018" list. In addition to her scholarly contributions to anthologies and journals, Dr. McGinity's advice and opinions have appeared in *Contact, Forward, Lilith, Moment, New York Jewish Week, Ritual Well, Sh'ma,* the *Times of Israel,* and *eJewishPhilanthropy*. Dr. McGinity serves as an ombudsperson for the Association for Jewish Studies Committee on Sexual Misconduct and on the Academic Advisory Council of the Jewish Women's Archive.

Fanni Muñoz Cabrejo studied sociology at the Pontifical Catholic University of Peru (PUCP) and received her PhD in history at the Colegio de México in Mexico City. Throughout her academic life, she has investigated the intersections of gender and education in education policy and management. Her papers have been published nationally and internationally in countries such as Argentina, Brazil, Mexico, and the United States. She has worked as a project manager for the International Cooperative. She is currently professor in the Department of Social Sciences at the PUCP, founding member of the Society for Permanent Research in Education, and associate of the Educational Forum. She promoted the creation of the master's degree in gender studies at the PUCP, of which she has been director since 2012. She has published on issues of educational decentralization, gender violence, gender and education, and cultural history.

Kammila Naidoo is based in the Sociology Department at the University of Johannesburg (UJ), South Africa, where she also serves as executive dean of the Faculty of Humanities. Prior to joining UJ, she taught at the University of Pretoria and the University of South Africa. Her doctoral work, which was completed at the University of Manchester, was an ethnographic study exploring family dynamics and relationships and the ways in which domestic violence reworks intimate unions. She has published in the areas of family life, poverty and inequality, gender-based violence, and sexual and reproductive health. She is currently a project investigator in the GendVProject titled "Urban Transformation and Gendered Violence in India and South Africa."

Ruth Preser is assistant professor at Tel Hai Academic College. She is a scholar in the field of cultural studies, combining feminist and queer theory and empirically informed inquiry. Dr. Preser studies forms of citizenship, the public sphere, and politics of belonging in the context of kinship, migration, diasporic cultures, and urban environments. She is a cofounder of the Haifa Feminist Institute Archive, Library, and Research Center and a member of the Lexicon for Political Theory research group at the Minerva Humanities Center at Tel Aviv University.

Rukmini Sen is professor in sociology in the School of Liberal Studies at Ambedkar University, Delhi. She has a master's degree from Jawaharlal Nehru University and a PhD in sociology from the University of Calcutta. She has taught at the WB National University of Juridical Sciences, Kolkata, India; has worked at the Centre for Women's Development Studies, New Delhi; and is currently teaching courses in sociology and gender studies at Ambedkar University, Delhi. She teaches and researches issues around sociology of law, feminist pedagogy, relationships, and intimacies in contemporary India. She is part of a UGC-UKERI collaborative project (2017–2019) titled "Feminist *Taleem:* Teaching Feminisms, Transforming Lives," in conjunction with the University of Edinburgh (https://feministtaleem.net/). Her publication "Reading the *Social* in Autobiographies: A Glimpse into Everyday Life and History" is part of the edited volume *Knowing the Social World: Methodologies in Sociological Research* (2017). She has coedited two journal special issues: "Indian Feminisms, Law Reform, and Law Commission of India: Special Issue in Honour of Lotika Sarkar" in the *Journal of Indian Law and Society* (vol. 6, 2018) and "Power and Relationships in the Academia: Feminist Dilemmas beyond the List-Statement Binary" in *Economic and Political Weekly Engage* (vol. 42, no. 50, 2017). Her most recent coedited book (with Prasanta Ray) is *Trust in Transactions* (2019).

Paula-Irene Villa is professor of and chair for sociology and gender studies at Ludwig Maximilian University, München. Since 2021, she has been the president elect of the German Sociological Association. She also served as an elected board member of the German Association for Gender Studies, which she cofounded, from 2010 to 2014. Her research focuses on the analysis of biopolitics, cultural studies, care and gender, and gender in (populist) politics. Dr. Villa has published widely on gender/social theory, the sociology of embodiment, beautification and normalization, feminist body politics, and German and European "antigenderism" as part of new nationalist populism. She has authored, coauthored, and edited eleven books and more than fifty chapters in books and papers in academic journals such as *Österreichische Zeitschrift für Soziologie, Gender, Soziologische Revue, Zeitschrift für Sexualwissenschaft, body politics, EMBO, Soziologie,* and *Soziale Welt.* Dr. Villa has directed funded empirical research (e.g., for the Deutsche Forschungsgemeinschaft/National Science Foundation, Volkswagen Foundation, and Humboldt Foundations) on cosmetic surgery, food/fitness, comparative analysis of gender-equality programs in academic capitalism, and popular culture. She writes op-ed pieces in German and international media (e.g., *FAZ Quarterly, taz,* the *Washington Post*). Her recent books include *The Future of Difference* (2020, with Sabine Hark; Spanish translation, 2022) and *Anti-Genderismus: Sexualität und Geschlecht als Schauplätze aktueller politischer Auseinandersetzungen,* coedited with Sabine Hark (2015, 2nd ed. 2017).

Elizabeth Whalley is assistant professor of sociology at Framingham State University. Her research and teaching utilize critical feminist criminology to examine cultural and institutional responses to sexual violence. She uses ethnographic, community-based, transnational, feminist, and mixed methods in her work. She has recently published research on carceral feminism, rape crisis centers, incarcerated women's mental health and sexual trauma, prison abolition, and transformative justice.

Index

233

Ingram Content Group UK Ltd.
Milton Keynes UK
UKHW042301090523
421481UK00003B/44